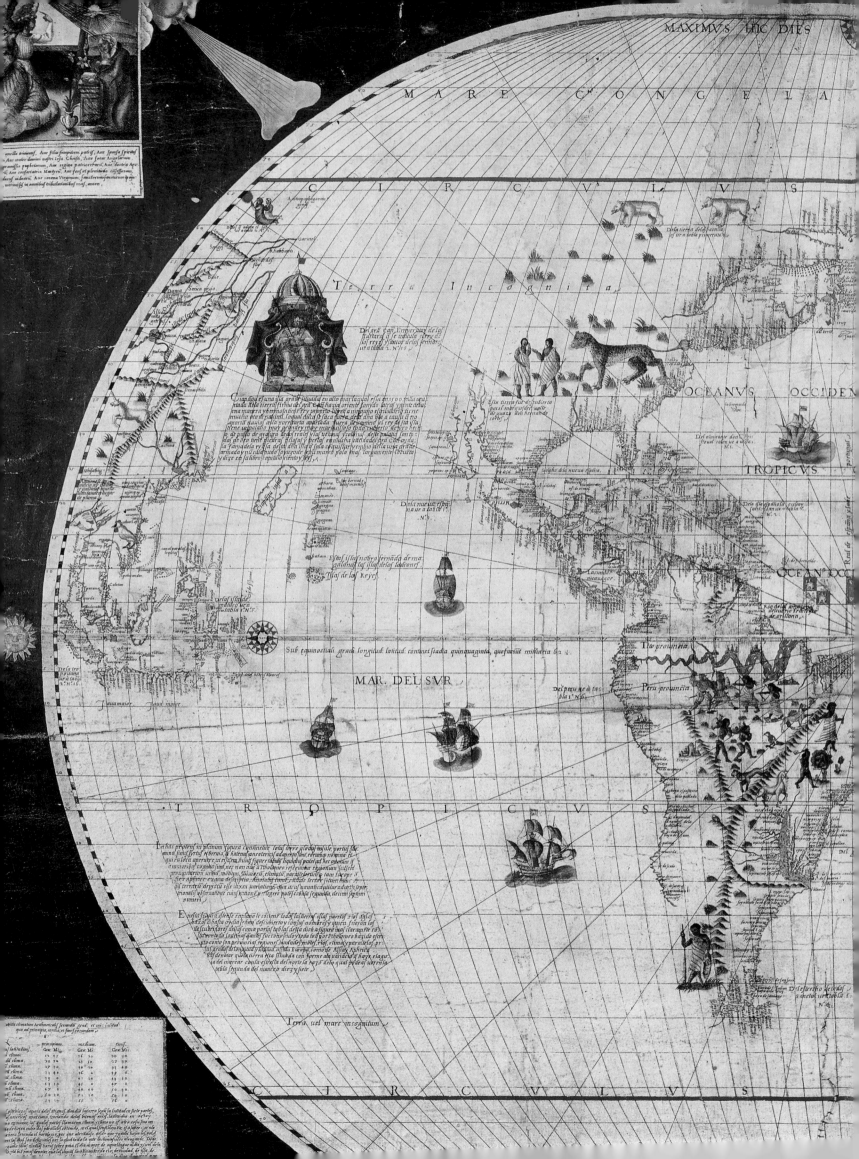

Americas Lost

1492–1713

The first encounter

Americas Lost

1492–1713
The first encounter

Edited by Daniel Lévine
Foreword by Claude Lévi-Strauss

Ricardo Avila Palafox, Michael Barry, Georges Baudot,
Jean-François Bouchard, Christian Duverger, Philippe Jacquin,
Miguel León-Portilla, Eduardo Matos Moctezuma
Anne Vitart

Maryse Delaplanche, photographer at the Musée de l'Homme

Translated by John Fergusson and Michael Barry

Bordas

Publication conceived and produced by Odile Berthemy
Editorial Manager: Dominique Wahiche
Design: Jean Castel
Production: Claire Svirmickas
Picture Research: Laurence Vacher
Maps: Graffito, Françoise Monestier
Index: Gilles Le Jeune

Texts by C. Lévi-Strauss, E. Matos Moctezuma, J.-F. Bouchard, C. Duverger, P. Jacquin, G. Baudot, R. Avila Palafox and M. León Portilla translated by John Fergusson, edited and typeset by Nicolas Andrews for the Book Creation Company.
Texts by M. Barry, D. Lévine and A. Vitart translated by Michael Barry and typeset by Nicolas Andrews for the Book Creation Company.
Index of the English edition by Kathy Gill.

Endpapers: *Mappemonde,* by Sébastien Cabot, 1544. [Bibliothèque nationale, Paris. Photo © Bibl. nat.-Arch. Photeb]

Picture Reproduction: Atelier Euresys
First printed in 1992
Printed in Italy by GEA Milan
ISBN 204014499–4
Copyright registration: April 1992
© Bordas SA 1992 for French edition
© Bordas SA 1992 for English edition

Home of the Brave

GLASGOW MUSEUMS
FONDS D'ACTION MECENAT SCIENCE ET ART, Strasbourg
BIBLIOTHEQUE NATIONALE, Paris

Loans

UK Museums: National Museums of Scotland, Edinburgh; Ashmolean Museum of Art and Archaeology, Oxford; Pitt Rivers Museum, Oxford; University Museum of Archaeology and Anthropology, Cambridge; Horniman Museum, London; Derby City Art Gallery and Museum

French Museums: Bibliothèque Nationale et Universitaire, Strasbourg; Muséum National d'Histoire Naturelle, Paris; Musée de l'Homme, Paris

Mexican Museums: Instituto Nacional de Antropologia e Historia, Mexico; Museo Nacional de Antropologia e Historia, Mexico; Museo Templo Mayor, Mexico; Museo Amparo, Fondation Amparo, Puebla

Swiss Museums: Musée d'Ethnographie de Genève

Private Collections: Fonds d'Action Mécénat Science et Art, Strasbourg

Creative Team

France: Fonds d'Action Mécénat Science et Art – Hubert Bari (project coordinator), Guy Hildwein, Jean-Baptiste Mantienne, Jean Bermon, Christophe Hener
Great Britain: Glasgow Museums – Seonaid Cowie, Geraldine Glynn, Jim Dryburgh, Deborah Haase, Joe Kelly, Antonia Lovelace, Carol Maconachie, Tamara Lucas, Julian Spalding (Director), Judith Wilder

Financial Support

Glasgow Museums supported by Strathclyde Regional Council; Conseil Régional d'Alsace; Conseil Général du Bas-Rhin; Ville de Strasbourg; Ministère de la Culture et de la Communication (Délégation aux Célébrations Nationales), Paris; Ministère de la Recherche et de la Technologie (D.I.S.T.), Paris

Production Team

Pittiwaf Nelson Pictures, Strasbourg (Video film); Bernard Desfarges Construction de Décors, Strasbourg (Sets); Philippe Eidel for Virgin Sound, Paris (Music); Sycomore, Ermont (Soundtrack); P.R. Consultants, Glasgow (Public Relations)

Coordination of Scientific Team

North America: Philippe Jacquin (Senior Lecturer at Université de Lyon)
Central America: Christian Duverger (Senior Lecturer at the Ecole Pratique des Hautes Etudes, Paris) and Daniel Lévine (Senior Lecturer at the Musée de l'Homme, Paris)

Curatorial research:

Antonia Lovelace, Glasgow; Philippe Jacquin, Lyon; Marie-Carmen Serra Puche, Mexico; Felipe Soliz, Mexico; Bertina Olmedo Vera, Mexico; Roberto Garcia Moll, Mexico; Mario Vazquez, Mexico; Angeles Espinosa Yglesias, Puebla; Daniel Lévine, Paris

CONTENTS

FOREWORD

America has been decribed as 'the unexpected continent', for it was discovered instead of the one that the explorers were attempting to reach from a new direction. And yet the two halves of humanity brought together as a result of this confusion regarded the event as entirely predictable – even though they knew nothing about each other.

Contrary to what might initially be thought, in the first few decades following Columbus' discovery of America, the event had scarcely any impact on European consciousness. For years, in fact, cosmographers took no account of the New World and its inhabitants. In the opinion of the Renaissance men, it was of considerably less importance than the discovery, a century or so earlier, that knowledge of the ancient civilizations could be acquired through the great Greek and Roman authors. This was the mirror in which scholars of that time first began to study America. The Indians quite naturally took their place among the strange races which had already been described by Pliny. The New World was merely another example of those wonderful concepts imagined by the Ancients: the Garden of the Hesperides, Atlantis, the Fountain of Youth or the Fortunate Islands. Perhaps Renaissance minds even identified America as one of them, miraculously rediscovered.

The new lands and peoples thus merely corroborated already familiar traditions. That the Amerindians should exist went without saying; knowledge of their customs revealed nothing really new. One only had to open the works of the Greek and Latin writers to meet people like them. Full of their book-based learning, convinced that they had nothing more to discover – or else trapped in their bigotry – at the turn of the sixteenth century the educated minds of Europe were in no way disconcerted by the evidence that they comprised only half of the human race. Their first reaction was to withdraw into themselves, in a kind of deliberate blindness.

For their part, the Indians were not surprised by the arrival of the navigators from Europe, because they thought they recognized in them their own ancient divinities. According to their traditions, these gods had left them in times past, promising to return one day from the countries of the rising sun. There is ample evidence for such beliefs, which were particularly enduring in Central America, among the Aztecs and the Mayans. They exist also in Peru, and there are traces of them in other places. This illusion explains to a great extent the confused welcome given to the conquerors by the Aztecs and Incas, their clumsiness in organizing resistance when they realized the truth, and the rapid collapse of this resistance.

These strange beliefs have intrigued historians for a long time; in fact, they are deeply rooted in the natural philosophy of the American Indians. Even the cultures which had a lower level of technology and economy than those of Mexico, Central America and the Andes – whether in North America or in the lowlands of South America – believed that objects and beings originated as a series of two-part phenomena. The first, or one of the first of these, resulted in non-Indians being placed alongside Indians. But in this case, as in all those which followed, there was never total equality between the two parts: one was always superior to the other. At the core of the Amerindian philosophy, therefore, lives this idea: that the poles between which natural phenomena and social life operate – heaven and earth, fire and water, near and far, Indians and non-Indians – do not and cannot ever coexist on equal terms, even though one implies the other. It is from this dynamic imbalance that the smooth running of the universe is derived.

As part of this concept, history determined that in the case of the Whites and the Indians the former would heavily influence the destiny of the latter. The Indians did not realize this immediately, because the idea of another race was a metaphysical presupposition in their culture. This explains why, from one end of the New World to the other, the Indians welcomed the Whites, handed over their lands and provided them, often to excess, with everything that the newcomers said that they required. Starting with Columbus in the Bahamas and the Caribbean islands, this was also the experience of Cortés in Mexico, of Pizarro in Peru, Cabral and Villegaignon in Brazil, and of Jacques Cartier in Canada. The fundamental reason is that, long before the arrival of the Whites, the Amerindians believed that their own existence also implied the existence of non-Indians. By their way of thinking, this opposition, which was also a complementary concept, transcended the opposition between them and their enemies, such as neighbouring hostile tribes.

The familiar Mexican and Peruvian traditions therefore acquire a fuller meaning when they are placed in the context of an ideology common to all the peoples of the New World. It enables us to understand more clearly why the Indians were, in the purest sense of the word, *demoralized* when they saw that the Whites, as slaughterers and oppressors, had no connection whatsoever with the image anticipated. The Amerindians' whole concept of the world was destroyed.

In both Americas, these white men effectively saw a table set for them where they could satisfy their rapacious appetite. Is there any need to recall the gigantic profits which they made? First, they removed the mineral treasures, which provided such an impetus to world trade that the coins minted in the gold and silver of the New World spread eastwards with astonishing rapidity to India and even China, as a means of payment for precious goods. The diet of the Old World was transformed by the introduction of plants developed and cultivated by the inventive genius, science and patience of the American Indians – maize, potatoes, tapioca, beans and gourds, tomatoes, peppers, groundnuts, pineapples, avocados and so on. Moreover, there was chocolate, tobacco and, for industrial purposes, rubber. Finally there were medicinal substances, chief among which were coca, the source of cocaine, and curare, a poison used as a muscle relaxant; and cinchona, from which quinine was derived. The Peruvians were not alone in possessing such a varied and complex pharmacopoeia based on animal, vegetable and mineral products; one of the first tasks of the conquerors was to compile an inventory of it. In the savannas and forests of tropical America there still survive – but for how long? – tribes whose knowledge we have hardly begun to grasp.

As soon as the accounts of travellers and missionaries provided European thinkers with direct knowledge of the customs of the Amerindians, and of the similarities and, more often, the differences that existed between these and their own, the reasoning devised by the humanists to protect the pagan Romans and Greeks against the antipathy of the Church acquired a new vigour. Throughout his *Essays*, the French writer Montaigne (1533–92) reinforces the defence of the customs of antiquity by citing those of distant peoples: he uses one to justify the other. However, ancient customs were known only through books, whereas living eye witnesses had described the ways of the American Indians. It was the arguments based on this first-hand information which undoubtedly made the greatest contribution to developing the relativism which would become, alongside the universalism of the philosophers of the eighteenth-century Enlightenment and yet often in direct contradiction of it, one of the two significant components of the political and moral thinking of modern times.

These material and intellectual gains had, as their counterbalance across the Atlantic, the destruction of countless human and natural riches. The extermination of the North American bison, the pillaging of the primeval forests, the enslavement of rivers by means of dams were all fatal to traditional ways of life, and some of these activities are still going on. More effectively than massacres – and there was no lack of those – hitherto unencountered infectious diseases and the religious intolerance introduced by the newcomers inflicted mortal blows on Amerindian society. Entire nations disappeared within a few decades; others saw their populations decimated; others still, saved from annihilation by their size, were brutally subjugated. Extermination of the people, appropriation of their lands, destruction of their monuments and their works of art, eradication of their moral and spiritual values: that was the fate of the conquered races.

The exhibition organized by the Musée de l'Homme, and this book, are intended to commemorate the discovery of the New World; but neither would wish to glorify the spirit of enterprise of the European nations at that time. Europe has at long last realized that the invasion of Western civilization set in motion a cataclysm affecting half of mankind; and Western civilization, in spite of the many virtues which it boasts, remains indelibly tarnished by that act. The aim of this book is to recreate, objectively, the circumstances which enabled or compelled the meeting of the two worlds, to retrace the stages in the defeat of one and, on occasion, the merging of both. Above all, the aim is to offer readers an opportunity for some serious, dignified and solemn reflection on an event which, in both its brightest and darkest aspects, was perhaps the most important in the whole history of the human race.

Claude Lévi-Strauss
Académie Française

'AS INDIAN MOORS OBEY THEIR SPANISH LORDS'

MICHAEL BARRY

The Catholic Sovereigns and Cardinal Cisneros at the surrender of Granada. *Relief on the altar of the Royal Chapel, Granada, by Felipe Vigarny, 1520. Equal partners in a royal marriage, Isabella of Castile and Ferdinand of Aragon united their Kingdoms in 1479. By capturing the last Islamic stronghold in Spain in January 1492, the Sovereigns completed the Christian Reconquista of the Peninsula. Granada's fall was the preliminary condition to their support for Columbus' venture. [Photo Oronoz, © Arch. Photeb]*

At the dawn not only of the New Year of 1492, but of what also turned out to be a new era in the history of the world, the last Moorish ruler in Spain surrendered the keys of his stronghold to King Ferdinand and Queen Isabella sitting on splendidly caparisoned horses outside the walls of the Islamic citadel of Granada: Christopher Columbus was in the crowd to witness the event. Described in the chronicles of the age as tall and ruddy with lank red hair already turned almost entirely white (although he was then only between forty and forty-two years old), the lean, earnest adventurer from Genoa jostled that morning of January 2 1492, among hundreds of onlookers all equally keen to see the culmination of eight centuries of Reconquest in the name of Christ – as they pressed behind the pikes of Captain Gonzalvo de Córdoba's formidable 'Castilian infantry: Catholic Spain's tough, stalwart soldiers, famous throughout Europe of the day and soon to drive rival France's knights

out of Italy by the start of the following decade. Columbus had been waiting in Castile for seven years to see Granada yield. Not until the Moorish fortress capitulated would the Catholic Sovereigns show any hurry to endorse his project for exploring a new western route to India across the Atlantic Ocean. Columbus had spent nine frustrating years in neighbouring Portugal between 1476 and 1485, trying to enlist King John II's support. Then Lisbon's ruler had finally and categorically rejected his plan. This morning, Granada's fall would cause a decisive break in Columbus' luck. As he wrote at the beginning of his sea-diary on August 4 1492: 'Your Highnesses have brought to an end the war with the Moors who reigned in Europe and finished this war in the great city of Granada where in this present year, on the second day of the month of January, I saw planted the royal banners of Your Highnesses by force of arms on the towers of the Alhambra, which is the fortress of the city,

and I did see the Moorish king leave by the gates of the city and kiss the royal hands of Your Highnesses and of His Lordship the Crown Prince.'

By completing their conquest of the Moorish emirate of Granada in early 1492, the two Spanish monarchs, Isabella of Castile and her husband Ferdinand of Aragon, had just reached – or so it yet seemed – the pinnacle of their power. The marriage in 1469 of these fully equal royal partners, heirs to the hitherto separate kingdoms of Castile and Aragon – with Isabella acceding in 1474 to the former and Ferdinand in 1479 to the latter – united into a single strong Spanish realm of some nine million inhabitants the centre and the eastern coast of the Peninsula. The claims to the throne of Castile – and thereby to Iberian overlordship – by King Alfonso V of Portugal, a kingdom rich in trade and ships but weaker in manpower (with only one million subjects), were shattered by Isabella's knights on the battlefield of Toro in 1476.

The new-found might of the Dual Monarchy of the 'Catholic Sovereigns' – Pope Alexander VI would confirm this proud title they claimed in 1494 – already made itself felt in European affairs. Ferdinand inherited for his part a great Catalan kingdom in the Mediterranean and all the rights of the house of Aragon over Sicily, Sardinia and shortly Naples: thus the King of Aragon was also the most powerful prince in Italy with whom the Papacy, Genoa, Venice, Florence, Milan and the king of France all had to reckon. In contrast, Isabella's Castile looked out towards the Atlantic: fifteenth-century Spain's chief export, wool, passed through the great sheep fairs of Burgos and the ports of the Asturias to the mills of the Northern European merchant cities of Bruges, Antwerp, Ghent and Brussels. This close trading link between Iberia's wool-producers and their Flemish markets would be powerfully and purposefully reinforced at the start of the next century by a full

The last Moorish King of Granada surrenders to the Catholic Sovereigns. *Relief on the altar of the Royal Chapel, Granada, by Felipe Vigarny, 1520. Christopher Columbus was in the crowd which witnessed the surrender of the emir Abû 'Abdallâh, known as 'Boabdil' to the Christians. [Photo Oronoz, © Arch. Photeb]*

11

dynastic alliance between Castile and the duchy of the Flanders effected in the person of Charles V, who was both grandson to the Catholic Sovereigns and heir to the house of Burgundy's domains in the Low Countries. But late fifteenth-century Spain was already deeply influenced by Flemish civilization and fashions in many fields – far more so than by the culture of contemporary Renaissance Italy – as could be seen in the Late Gothic symbolism of her architecture and sculpture, the austerely devotional style she favoured in her oil paintings, and the new form of Christian mysticism (Thomas à Kempis' *devotio moderna*) she mainly derived from the teachings of Flemish divines.

In 1482, having dealt with rival dynastic claims and suppressed the last uprisings of feudal magnates, Ferdinand and Isabella felt confident enough to throw their turbulent warrior class against the remaining Islamic enclave of Granada. The conquest of the Moorish kingdom ten years later closed the grip of the royal couple over all of Spain, but even they could hardly have foreseen the new and enormous realm across the seas which Christopher Columbus was shortly to give them.

Religious takeover

While Ferdinand and Isabella proclaimed themselves devoutly respectful of the supremacy of Rome, they jealously maintained authority over their own religious hierarchy and appointed their own Bishops whom the Pope was content to confirm, so creating a state church which would always remain, even in America, a pliant instrument of the Spanish monarchy. It was Isabella and Ferdinand who imposed – and indeed, wrested from Pope Sixtus IV – the reestablishment,

from 1478 onwards, in Castile and then in Aragon, of the Court of the Inquisition, tightly linked to the crown under its first president, the redoubtable Dominican, Tomás de Torquemada.

For all its talk of defending the purity of the Faith, the Inquisition provided the Catholic Sovereigns with an excellent bureaucratic and intelligence-gathering tool by which to pry into the life and privacy of potentially every subject in their realm, whatever his aristocratic or even ecclesiastical rank, a religious device through which to spy and inform in depth: thus giving the Spanish monarchy a new, centralized and uniform administration superimposed upon the old feudal order of Spain – with what to the Sovereigns remained as irksome pockets of local freedoms, quasi-independent baronies, municipal autonomies, regional parliaments and the like. Eventually, once she had tapped the mineral resources of the 'Indies', Spain would emerge as the greatest Catholic power in the world to whom even the Pope had to yield. The sack of Rome by Charles V's German mercenaries in 1527 punished the Holy See for its equivocations in favour of France in a desperate attempt to break the stranglehold of Spanish domination. In 1530, in the cathedral of St Petronius in Bologna, a submissive Pope Clement VII crowned Charles V, ruler of Castile and Aragon, of Flanders and the Germanies, of the Two Sicilies and Milan, and of the 'Indies', as Holy Roman Emperor.

The capture of Granada, the prelude to all this grandeur, not only ended medieval Iberia's unique cultural tradition of (somewhat uneasy) co-existence between the Three Faiths: Christianity, Judaism and Islam; it also removed the final obstacle to the Catholic Sovereigns' support for Columbus' ocean project. Bartolomé de Las Casas

---

THE *REQUERIMIENTO*, OR CALL TO CONVERSION

Many odd quirks in sixteenth-century Spaniards' behaviour on New World battlefields find explanation by reference to the model of Islam's jihâd, the Holy War of their sworn enemies for close on eight hundred years. Such was the custom of the requerimiento *or 'requirement' made mandatory by a decree of King Ferdinand in 1513: before attacking any group of 'Indians', a member of the expeditionary force had to read a document aloud, whereby he summoned them to embrace Christianity and acknowledge the suzerainty of the King. If they refused or gave no response, attack was legitimized: hence the justification for the charge of the Castilians against the Inca in 1532 when the Peruvian ruler proved incapable of grasping what Pizarro's chaplain was asking for. In his* Brevísima relación de la destrucción de las Indias, *Bartolomé de Las Casas (1484–1566) ridiculed this custom, especially when the herald responsible shouted the* requerimiento *at a safe distance and in a language which the locals could not understand. By way of theological justification, the author of Ferdinand's edict, Martín Fernández de Enciso, referred to Deuteronomy 20:10-14: 'When thou comest nigh unto a city to fight against it, then proclaim peace unto it. And it shall be, if it make thee answer of peace, and open unto thee, then it shall be, that all people that is found therein shall be tributaries unto thee, and they shall serve thee. And if they will make no peace with thee, but will make war against thee, then thou shalt besiege it: And when the LORD thy God hath delivered it into thine hands, thou shalt smite every male thereof with the edge of the sword: But the women, and little ones, and the cattle, and all that is in the city, even all the spoil thereof, shalt thou take unto thyself.' The* requerimiento *probably also parodied medieval Muslim laws of war which specifically enjoined an elaborate invitation to surrender and pay tribute (but not necessarily to convert: that was the harsh Castilian crusading touch). When the Ottomans captured Constantinople in 1453 they first offered terms of surrender and tribute to the Byzantines according to a prescription of the Koran.*

(1484–1566), in many ways the most accurate and certainly the most profound and moving of the Castilian chroniclers of the first European encounter with the New World, thus described the political mood in Spain on the eve of 1492: 'The preoccupation of the Sovereigns in those days, as it had been for many years, was the siege which they had installed before Granada; for when princes are occupied at making war, neither sovereign nor kingdom is at peace, with but little attention being given to the most urgent things in life; the ears of men at court are filled only with counsels, consultations and battle plans, and so this single affair does suspend all others and imposes silence upon them.' (*História de las Indias*, I, XIX.) The national preoccupation with Granada explains why Columbus had been so anxious to see the little Islamic kingdom reduced: only a successful outcome to the siege of Granada would remove the last barrier to achievement of his life's ambition.

But the surrender of the emirate on January 2 unleashed a flurry of events, like the release of pent-up forces, which continued throughout 1492, to such an extent that Catholic Castilians would refer to it as the *annus mirabilis*, 'the year of wonders'. The sharpest political observer, Niccolò Macchiavelli of Florence, detected the craft underlying King Ferdinand's distinctive rush to act: 'He has always done and planned great things, which keep in suspense and excite the admiration of his subjects as they contemplate each event. He has linked his actions together in such a way that he leaves no time-gap between them for any man to thwart him.' (*Il Principe*, XXI.)

On 30 March 1492, in the palace of the former Moorish kings of Granada, Ferdinand and Isabella signed the decree which expelled all unconverted Jews from Spain. This measure foreshadowed the ban upon Islam which shortly followed in 1499. This 'pious cruelty' (the phrase is Macchiavelli's) brutally ended the traditional claim of Castilian monarchs to be protectors and 'Emperors of the Three Faiths'. Henceforth there would only be one religion in the Spain of the Catholic Sovereigns, and total obedience to it.

On 17 April 1492, still in Granada but in the fortified camp of Santa Fe (the 'Holy Faith') in view of the ramparts of the Moorish citadel, the sovereigns at long last gave formal approval to Columbus' enterprise. The chronicle of Las Casas puts it romantically, describing how the admiral-to-be was hastily recalled by an *alguazil*, or mounted police-officer, at a few hours' gallop from Granada, just as the disappointed adventurer was riding off to submit his plan at all odds to the kings of France or England. His brother Bartolomeo had preceded him, and after undertaking a fruitless visit to Henry VII in London, had taken up residence in the court of Charles VIII in Paris.

On 3 August, the round-shaped *nao* and the two lighter caravels of the explorer – newly ennobled and promoted to Admiral and Viceroy of all lands in the 'Indies' to be discovered – weighed

Map by the Arab geographer Al-Idrîsî (*1100–1160*). *Frontispiece illustrating the* Muqaddimah, *or 'Introduction to the Science of History', by the fourteenth-century Tunisian philosopher-historian Ibn Khadûn. Originally from Ceuta on the Moroccan coast, Al-Idrîsî lived at the court of the Norman Kings of Sicily, Roger II and William I, and has become a symbol of the immense influence exerted by Islamic culture on Latin-Christian civilisation in the twelfth century. His representation of the known world, from his* Kitâb Rujâr, *or 'Book of Roger', remained authoritative not only among Muslims but also in learned Christian circles until the Renaissance. Al-Idrîsî's map preserves the basic outlines of Greek cosmography, but ignores the tripartite division of the land-mass – into a 'Europe', an 'Asia' and an 'Africa' (or 'Lybia') – imagined by the Greeks. In Al-Idrîsî's view, the land-mass was a single occumene, or inhabited World-Island, gouged by deep gulfs and encircled by a single ocean (borrowed from the Ôkeanos of the Greeks, becoming Ûqiyânûs in medieval Arabic). According to medieval Arabic mythology, the farther shore of the ocean was the outer rim of the world, marked by a chain of magic mountains, known as Qâf, consisting of magnetic rocks which caused compass needles to go wild and sucked the iron nails out of ships, causing vessels to disintegrate and sink. Other names for this feared ocean were al-Bahr al-Muhît, 'the all-encircling sea', and Bahr az-Zulumât, 'the Sea of Darkness'. It should be noted that Al-Idrîsî's map shows Africa as a stylized body of land, shortened, rounded, and theoretically circumnavigable since it appears bathed by the same ocean as the shores of India: a world-view accepted by the fifteenth-century Portuguese, who believed that if they sailed around Africa, they could reach the Orient. [The Bodleian Library, Oxford. Photo © the library, Arch. Photeb]*

anchor in Palos, a small port on the Atlantic coast of Andalusia. On 6 September, these ships left the Canary Islands. The Canaries were a Castilian possession on what were at that time the known limits of the western ocean. The islands had been discovered in 1405, and the Castilians had then proceeded to conquer and enslave the islanders with grim thoroughness. The Guanchos of Berber stock had still been following a neolithic way of life in the early fifteenth century, depending for their food and clothing on herds of goats; their sole means of defence against the steel-clad invaders had been their spears, whose tips were hardened in fire. The fate of these natives of the Canaries foreshadowed what would happen all too soon to the natives of the Antilles.

The cultural outlook

Columbus' project and the adventure of 1492 were the culmination of a complex pattern of events, not only social, commercial and technological in nature, but also politically and religiously deeply felt, that characterized Latin European civilization generally at the close of the Middle Ages. The

Our Lady of the Navigators, *by Alejo Fernández (1477–1545). Is the figure on the extreme left the real Christopher Columbus? This was a theory suggested by Samuel Eliot Morison in 1942. Certainly the bearded, angular features correspond more closely to Las Casas' descriptions than other conventional representations. 'The Indians approached the Admiral, who they took to be the leader because of the eminence and authority that exuded from him…and they reached out and touched his beard in amazement.' [Alcázar, Seville. Photo © G. Dagli-Orti]*

their activities in 'the Indies' to certain cultural priorities which may surprise us.

The armoured and mounted Spanish lancers shortly to descend in a burst of steel and powder upon the peoples of the New World – Columbus himself landed his first shipment of warhorses in Haiti in 1493 in order to enslave the natives – were essentially knights: a breed of equestrian warrior no different from the class of men who had ridden through the horseshoe-arched gates of the Alhambra only a few months before under a blaze of Aragonese and Castilian heraldry – banners of Crosses of Saint James and coats of arms displaying paly of gules and gold, towers and lions rampant.

For Castilians, no break appeared to have occurred between the taking of Granada on January 2 1492 and Columbus' first anchorage off the Antilles on October 12. Cortés stressed this continuity of conquest between the Old World and the New when he wrote to Charles V about his first entrance into a large Mexican town: 'It is almost unbelievable, but this place is much larger than Granada, much stronger, endowed with buildings which are just as handsome, and far more populous than was Granada when she was taken. (*II Carta de Relación,* 30 October 1519.)

Castile in 1492 – legally speaking, Columbus' enterprise was placed under the sole jurisdiction of the crown of Castile, not that of Aragon – was a horseman's country, looked landwards, was the least endowed with seafaring tradition of the three Iberian nations of the fifteenth century. Columbus brought with him a naval technique and a vision of things maritime acquired partly from his native Genoa and most especially in Lisbon, capital of the most enterprising seafaring nation in the fifteenth-century world. Castile's caravels always remained vessels of pure Portuguese design. In the sixteenth century their main purpose was to discharge a class of landlubber Spanish knights who endeavoured to re-create and exploit in the New World the agricultural, herding and mining society from which they came in the Old. The Portuguese colonial venture differed sharply from that of contemporary Castile. Portugal's expansion round the shoreline of Africa, then on to the East Indies and ultimately to Brazil, was that of a seagoing mercantile empire under a crown monopoly dependent on a far-flung network of ocean-side trading posts that ranged virtually around the world by the middle of the sixteenth century. Lisbon's fifteenth- and sixteenth-century school of cartography embodied an intellectual revolution in its new oceanic conception of the world that still represents the supreme scientific contribution of any of the Iberian nations to the culture of the European Renaissance. When Columbus resided and learned most of his trade in Lisbon in 1476–1485, Portugal, not Castile, was the true explorer-kingdom. Castile stumbled into its share of maritime empire through the fortunate accident of the Catholic Sovereigns' endorsement of Columbus' project. What is no accident is that it

Genoese navigator, not only through his actions but in his surviving writings as well – as collected by Las Casas – mirrors the main cultural preoccupations of his age. Numerous elements obviously went in to making the world revolution of 1492. Its most important immediate result, apart from the wholly accidental discovery of the New World, lay in Western Europe's technological surge forward through every ocean of the globe: a triumph whose price was paid on American soil, as we know, in the unspeakable suffering of the native peoples – which the coastal peoples of West Africa in turn came quickly and closely to share, through slavery, by the opening decades of the sixteenth century. Nonetheless, late fifteenth- and early sixteenth-century Europeans consciously ascribed was naval expeditions flying the Portuguese flag which first established that the land mass glimpsed by Columbus was truly a New World and not, as the Genoese navigator continued stubbornly to believe until his death in 1506, an outlying peninsula of Asia. Sailing in Vasco da Gama's pioneering wake of 1498, the Portuguese commander Perálvares Cabral clearly realized that he had touched upon the shore of an entirely new body of land when he sighted the eastern tip of Brazil in 1500 in his great loop across the south Atlantic which eventually allowed him to round the Cape of South Africa and proceed to India (the real India). This first Brazilian sighting was followed by the coastal explorations of the Florentine Amérigo Vespucci in Portuguese service in 1501–1502. This is why, in 1507, the German cartographer Martin Waldseemüller gave the latinized name of Amérigo to the new continent. The terms 'Indians' and 'West Indies' perpetuate Columbus' enormous ethnographical and geographical error; yet such was the magic associated at the turn of the fifteenth and sixteenth centuries with the name 'India' that the Spanish Empire in the New World chose to continue to cloak itself in an utterly phantasmagorical self-designation as *Las Indias*: a parody, as it were, of the real maritime Indian empire of the age, the one which the sixteenth-century Portuguese were staking out for themselves with trading posts along the coastal fringes of authentically Muslim and Hindu Asia.

Lisbon's initial cold-shoulder attitude towards Columbus was partly due to the fact that, as the European protagonist of nearly all oceanfaring exploration throughout the fifteenth century, the Portuguese crown was continuously pestered by cranks from every corner of Western Christendom asking for ships, crew, and financial backing for harebrained schemes of 'discovery'. In 1485, in the same year that King John II turned down Columbus' project as cartographically impossible, he also rejected a fantastic plan submitted by a Flemish adventurer, Ferdinand Van Olmen, proposing to search for the mythic Seven Cities of Cíbola far out in the Western Ocean. Hard-headed John II was then committing his capital to finding a practical route to India by rounding Africa. The Portuguese captain Bartolomeu Dias carried out the first part of this programme by reaching the Cape and sighting the Indian Ocean in 1487. Under John's successor, King Emmanuel I, Vasco da Gama completed the planned work of exploration, rounded the Cape and crossed to the port of Calicut in South India in 1498. However the Portuguese also had sound theoretical reasons for refuting Columbus' plan. John II's cartographers were perfectly aware that the world was round: this had been common knowledge among all learned men since the astronomical calculations of the Alexandrian Greeks. But furthermore, in the opinion of the King's advisers, Columbus seriously underestimated the surmised circumference of the

Polyptych of St Vincent: Panel of the Infante *(c. 1460). King Alfonso V of Portugal and his royal family in prayer before the patron saint of navigators. Near the kneeling young ruler, on the right, stand the youthful Crown Prince and future King John II, and Alfonso V's famous uncle, the Infante Prince Henry the Navigator – whose intense expression, seamed features, clipped moustache and turban-like chaperon headdress (fashionable in mid-fifteenth century Europe) were easily identified, when this polyptych was rediscovered at the end of the last century, from a similar-looking miniature in Azurara's Chronicle of the Deeds of Guinea. This oil is attributed to Nuno Gonçalves – the figure in the upper left-hand corner may be his self-portrait – who ranks as the greatest painter of fifteenth-century Iberia. The Flemish influence, with its late medieval mystic fervour, remained far more marked than that of Italy in the painting of Spain and Portugal in Columbus' generation, just as architecture was still Late Gothic – although interpreted with increasing flamboyance not devoid of Moorish touches (known as the 'Manueline' style in Portugal from the name of King Emmanuel, reigned 1495–1521, and as the 'Plateresque' in Castile, from the Spanish platero meaning 'silversmith'). Gonçalves' panels depict the entire range of fifteenth-century Portuguese society including, in other sections not reproduced here, knights, clerics, fishermen, sailors, and even a helmeted and bearded Moorish vassal and a Rabbi (somewhat cruelly caricatured) holding his open Torah. Such figures as a Muslim tributary emir or a Jewish dignitary in a Christian Iberian court would no longer be acceptable by the end of the fifteenth century, after the expulsion of all unconverted Jews from Castile in 1492 and from Portugal in 1496 (under Castilian pressure), followed by the prohibition of Islam throughout Spanish territory in 1499. [Museu de Arte Antigua, Lisbon. Photo María Novais, © Arch. Photeb]*

globe and the distance westwards between the Iberian peninsula and the coast of Asia. They were, of course, right.

The conquerers' make-believe world

While fifteenth- and sixteenth-century Iberians charted the coasts of the New World with commendable accuracy, their descriptions of local human realities were warped to fit into their own frame of mind, characterized by the knightly ethic and crusading zeal.

Christopher Columbus insisted until the end of his life that the main purpose of his expedition was to finance the Christian reconquest of Jerusalem by finding gold in the Indies. In his will, drawn up in 1505, he writes: 'At the time that I left to discover the Indies, I did so with the intention of beseeching the King and Queen our Sovereigns that, from the income that their Highnesses would derive from the Indies, they should determine how much they should disburse for the conquest of Jerusalem. Thus did I entreat.'

The Iberian peninsula in 1492 was steeped in crusading fervour following the capture of Granada. The eminent French scholar Marcel Bataillon has brought to life some of the more agitated figures of the period, such as the popular preacher Fray Melchior, who interpreted the recent fall of the emirate as an apocalyptic sign forecasting the imminent liberation of Jerusalem, the downfall of Islam throughout the world, and finally the approaching End of Time. The Flemish cleric, Charles de Bovelles, repeatedly urged the Spanish monarchs to undertake a total holy war against the Muslims and reminded Cardinal Cisneros of this miracle: after the surrender of Granada, workmen were said to have found in the ruins of an old church in Toledo a vase decorated with paintings of fallen Moors, with the inscription: 'When this will be seen by the eyes of man, destruction will be imminent for those hereon depicted'. Religious excitement hardly spared the Catholic Sovereigns themselves after they entered Granada, and certainly spurred their agreement to Columbus' scheme, which had been considered little short of insane as late as 1490 by the wisest brains of the Castilian Royal Council, presided over by the learned ecclesiastic Talavera, who was well informed about the cartographical science of neighbouring Portugal.

Cardinal Cisneros for his part pressed King Ferdinand to pursue the Granada crusade across the straits to Africa, just as the Portuguese had been harassing the Moroccan sultanate for decades and setting up impregnable fortresses along this shoreline. In 1509, Cisneros was granted his wish and personally led the victorious naval expedition which captured the coastal town of Oran, successfully held by Spain for more than two centuries against the various Islamic powers which succeeded one another in Algiers. On his return from the conquest of Mexico, Cortés, by then more than fifty years old, fought again beneath the walls of Algiers in 1541. However, staunch resistance by the mountain Berber tribal peoples, and the growth of Ottoman naval power in the Mediterranean, effectively checked any Iberian expansion in North Africa and helped to divert it towards shores infinitely more remote.

The tradition of a magic painted vase invoked by the cleric Charles de Bovelles, thought to have been found in 1492 in the ruins of a Toledo church and believed to predict the coming downfall not only of the North African Muslims but of infidels everywhere, was actually still another example of heavy but unusually unconscious medieval Christian Iberian cultural borrowing from the folklore of the Spanish Moors themselves. The Arabic chronicles of the Islamic conquest of Spain, in the eighth century, had been full of very similar stories telling of magic mirrors and frescoes with doom-laden inscriptions

THE CURSE OF
KING RODERICUS
The Arabic folk tales which related the Islamic conquest of Spain passed virtually intact from Moorish into Spanish Christian literature at the turn of the eleventh and twelfth century and formed the core of what became the national mythology of medieval Christian Spain, as in the popular songs of the fifteenth-century Castilian *Romancero*: a legendary cycle mostly centered around the figure of the last Gothic king of Spain, Rodericus or Rodrigo, shown as overwhelmed by various omens foretelling his own downfall and the Arab conquest as a punishment for his sins. Castilian and Portuguese chroniclers regarded the curse brought upon Spain by the sins of King Rodericus as having finally been lifted with the triumphant recapture of Granada, and they thoroughly Christianized these tales in order to turn them against their own enemies, the Moors themselves at first, and then even against the native rulers of the New World.

discovered in old palaces, warning the arrogant and infidel Christian kings of Toledo of their impending destruction at the hands of the Arab warriors of the True Faith.

Such underlying Moorish literary influence is very evident in several of the Spanish chroniclers' depictions of the sixteenth-century America. In Mexico, the Franciscan friar and chronicler, Bernardino de Sahagún (1499–1570), who usually shows considerable sensitivity to the subtleties of the local culture, mingles an obvious Spanish-Arabic motif with authentic Aztec lore in his account of the prophecies which were supposed to have warned the last Aztec ruler of the imminent destruction of his empire: for example, where he tells the story of the magic mirror of black obsidian borne upon the head of a bird, wherein Moctezuma ('Montezuma') deciphered within the sombre reflections of the polished stone the melancholy prediction of his own overthrow. Regarding Peru, the aristocratic historian Garcilaso de la Vega

Castilian cavalry before an assault against the Moors of Granada. *Painted in the Palace of the Escorial for King Philip II about 150 years after the event but scrupulous in its depiction of the equipment and equestrian style of contemporary Spanish knights. The knights ride 'long', as befits lancers, in the manner of all heavy European cavalry of the day: that is, with stirrup leathers left so long that a rider's legs were stretched full length, feet pointed well forward and body braced against the high steel-plated cantle of the saddle, in order to absorb the terrific shock of the lance-thrust: driven home with the irresistible force of mount and knight together behind it. What is known as the modern 'Western' style of riding, bequeathed by Mexican cattle-herders to Texan and other US cattlemen, actually has faithfully preserved to this day the 'long' leg of Cortés and his sixteenth-century conquistadores. By contrast, in the lower part of the painting, the King's Christian scouts ride a la jinete, that is, in the 'Moorish' style borrowed from their opponents: stirrup leathers here are pulled up short, allowing the lightly armed horseman to rise from his saddle and virtually stand in his stirrups, the better to slash with his sabre, loose an arrow or cast a javelin. This manner of riding 'short', in fact, corresponds more closely with the modern balanced 'English' style of horsemanship. In present-day Spanish, the very word jinete has come to mean, simply, 'horseman'. But fifteenth-century Spanish knights in the Wars of Granada learned to use both styles of horsemanship: that is, the 'short' to reconnoitre and harass, and the 'long' to charge and crush. Spain's superb cavalry was one of the reasons she conquered the New World so rapidly. [Fresco in the Hall of Battles, Escorial Palace, near Madrid. Photo © Oronoz, Artephot]*

(1539–1616), the son of a Castilian knight and an Inca princess, evokes similar omens at the beginning of his own chronicle: according to Garcilaso, three years before the first landing of the Spaniards in 1531, the sky above Peru was streaked with comets, the mountains were shaken by earthquakes, the sea began to boil, the Inca Huaina Capac saw an eagle attacked by vultures fall at his feet, and the moon appeared encircled by three rings – blood-red, green and smoky black – which signified for the royal soothsayer a wave of blood, then the fall of the Empire, and finally the dispersal of its glory 'like so much smoke'. For Garcilaso, 'this showed the mercy of the Lord who took pity on the Gentiles of the New World, which is why he inspired so much zeal and courage in the hearts of the Spaniards who brought to them the light of the Gospel.' (*Comentários reales*, bk X.)

This is why caution is in order when reading the accounts of New World civilizations transmitted by sixteenth-century Iberian chroniclers whose minds were soaked in the imagery of their own traditional crusading and knightly lore. At the turn of the fifteenth and sixteenth centuries, as is well known, the popular craze for romances of chivalry was probably at its height throughout the Iberian world – Cervantes' devastating satire of these novels would only come out some four generations later, in 1604 – and was satisfied at relatively cheap cost by the new printing presses set up by the German immigrant, Hans Cromberger, in Seville (in spite of the grumblings of the Inquisition: both Charles V of Spain and Emmanuel I of Portugal were avid readers of his kind of books). The present-day map of America is littered with colourful names which are none other than the projection of the epics and fantasies of Castilian chivalry. Entering Mexico-Tenochtitlán with Cortés in 1519, Bernal Díaz del Castillo uttered a famous sentence when he saw the splendours of the Aztec capital: 'We were lost in admiration and said to one another that everything resembled the enchantments told of in the book of *Amadís*.' (*Historia Verdadera de la Conquista de Nueva España*, ch.87.) The imagination of the conquerors fed on the *Amadís of Gaul*, the *Romancero of King Rodericus*, and various adaptations of the *Alexander Romance*.

Gold and the cross

In such a cultural context, Columbus' conception of his expedition as a crusade was by no means out of touch with the temper of his times, and certainly no mere cynical mask for empire-building. No doubt economic needs were a driving force, then as now, but prevailing religious attitudes coloured and modified patterns of behaviour deeply. As a warlike manifestation of an older form of European civilization, the Crusades may not be reduced to a simple list of military expeditions to Jerusalem, but correspond rather to a permanent state of mind in traditional Western Christendom: where medieval trends of thought lingered down to at least the middle of the seventeenth century.

The 'Crusade' under such a name was first preached by Pope Urban II at Clermont in France in 1095, when he called upon Christian knights to deliver Jerusalem from the infidel with a string of quotes from the Old Testament (none from the New) and especially from Deuteronomy. Justifying defence of the cross by means of the sword for the greater good of the Church, the Pope's sermon became the model for all later medieval homilies preached on behalf of Crusading (with identical citations from Deuteronomy). The Crusade implied perpetual readiness for holy war, at first directed against Islam but then also against other creeds or heresies: whether Jews, Albigensians, Greek Orthodox Christians, or eventually 'pagans' in the New World.

The Crusade for Jerusalem and the Spanish *reconquista* constituted rigorously equivalent holy wars, however, in the eyes of Urban II, who specifically exempted Iberian knights from fighting in Palestine: their services were far too urgently required against the Andalusian Moors. Moreover knights from other European lands also participated in the Iberian Crusade: the country of Portugal, for example, was founded in the twelfth century on a strip of territory seized from the Moors by an expatriate French knight, and in 1147, an Anglo-Norman fleet en route to Jerusalem helped capture what became its capital city, the emirate of Lisbon. Apart from material improvements in the quality of their ships, harness and weaponry with the obvious addition of fire power (which ultimately made knighthood obsolete but not quite yet at this date), very little still distinguished late-fifteenth- and sixteenth-century Iberian *conquistadores* from their medieval forebears, and certainly nothing in their general religious outlook or knightly moral code. Compared to any one of the more famous twelfth-century Crusaders in

Palestine (Godfrey de Bouillon wading his horse through the blood in Jerusalem's streets, for example, or the robber baron Renaud de Châtillon), Cortés or Pizarro in America cannot be said to show any real decline in ethical standards, and broadly display very similar behaviour: self-assured religious zeal mingled with frozen cruelty towards a dehumanized enemy; identical cynicism in striking deals or even forming alliances with the same enemy where circumstances demanded; comparable lust for booty in the name of a sacred cause; and most especially, a craving for fiefs (with attached serfs) to be carved out of conquered territory in order to ensure one's livelihood and knightly social status and cut a name in the world.

Even sceptical modern historians on the alert for economic motives confess how hard it is to separate the tightly intertwined motivations of greed and religious faith amongst the *conquistadores*. Cortés and his men trapped and slaughtered with matchlock fire a dense crowd of unarmed natives in the public square of Cholula in Mexico in 1519; then the same Cortés raised a wooden cross on the highest pyramid and, with regard to the survivors, 'made known most clearly to them all things concerning the Holy Faith, that they should cease to worship idols and no more sacrifice nor eat the flesh of man' (Bernal Díaz ch.83). Thus not only Castilians. No sixteenth-century Iberians kept out a sharper eye for a hard bargain to be struck in the spice trade with whatever local commercial partner – Hindu or Muslim – than King Emmanuel's shrewd governors in the Portuguese East Indies. The same officers also thought nothing of turning into outright pirates at the expense of Arab shipping in the Indian Ocean, confiscating cargoes of pepper and cinnamon, ordering the cutting off of the hands and feet of captive crews, shutting them up in the holds of their vessels and burning them alive. Yet after leaving in his wake a swathe of sunken Muslim *dhow-s* and devastated villages along the southern coast of Arabia, governor Albuquerque dropped to his knees on his deck in ecstasy before his vision of a cross of light filling the skies off the beach of Ethiopia in 1513: 'It was seen from numerous vessels, and many were those who knelt to worship it, shedding tears of devotion all the while' (Letter to King Emmanuel I, 4 December 1513). Modern-minded Portuguese historians now minimize this crusading aspect of their nation's expansionist past to stress its cooler economic drives. They have a point. But the knightly ethic did not necessarily always coincide with mercantile motives or even with common sense, and economic rationalization can do little to explain away the fact that the young and childless King Sebastian in 1578 led the flower of Portuguese chivalry to their deaths, against all better advice, in a suicidal crusading attempt to conquer the mountainous Moroccan interior: resulting not only in his own demise without issue but in the political collapse of Renaissance Portugal and its annexation by Castile.

St James of Compostela, Killer of Moors, *by Juan de Flandes, 1500. 'Santiago Matamoros' rides to the rescue of Christian knights, sword in hand, just as the battle seems lost. The contemporary Spanish essayist Américo Castro has pointed out that traditional Iberian painters depict the Apostle with the same face as Christ: St James the Major is the Saviour's twin brother, but mounted and armed. According to Castro, the Spanish medieval cult of Santiago reflected the desperate need of the Christian North to give itself a protective warrior-saint to stand against the armed Prophet of the Islamic South: St James on horseback, according to Castro's thought-provoking view, was essentially a mirror-image of Muhammad. The conquistadores who followed Cortés often thought they saw Santiago on Mexican battlefields; in the words of the chronicler Oviedo, 'they affirmed that one saw the Apostle St James fighting on a white horse in favour of the Christians; and the Indians said that the horse, using his hooves and teeth, killed them too.' Horses and steel swords, caravels and artillery pieces, unshakeable faith in Santiago, and finally the virus of smallpox, of which the Spaniards were unconscious and immunized bearers, together account for the shattering impact of the Iberian assault upon the New World. [Museo Lázaro Galdiano, Madrid. Photo Oronoz, © Arch. Photeb]*

The Fountain of Youth, *by Hieronymus Bosch (1450–1516). Detail from 'The Garden of Delights', a painting which once belonged to King Philip II of Spain. This Old World myth was fantasized and projected upon the map of the New by the governor of Puerto Rico, Don Juan Ponce de León: in the course of his futile search, he discovered Bimini and Florida in 1511–1512. [Prado, Madrid. Photo Ornoz, © Arch. Photeb]*

In the theological view of the age, crusading and plunder were no contradiction in terms, but complemented one another: for only gold or the profit from traffic in spices or slaves could provide the sinews for the ultimate liberation of Jerusalem.

In a letter to King Ferdinand and Queen Isabella sent from Jamaica (which he still thought was somewhere in the East Indies) on 7 July 1503, Christopher Columbus himself provides us with the most eloquent – and fervently believed – religious rationalization of the economic aspect to crusading perhaps ever written in his century: 'The Genoese, the Venetians, and all the nations who have ever possessed pearls, precious stones or other things of value, have all carried them to the farthest ends of the earth to barter and convert them into gold; for gold is a most excellent thing; it is with gold that one constitutes treasure; he who possesses gold may do whatsoever he wishes in the world, and thereby even lead souls to Paradise.'

Given that the *conquistadores* made no secret of their lust for gold, it is, of course, legitimate to consider the Crusades as large-scale plundering expeditions. Viewed in such light, the first Crusades of the eleventh and twelfth centuries do appear as a continuation of the great migration of Northern European warrior peoples at the expense of the richer and more civilized lands of the southern and eastern Mediterranean, which had accepted Islam in the early Middle Ages. The vast majority of Spanish Muslims were of course local converts, as is clear from the language which most of them spoke at the time of the fall of Granada: not the classical Arabic of their higher culture and liturgy, but a Romance dialect close to Castilian, *aljamiado*, mixed to be sure with many Arabic words. Early medieval Moorish Spain included the most populous cities and fertile portions of the Peninsula, and excited the envy and hatred of the small, barbaric, rural and poverty-stricken Christian kingdoms to the north.

If any one date may be retained to mark the beginning of the end of the age of chivalry, Sebastian's Moroccan disaster of 1578 is as good as any; (Castile's own knightly pride was soon sapped by the catastrophe to its Armada in 1588, and the generation of Cervantes matured in the shadow of these twin Iberian defeats.)

But in the age of self-confident Iberian exploration and conquest, that is, down to roughly the third quarter of the sixteenth century, knightly visions of gold and the cross remained blended, as in the celebrated remark made by that archetypal *conquistador*, Bernal Díaz, in Mexico: 'I have always shown zeal as a good soldier to serve God and the King our lord by striving to gain honour as should any nobleman, and also to wax rich' (ch. 1).

THE FOUNTAIN OF YOUTH

This was originally an Arabic motif transmitted to Christian Spain through one of the Islamic versions of the Alexander Romance. The pseudo-Callisthenes Alexander Romance was popular in Western Christendom and among medieval Muslims, who read the tales in Arabic translation and added motifs of their own: notably the story of the Fountain of Life, a tradition of Mesopotamian origin which reappears in the Koran, and was much meditated upon for its rich spiritual symbolism by Muslim mystics in Spain and elsewhere. According to the Arabic version, beyond the darkness wherein the sun sets, exists a miraculous fountain: whoever finds and bathes in it gains eternal life. Absorbed into medieval Christian folklore, this theme notably figures in that book of fantastic Travels, attributed to Sir John Mandeville, a fourteenth-century Anglo-Norman knight supposed to have returned after a pilgrimage to Jerusalem from a journey across Asia. Columbus had been an avid reader of the book. As Mandeville told it, he who bathed in the Fountain secured, not only eternal life but also everlasting youth. In 1512–1513, Don Juan Ponce de León left Puerto Rico to look for this magic Fountain among the Bimini Islands, apparently having misunderstood what the Carib natives were telling him. According to the chronicler Oviedo, 'it was so often repeated and assured by the Indians in these regions that the caravels of Juan Ponce and his men became lost for more than six months in these islands, in search of this Fount: which was a great deceipt on the part of the Indians, and an even greater extravagance (desvarío) in believing them on the part of the Christians.' (História general y natural de las Indias, XVI, xi.) Nevertheless, Ponce de León discovered the peninsula which he named 'Florida', in honour of Flower Sunday, or Easter.

The splendour and plunder of Spanish Islam

In northern Christian eyes, Spanish Islam at the height of its power in the tenth and early eleventh centuries appeared to gleam with wealth. The monetary economy of the caliphate of Cordova remained solidly based on a gold standard and was integrated into that of the Islamic world as a whole; the Spanish caliphs minted magnificent gold coinage stamped with distinctive calligraphic emblems at a time when the petty Christian kingdoms of Castile or León bartered in kind or in small silver coins alone. Islamic Andalusia, *Al-Andalus* in Arabic, lay on the European end of the trail of African gold dust, transported by caravans from the shores where it was panned along the bends of the River Niger. The Muslim dynasties of Cordova and then Seville maintained vital political and military connections with the Moroccan hinterland, whose markets linked with the lucrative gold-trail across the Sahara and whose tough mountain tribes provided the shock troops necessary to counter any attacks from the northern Christians. During intervals of peace, Al-Andalus played a key rôle as one of southern Europe's major commercial centres, where crude Northerners exchanged their raw materials for export to the Islamic world: wood, furs, silver ingots, and even (down to the eleventh century) slaves of European stock. In return, Cordova sold to barbarian Europe a variety of precious foodstuffs from the Islamic world (including Indian spices transported through Alexandria) as well as its own fine crafts and – most important of all – the gold dust from the South melted into the caliphate's splendid coinage.

Down to the mid-eleventh century, the relationship of the bleak Christian baronies of the North to the glittering caliphate of the south remained one of close economic dependence, accompanied by a sense of admiration tainted with jealousy and fear – negative emotions which the northerners sublimated and self-justified in marked religious hatred for Islam (a situation not dissimilar – in reverse – to feelings entertained in much of today's Islamic world in regard to the modern West). As far as medieval Muslims were concerned, Al-Andalus stood, for all its fertility, culture and wealth, as a vulnerable frontier outpost of their civilization. Christian warbands continually raided Muslim border settlements in order to plunder the caliphate's precious coins that were so much in demand in the gold-starved north. 'You are worthy to lead men into Moorish territory by night' – *bueno eres para regir gente en tierra de moros de noche* – became a standard Castilian proverb once applied to marauding knights but attested in later fifteenth-century literature – as in Fernando de Rojas' *La Celestina* – simply to designate the all-around qualities of any well-appointed Christian Spanish gentleman.

While the northern Christians expressed detestation for the Islamic South, they were drawn to its civilization and inadvertently imitated many of its outward forms. From this mixture of conscious repulsion and unconscious attraction regarding Islamic civilization were born, indeed, the characteristically variegated traits of traditional Spanish Christian culture. The contemporary Spanish essayist Américo Castro, in his key study of the fervent medieval Iberian cult of *Santiago*, Saint James the Apostle, at the northern Spanish shrine of Compostela, believes that 'Santiago' represented something more than just another of the many armoured saints of the Middle Ages (St Michael, St George and the like) whose images served to glorify and sanctify the knightly class. In medieval Spanish eyes, St James appeared as the twin brother of Christ, but mounted and armed with a sword, an Apostle not of Peace but of War, who could, when invoked, miraculously intervene in battle against Moors – or later, in the New World, against Aztecs. Castro sees this cult figure of Santiago as an unconscious reproduction, as it were as a needed psychological counterpart, among northern Christians, of the Armed Prophet of their Muslim opponents. Indeed the very notion of the Crusade may have been, again, a crude retort to, and unconscious parody of, Islam's *jihâd*.

Morally fortified with what was, in any case, their psychological equivalent of the *jihâd*, the Castilians pierced through Muslim defences by taking Toledo in 1085: this irretrievable disaster for Spanish Islam was followed, like knells, by the fall of Lisbon in 1147; then the battle of Las Navas de Tolosa in 1212 where the allied knighthoods of Castile, Aragon and Portugal broke the military backbone of Andalusian resistance; and finally the surrenders: Valencia to Aragon in 1238, Cordova and then Seville to the Castilians in 1236 and 1248 respectively. From then on there remained only the emirate of Granada, usually as a tributary state to Castile, and only internal feuds and dynastic troubles in Castile spared this last hold out of Spanish Islam until the final ten-year assault by Ferdinand and Isabella in 1482–92.

From their capture of Toledo in 1085 down to their final entry into Granada in 1492, Castilian rulers invariably retained and consciously imitated the administrative practices of the Moorish princes, again in a rather crude empirical manner. Subject religious communities, Muslim and Jew, were granted toleration in return for tribute, accepting inferior status and relinquishing the right to proselytize, for such had been the rule of the caliphate with regard to Christians and Jews. But medieval Castilian tolerance for the other two faiths, so long as such forbearance lasted (down to 1492 for Jews and 1499 for Muslims), was relative and based on hard pragmatism. Jews, whose knowledge of Arabic gave them access to Muslim administrative experience, were forced into service in an ambiguous status as the king's main tax-collectors because as the most vulnerable group in the realm, they depended on the monarch's protection alone and he could mercilessly control them: moreover popular discontent could always be deflected against Jews when taxes rose, thus screening royal prestige. Moors, in fact, were humiliated far more than Jews in medieval Castile because they were retained as serfs.

The Christian conquest of Islamic Spain at long last placed enormous reserves of African gold in the hands of northern monarchs, and the thirteenth-century minting of yellow bullion by Western European rulers for the first time since the fall of the Roman Empire was a telling sign of Latin Christendom's resurgence in the Mediterranean. But even by the end of the fifteenth century, Christian Europe had not yet slaked its thirst for precious metal. The Portuguese on the coast of Guinea hoped to tap African gold production at its source. Ultimately only America's mines provided Europe with the bullion it wanted.

The agricultural plundering of Andalusian Islam not only gave Christendom its taste for new foods such as sugar cane, oranges, lemons, apricots, rice and mulberries, but also provided Christian barons with a skilled new Muslim workforce on the land, subjugated and exploitable. Large-scale enfeoffment of Moorish lands with enslaved peasants by Aragonese, Castilian and Portuguese knights in thirteenth-, fourteenth- and fifteenth-century Valencia, Andalusia and the Algarve, closely prefigured future *conquistador* practice in the Antilles, Mexico and Peru.

The thirteenth-century breakthrough of the *Reconquista* did, however, present the Castilian Kings with an immediate political paradox: their effective royal power was actually weakened. For Castile's monarchs had only been able to break down Muslim defences by recourse to feudal levies among their barons and through the key military support provided by the Masters of the three main orders of Spanish chivalry: the Knights of Santiago, Calatrava and Alcántara. Conquered territories were rewarded by the monarchy as autonomous fiefs to those knights who operated as 'advanced' or frontline military leaders (*adelantados*). Such knights swore oaths of fealty, but ruled in virtual independence over vast new estates in the south where the King's writ ran little. The Masters of the military Orders enjoyed similar autonomy: the Brethren were endowed by the monarch with 'entrusted' lands, *encomiendas*, with allocations or *repartimientos* of Moorish peasants compelled into forced collective labour, for whose souls the knights assumed responsibility before the King with the charge of ensuring their gradual conversion to Christianity.

Most of these social patterns were, from the very first, transferred intact to sixteenth-century Spanish America.

Islamic practices were suffered to linger longer among *Morisco* serfs under the more tolerant Aragonese nobles of the Valencia region – into the seventeenth century, in fact – than in sterner, Castilian-ruled Andalusia: but the important thing for Castilian or Aragonese grandees alike was that *repartimientos* of Moorish peasants represented their main source of wealth: 'The more your Moors, the more your winnings' (*Más moros, más ganancias*), according to another brutal proverb quoted by Fernando de Rojas in 1499.

Transplanted fiefs

Three years after the surrender of Granada, in the island of Haiti in 1495, the first two captains of *conquistadores* in America – Christopher Columbus in his position as Viceroy and his brother Bartolomeo – fully recreated the Old World system of *encomiendas* with *repartimientos* or distributions of captured and enslaved natives – entailing, of course, the responsibility of their masters to

---

THE MYTH OF THE AMAZONS

The Alexander Romance was the source for the myth of the Amazons. This legendary biography of the Macedonian conqueror went back to a popular Graeco-Egyptian anonymous text of the third century AD. Medieval and Renaissance writers plundered the book's themes – including that of the legendary kingdom of the 'Amazons' or warrior women – to provide exotic settings for their knights-errant. In January 1493, we find Columbus, in the Antilles, affirming that his Indian guides 'told him that by following this sea-lane he would find the island of Matinino (Martinique), adding that it was inhabited by women who lived without men. Las Casas comments sceptically: 'The guide spoke to him of an island called Matinino, on which was hidden much gold, and which was inhabited by women alone, to whom men came at certain times of the year, and if a daughter was born to them, they kept her, but if it were a boy, they sent him back to the island of the men. Now it has never been verified since, it should be known, that there were ever solitary women in any land in the Indies, and that is why I think that either the admiral did not properly understand what they were saying, or else that they were telling him tales.' (I,lxvii.) Nonetheless, in 1542, the South American expedition of Don Francisco de Orellana merely needed to see a few armed native women on a river bank for the legend to find confirmation in the eyes of the group's chronicler, the monk Gáspar de Carvajal, and for the name 'Amazon' to be given to the great body of water in what became Portuguese America. In the same year, Don Juan Rodríguez Cabrillo, sailing along the north-western shore of Mexico, gave the appellation of 'California' to what appeared to be a long and unending island, borrowing from the name of a character in the romance Las Sergas de Esplandián *by Ordóñez de Montalvo:* Calafia Queen of the Amazons.

convert them – among the new Spanish colonists in the Caribbean. This replicated transfer of the serfdom of Iberian Moors among the 'Indians' of the New World by no means escaped the attention of other Renaissance Europeans. On the Elizabethan stage, Christopher Marlowe slyly juxtaposed ethnic terms from both shores of Castile's Atlantic empire in his scene from *Doctor Faustus* (1592), where diabolic tempters of the magician suggest that he be served by spirits 'as Indian Moors obey their Spanish Lords'.

That, however, is where the shoe pinched. When Queen Isabella learned in 1499 that Columbus in Haiti, acting on his own authority in his remote island like an Andalusian grandee in the early days of the *Reconquista*, had enslaved and shared out three hundred natives as parting gifts to fellow-colonists returning to Spain, she uttered a sharp query whose words betray her stab of anger: 'By virtue of what power does my own Admiral give away my own vassals to anyone at all, *a nadie?*' (Las Casas, *op. cit.*, ch. I, CLXXVI.)

Fiefs and serfs, *encomiendas* and *repartimientos*, won with their own swords by Castile's knights in Andalusia against the Moors during the climax of the *Reconquista* of 1212–1248, were precisely what had so dangerously swelled the power and virtual independence of the new land-owning grandees, weakened royal authority, and nourished the feudal disputes and dynastic struggles which so tormented Spanish history throughout the fourteenth and fifteenth centuries down to the accession of the Catholic Sovereigns, with each aristocratic faction vying for influence by supporting its own candidate to the throne. The very existence of Portugal showed the example of how a baron, originally a vassal of Castile, was able to transform his fiefdom into a kingdom by 1143 by enlarging his domain, on his own initiative, at the expense of the Moors. The concern of the Catholic Sovereigns and of their successor Charles V as of 1516 would be to prevent repetition of such turbulent baronial independence on a far larger scale, and at a much greater distance, in the 'Indies'.

The last quarter of the fifteenth century meant not only for Spain under Ferdinand and Isabella, but also for contemporary France under Louis XI and England under Henry VII, a period of tremendous effort on the part of the monarchies to re-establish centralized royal control over the feudal grandees. The Catholic Sovereigns were able to exploit the banner of the crusade to achieve this end by renewing the war against the Moors in Granada, thus harnessing the warlike energy of their nobles and providing a holy outlet for it. Macchiavelli noted:

'We have in our time Ferdinand of Aragon, the present King of Spain. He might almost be called a new prince because although at the start a somewhat feeble monarch, he has become by reputation and glory the foremost King in Christendom; if you consider his actions, you will find them all marked by greatness, and indeed in

'The burning of heretics', or Auto de Fe, *by Pedro Berruguete. The scene shows an execution presided over by St Dominic, the thirteenth-century Spanish founder of the Inquisition, but the setting and costumes depicted are those of the late fifteenth century. The saint welcomes the repentance of the heretic (left) who is reprieved from being burned at the stake; the others, hardened in their errors, march to their doom wearing the* san benito, *or cap and tunic of infamy, painted with demons; the bearded prisoner is probably a Jew or a Moor. The helmeted alguazil does not realize it, but he rides in the style of a Muslim horseman, with 'short' leathers and bucket stirrups wide enough to stand in. It is hard to see how these 'acts of faith' could claim moral superiority over the human sacrifices of the Aztecs which so horrified the conquistadores. [Prado, Madrid. Photo Oronoz, © Arch. Photeb.]*

Just as forcibly converted Spanish Jews were popularly jeered at as *marranos*, or 'swine', so subjugated Moors were referred to by the pejorative term *mudéjares*, from Arabic *mudajjan*, 'domestic animal'. Christian feudal lords, from the king down, wished to retain on their lands only Muslims of the very lowest social orders – artisans, muleteers, peasants – while systematically driving out of the cities all potentially dangerous aristocratic and intellectual élites. It was mainly Jewish scholars under Christian rule who translated those recovered Arabic texts considered essential by the Church, such as the medical or astronomical treatises. During the final phase of the Reconquest, in 1490, Fernando del Pulgar, secretary to Ferdinand of Aragon, described how the king typically evacuated the Muslim population of three newly subjugated towns in the emirate of Granada: 'He ordered that there should be ejected from these three cities and from their suburbs all the Moors and Mooresses whom he had left there as *mudéjares*. And he gave them surety so that they might pass if they so wished to the parts of Africa; or if they so wished, they could remain with their families and their chattels in his kingdoms and domains, but then they must reside in the villages and hamlets, and not enter either into the cities or fortified towns.' (*Crónica de los Reyes Católicos*, ch. CCLXI.) Shortly after the fall of Granada, in 1493, the emir, his court, and the leading Muslim merchants and theologians were permitted, or rather encouraged, to sell their lands and leave for exile in Morocco. As of 1499 and the crushing of the Moorish uprising, those Muslims who remained in Spain – some 300,000 around Granada and perhaps half that number in the region of Valencia – had to practise their faith in secret. These were mostly agricultural labourers when not downright serfs. Among the conquerors of Granada, the knightly family of Don Antonio de Mendoza – future viceroy of Mexico in 1535 – received the largest *encomienda* with a huge *repartimiento* of Moorish peasants left to their fate by their traditional masters.

some cases extraordinary. From the start of his reign, he immediately attacked Granada: this enterprise laid the foundation for his State. He has conducted the war in all tranquillity and without fear of interference: by its means he has occupied the minds of those barons of Castile who, preoccupied by the war, no longer have thoughts of contesting his authority'. (*Il Principe*, ch. XXI.)

But because of its very conquests across the Ocean, the strong monarchy of the Catholic Sovereigns and of Charles V found itself immediately confronted in the New World with the same dilemma which had so nearly destroyed Castile's royal authority in the Old, in the tumultuous wake of the thirteenth-century *Reconquista*. The terms of the problem set before Spain's rulers were these: how to contain, satisfy and exploit the military skills of one's knights without rewarding them with fiefs? But at the same time, how to prevent the grant of such fiefs from encouraging their drive for ever greater autonomy and even independence? From the moment of his accession, Ferdinand took care to secure personal control over the great Spanish Orders of Knighthood and their fiefs whenever their Masterships became vacant through the deaths of their incumbents. But, after the capture of Granada, he found himself compelled to grant immense new *encomiendas* to the nobles who had fought on his behalf.

The Catholic Sovereigns were lucid rulers and clearly saw that identical social causes were bound to produce the same effects. Indeed, extension to America of the system of the *encomiendas* did provoke before the middle of the sixteenth century – in Peru – an explosive repetition of the baronial revolts of medieval Castile. From the very beginning of the adventure in the New World, the monarchs were justifiably worried about the feudalization of the discovered territories which risked rendering sovereignty of the crown over the 'Indies' and their inhabitants not only indirect but illusory. For this reason, by an edict of 21 May 1499, they relieved Christopher Columbus of his office as governor in the Antilles (with his bloated claims to permanent and hereditary viceroyship for himself and his family over the 'Indies'). They sent a royal officer to the islands who brought the deposed explorer back in chains, although Columbus subsequently received a title and pension by way of compensation and the right to lead further explorations.

It was obvious that the monarchs should wish to reimpose their authority in similar manner over the other conquerors in the New World, and why they chose to pay such careful attention to the strident denunciations by a handful of Dominican friars, among them the saintly António de Montesinos and Bartolomé de Las Casas, concerning the cruel excesses of the knights against the native serfs in their American *encomiendas*, especially in the Antilles where the rigours of slavery and the introduction of European diseases

had almost wiped out the original population by the second quarter of the sixteenth century.

And yet, when Charles V, urged on by Bartolomé de Las Casas who saw no other salvation for the natives except under the direct protection of the crown, tried by means of his 'New Laws' in 1542 to reclaim under royal monopoly all granted New World fiefs by compensating *conquistador* fief-holders with titles and pensions (as Ferdinand had done for the family of Columbus), he unleashed indignant protest by the Spanish knights in Mexico and, worse still, the open revolt of those in Peru: 'Is this the fruit of all our toil? Is it for this that we have poured out our blood like water? Now that we are broken down by hardships and sufferings, to be left at the end of our campaigns as poor as at the beginning! Is this the way government rewards our services in winning for it an empire? The government has done little to aid us in making the conquest, and for what we have we may thank our own good swords; and with these same swords we know how to defend it.' (Letter from Gonzalo Pizarro, younger brother of the conqueror Francisco Pizarro, in the name of the Castilian barons in Peru, to Pedro de Valdívia, 1543; William Prescott translation, *Conquest of Peru*, bk. IV, ch. VII.)

Only the immediate revocation by the king of the 'New Laws' or *Leyes Nuevas*, on the urgent insistence of the viceroy Don Antonio de Mendoza, soothed knightly outrage in Mexico. But it took the king's representatives a lengthy campaign, from 1543 to 1546, to reduce the secession of the *conquistadores* in Peru which threatened to turn the distant Andean province into a baronial kingdom as fully independent of Castile as medieval Portugal had ever become. The factions of knights who clashed on the bleak *Altiplano*, in support of the king's party or the rebellious Gonzalo Pizarro, revived a vision of the feudal civil wars which had torn Spanish society apart two centuries earlier.

So their hereditary *encomiendas* of 'Indian' villages were left to the barons as well as to the great religious orders – Franciscans and Dominicans – which settled in the New World. All that remained of the efforts of Las Casas on behalf of the 'New Laws' were a few clauses mitigating the servitude of the 'shared out' native peoples, as well as his lingering saintly influence at least among some missionaries who worked in the Mexican villages or in the remoter 'Indian' borderlands.

The crown did, however, take the precaution, during all three centuries of its American empire, of ensuring that its viceroys and other senior colonial administrators were always nobles born in metropolitan Spain – *penínsulares* – and not feudal landlords born in America – *criollos* or 'Creoles' – so as to retain what it could of its control overseas.

The cross and the sword

The monarchy retained its close alliance with the Church throughout. The ecclesiastical hierarchy provided the crown with its intellectual resource and also ensured the management of much of its bureaucracy and of nearly all its social services (schools, hospitals) in both the Old World and the New. In addition, the clergy, by its teaching – or indoctrination – eased integration of the native populations into the colonial system. The Church provided the moral and cultural framework of the Hispanic world, and while it had to come to terms with the interests of the temporal kingdom which defended it, had no intention of sharing its absolute dominion over souls.

Nonetheless, since the Spanish Church at the turn of the fifteenth and sixteenth centuries still included the majority of the kingdom's intellectuals, it also embraced some highly contradictory philosophies all claiming to speak in its same name. Members of the clergy ranged from ferocious military totalitarians blindly loyal to the crown, to disinterested humanists profoundly influenced by the new *devotio moderna* of contemporary Flemish mysticism. Among the populace, hatred of Muslims and Jews – whose dislike for graven images was well-known – encouraged a veneration of religious paintings, relics and holy statues, which by 1492 was scarcely to be distinguished from any so-called 'idolatry' or 'fetishism' which Iberian *conquistadores* thought they were morally entitled to condemn in Africa or the New World.

The crusade, once transferred from the Old World to the New, no longer concerned itself with liberating Jerusalem but served instead to establish, on American soil, a feudal order fully as rigid as anything in its medieval Castilian model, if not more so. Once the storm of conquest had passed, the Empire settled into an inflexible three-tiered social structure: one class prayed, another fought and the third laboured (*oratores, bellatores, laboratores*) in accordance with the most immutable of medieval European schemes. The Inquisition opened in Santo Domingo in 1517, in Mexico City and Lima in 1569 in order to watch over Spaniards and half-castes. Only the native population escaped its iron rule because considered inferior beings and child-like, although Pope Paul III (reigned 1534–1549) had acknowledged the full

humanity of the 'Indians' and hence their fitness to be converted to Christianity. The outcries of the humanist friars such as Las Casas or some of the Franciscan missionaries in Mexico against the degradation of the 'Indians' provided some solace to the native flocks they laboured to protect, but were powerless to change the social order and ultimately remained isolated. Lewis Hanke has collected the papers of those Spaniards most vociferously opposed to Las Casas. As spokesman for the conservative hierarchy of Mexico, the Dominican friar, Domingo de Betanzos, protested in 1541 against the proposal of the 'New Laws' by referring to the traditional political wisdom of Aristotle, as encapsulated in the *De regimine principum* ('Concerning the Rule of Princes') by St Thomas Aquinas: no society may tolerate equality between all its members without descending into anarchy; just as in Aristotle's view of slaves, Mexico's native peasants are brutes by nature, they are mere organs whose task it is to labour in the service of the vast natural body which constitutes the State – itself directed by the Intellect as symbolized by the clergy who pray, and defended by the warriors who make up the skeletal framework holding it together.

After the annulment of the *Leyes Nuevas* in 1542, the Spanish-Mexican clergy passed a final satisfied judgement in praise of the class of knights, who had delivered to them, after all, a rich haul in American souls: 'In a well-ordered republic, it is necessary that there should be rich men so that they may offer resistance to enemies and so that the poor of the land may live under their protection, as is the case in all civilized nations where there is good order and stability, in Spain as in other kingdoms. If this country is to survive, it is a great error to think that all its inhabitants should be equal. Neither Spain nor any other kingdom could preserve itself without noblemen and princes and rich men. And in this country there can be no rich or powerful men without peoples placed in *encomiendas*, as they are popularly called: because all labouring and harvesting is ensured by the Indians in the villages placed in *encomiendas* by the Spaniards: and outside of this procedure, there is no means of harvesting or storing anything at all.'

Marco Polo tells of the dog-headed Andaman islanders. *From the thirteenth to the very end of the sixteenth centuries, from Marco Polo and Sir John Mandeville to the Portuguese Duarte Pacheco in Africa and Sir Walter Raleigh, not to mention Shakespeare's Othello, European travellers all have stories of monstrous semi-humans (one-legged men, headless savages with faces set in the middle of their chests etc.) thought to live in territories just beyond the lands they themselves explored, on the edge of the known world. The myths of such creatures were handed down from the traditions of classical antiquity. Livre des merveilles, late fifteenth century. [Bibliothèque Nationale, Paris. Photo © Bibl. nat.-Arch. Photeb]*

THE MYTH OF THE ANTILLES

The myth of the 'Antilles' and of the 'Seven Cities of Cíbola' goes back to a Portuguese version of the epic cycle of King Rodericus. According to the legend, seven Portuguese bishops and their flocks fled before the Arab invaders of 711 by taking ships across the ocean, and finally reached the 'opposite islands' (ant'ilia), where they built seven wonderful cities. According to Las Casas (I,xiii), the imagination of Columbus was fired during his stay in Madeira in 1484 by a story that several Portuguese sailors, blown off course in the days of Prince Henry the Navigator (1394–1460), had claimed to have landed at the Antilles of the Seven Cities, been welcomed by priests and shown magnificent churches and also clods of earth formed of gold dust. The Spaniards gave the name of Antillas to the Caribbean island chain, but failed to find any trace of the Seven Cities there and continued their search as far as the deserts of New Mexico.

THE ENCOUNTER

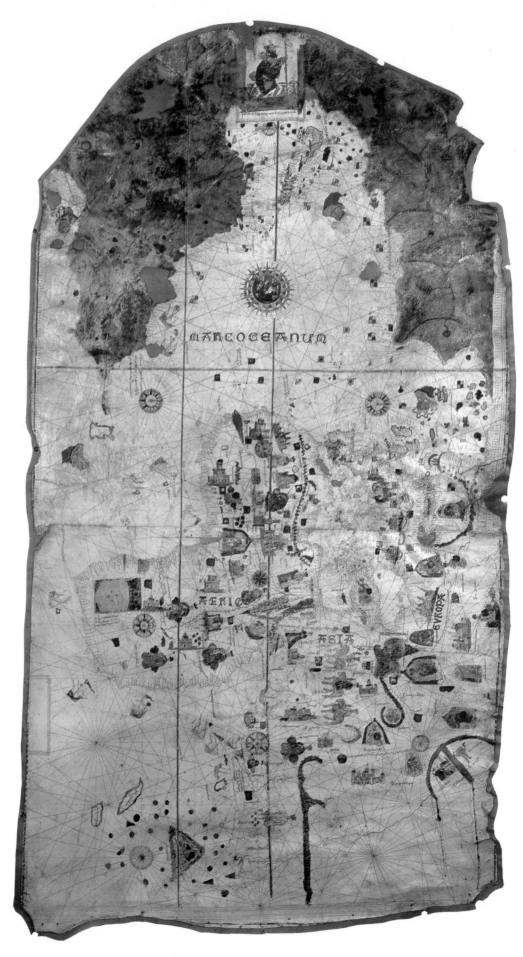

THE FIRST ENCOUNTERS WITH THE AMERICANS

DANIEL LÉVINE

The discovery of the Americas at the end of the fifteenth century is one of the most important events in the history of mankind. Never before had two civilizations so totally ignorant of one another been thus confronted. For the first time, worlds which had never imagined each other's existence clashed in mutual wonder. Columbus' landfall in the Bahamas in 1492 allowed the world to reintegrate an immense fraction of itself, of which it had hitherto known nothing. Only a few years were to pass before Spain's *conquistadores* sustained a second shock, when they encountered the two greatest native States in the Americas, the Aztecs of Mexico and the Incas of Peru. While the social resilience and power of these two indigenous empires posed a serious threat to the handful of Spanish conquerors, they reassured them as well by presenting them with an image of hierarchical organization and high civilization, which they could relate to their own European cultural background – in contrast to what they had found among the Taínos of the Greater Antilles. The adventure of the encounter between Americans and Europeans unfolded through various stages, in the course of which the conflicting civilizations, after a very brief period of mutual observation, met in battle, before mingling and giving birth to new cultural manifestations. Within decades, the uniform sable cloak of Hispanic culture seemed to have spread over and blanketed all the manifold expressions of Indian civilization; but soon enough, tears appeared in the sombre cape of Castile, allowing the rich warm tones of the Indian universe to emerge again into the light of the solar disc under which it yearned to live and which it so deeply venerated.

Still very much stirred by the crusading spirit which had marked the reconquest of their territory from the Muslims, the Spanish *conquistadores* attacked the New World in a spirit of mixed curiosity, fear, interest, wonder and greed. The Spanish conquest of America played itself out in two main phases. The first lasted from 1492 to 1518 and covers the period corresponding to the initial discovery of the West Indies (the Antilles) with the Spanish settlement of these islands. In turn, these islands served as rear bases for conquering expeditions launched against the continent in the course of the second phase, lasting from 1519 to 1550: marked by the shock of the encounter with the two great American empires, the Aztecs of Mexico and the Incas of Peru.

The fantasy of the Indies

In the fifteenth century, the learned were convinced that the Earth was round. Columbus fully shared this theory and believed it possible to reach the Orient by sailing due west rather than by circumnavigating Africa. The Portuguese had concentrated all their interests and efforts on this African sea route and when Columbus submitted his plan to King John II, Lisbon's ruler, who was already reaping much profit from his trade along the African coast, he rejected the Genoese navigator's proposal. Columbus had no further luck with his project with the rulers of Spain, England and France between 1486 and 1492. At length, however, by sheer stubbornness, and thanks to his relations with the Franciscan friars of the convent of La Rábida who cared for his young son Diego and whose prior Juan Pérez had once been confessor to Queen Isabella, Columbus was able to secure a new audience with the Catholic Sovereigns. After many discussions, and with support from Queen Isabella who saw in Columbus an instrument by which to spread the Catholic faith, the rulers granted him the capitulations of Santa Fe. By these, Columbus was appointed 'Admiral of the Ocean Sea, Viceroy of the islands and of the mainlands discovered or to be discovered'. The titles were supposed to be hereditary, and King Ferdinand signed such clauses with no great enthusiasm, foreseeing the problems that would arise from a document which so yielded sovereignty over distant lands to the members of a single family. Antagonism between Columbus and the Crown's officials, in fact, arose immediately.

With financial backing at long last for his expedition, Columbus left Spain on Friday 3 August 1492 with eighty-seven men aboard a round-shaped Galician *nao*, the *Santa María*, and two lighter caravels of Portuguese design, the *Niña* and the *Pinta*. Such ships had largely made possible Portugal's reconnaissance along the African coast. Fast and manoeuvrable, the caravel was the ideal tool in this age for exploration and discovery.

After a necessary stopover in the Canaries for supplies, repairs and rerigging of the *Niña* to make her more seaworthy, the little fleet sailed due west in the night of 8 to 9 September. Columbus piloted the *Santa María*, whose crew were mostly drawn

from gaols. On 22 September, the appearance of headwinds at last reassured the sailors, who had hitherto navigated with a constant fair wind astern, that they would be able to sail back to Spain. Columbus jotted down the event in his journal, noting the good news these headwinds meant for all concerned – both for the admiral's prestige and for his own men who now knew for certain that they would be able to travel home again. On 8 October, the crew saw migrating birds cross the sky southwards. At last, on the night of 11 to 12 October, a *Pinta* crewman, Rodrigo de Triana, made out the first strip of American land. The expedition had just touched upon an island of the Bahama group, either Watling Island or Samana Cay Island some sixty-five miles to the south: an

Coat of arms granted to Christopher Columbus by the Catholic Sovereigns, *displaying the arms of Aragon and Castile, the Admiral's anchors and the lands to be discovered.* Book of Privileges, 1503. *[Archivos de las Indias, Seville, Spain. Photo © G. Dagli Orti]*

Three-pointed stone, *Lesser Antilles, Dominica. Fifteenth century. [Musée de l'Homme, Paris]*

Right-hand page
Taíno zemi, *stone, depicting a skull, Greater Antilles, Puerto Rico. Fifteenth century. [Musée de l'Homme, Paris]*

island known to the people who dwelt there as Guanahani and which the Admiral christened San Salvador, 'Holy Saviour'. The first meeting between Americans and Europeans occurred on the morning of 12 October 1492. These first Indians encountered were the Taíno people, who inhabited most of the West Indies at the turn of the fifteenth and sixteenth centuries. Columbus offered them red sailors' caps, glass pearls, hawk-bells and other trinkets of little worth but which pleased them greatly. On 13 October, the Indians crowded the beach to see these strange creatures, the Spaniards. Columbus spotted several of them wearing a small piece of gold in their noses and asked them whence they procured this metal. From farther south, the Indians indicated – an answer the *conquistadores* were repeatedly to hear from the native peoples throughout the New World, where gold always seemed to come from some other place. Native wariness of the Spaniards would be justified soon

enough by Columbus' behaviour. Badly in need of interpreters for future Spanish expeditions and the propagation of the Faith, Columbus kidnapped a group of Indians who had come aboard his ship in all goodwill, to take them back to Spain and have them learn Castilian.

After scouting the shores of the Bahamas between 13 and 27 October, the little fleet discovered and reconnoitred the northern coast of Cuba down to 5 December. Columbus christened this new land Juana, in honour of the daughter of Queen Isabella. Between 6 and 16 December, Columbus skirted the northern shore of Haiti which he called Hispaniola, 'the Hispanic Island'. The Genoese navigator was convinced he had reached Asia and the fabulous empires described by Marco Polo. Thus he first identified Cuba with Marco Polo's Cipango (Japan), then, as the shoreline stretched, he told himself that this must be the coast of the mainland: Cathay itself

ORIGIN OF THE NAME AMERICA

In the year 1499, the navigators Alonso de Hojeda and Juan de la Cosa, accompanied by the Florentine Amérigo Vespucci, explored the northern shore of the South American continent from Venezuela to Brazil. Vespucci returned to these shores under a Portuguese flag in 1501-1502 and a map attributed to him and published in Florence in 1502 termed the new lands 'an unknown continent'. In 1503, the Florentine published a *Relation* of his voyage, claimed to have been made as early as 1497, and entitled *Mundus Novus*: the birth certificate of the 'New World'. In 1507, the German cartographer Martin Waldseemüller published, in the eastern French town of Saint-Dié, a map designating the new continent with Amérigo's name: *America*.

ALBERICA

'America' might just as well have been named 'Alberica'. We know that the cosmographer Waldseemüller was responsible for christening the new continent thus on the basis of the navigator Amérigo Vespucci's first name. This curious first name, however, is only a Tuscan dialect form of the Latin 'Albericus', itself derived from Germanic 'Alberic'. It is curious – and perhaps we should read here another sign of the emerging importance of the modern European vernaculars at the beginning of the sixteenth century – that Waldseemüller, who wrote in Latin, should have chosen a dialectical over a correct classical Latin form. The New World's vernacular name, 'America', in a sense marks the beginning of the end of Latin's monopoly as a learned language. America's naming is no neutral matter: it is a spectacular manifestation of the spirit of the Renaissance.
Christian Duverger

The 'West Indies'

(China), the realm of the Great Khan. Looking for gold among the hot, humid islands over the following weeks became an obsession with Columbus, who shared his age's belief that yellow metal was to be found in warm climates, and silver, under cooler skies. He did realize, however, that the natives of these regions possessed no more than small noseplugs or earrings made of gold (*caona*) or more often of *guanin*, an Antilles term designating an alloy of some gold and more copper.

The Spaniards received a particularly warm welcome from the Indians on the northern plain of the island of Hispaniola, near present-day Cap Haitien. Here the Europeans met their first important chieftain, the *cacique* Guacanagarí. While gold was not exactly abundant here either, neither was it altogether lacking, for the dignitaries surrounding the chief wore some hammered sheets of yellow metal in their head-dresses. Again Columbus asked through signs whence this gold came, and the name which most often came up in the Indians' replies was *Cibao*: a mountainous area of Hispaniola, but which the Admiral at once identified with Cipango or Japan. Columbus' error was perfectly compounded by the context of the cartography of his day, which placed the islands of Cipango (Marco Polo's Italianate transcription of the Chinese name for Japan, *Jih-Pên Kuo* or 'Sun Rise Land') on the same latitude as the Canaries, to the east of Cathay or China. Throughout his first voyage, Columbus carefully recorded every piece of gold he saw. On 24 December, the *Santa María* foundered on a reef. The Spaniards salvaged the

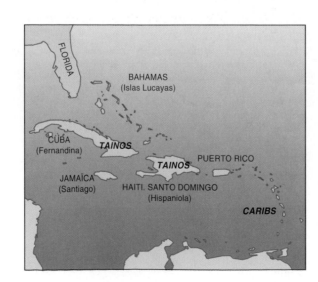

ship's wood and artillery, and, with the help of the Indians, built a small fort where forty volunteers elected to stay. On 16 January 1493, Columbus weighed anchor for Europe with the *Niña* and the *Pinta* and reached Lisbon on 4 March.

This first little fort in Hispaniola foreshadowed the island's imperial fate: to serve, as it were, as a launching pad for the conquest of the continent. Once in Spain, the Admiral attempted to share his enthusiasm for the beauty of the islands where he had spent some three months, emphasizing their beauty as tropical paradises and especially the docility of the natives. Since Columbus knew that his royal masters were somewhat irritated that so little gold had actually been found, he stressed another possibly profitable side to the discovery (thereby disclosing his own future intentions as governor of the colony): the Taínos, he pointed out, were a servile lot and could be turned into excellent slaves. In so far as he had discovered new lands and claimed them for the Spanish Crown, he had fulfilled his mission. The Admiral was duly received by the Court in April at Barcelona, where he presented to the rulers his Taíno Indian captives, along with some gold, samples of new foodplants including maize, and a number of native artefacts.

At the request of Spain's rulers, Pope Alexander VI Borgia officially recognized the rights of the Spanish Crown to the lands beyond the Ocean and to new subjects there, in order that they should be instructed in and converted to the True Faith. In March 1493, the Pope divided all newly discovered lands between the Spaniards and the Portuguese, granting to Castile those territories lying a hundred leagues to the west of a meridian line passing through the Azores and the Cape Verde Islands. The following year, the Portuguese demanded a more equitable share. On 7 June 1494, King John II of Portugal and the Catholic Sovereigns signed the Treaty of Tordesillas, which moved the dividing line to a meridian lying 230 leagues to the west of the Cape Verde islands: an agreement which, in time, would yield to the Portuguese legal claim to Brazil.

First portraits of the Indians

Columbus' geographical conceptions were an odd mixture of fact and fancy. In the entry to his sea-journal for 4 November 1492, he understood the

natives of Cuba, whose language of course he could not make out at all, to be telling him of the existence of men who had only one eye, and of others with the heads of dogs who lived on human flesh. Such descriptions which Columbus thought he heard really derived from late medieval European folklore – itself mostly inherited from Classical mythology – regarding the fantastic peoples supposed to dwell in the Far East. Even so, it remains possible to peer through the prose of Columbus' diaries, as transcribed and preserved for us by Las Casas, to try to form some idea of the first American Indians he saw.

Initial relations between the Spaniards and the Taínos – whom Columbus describes as cheerful and peaceful – seem to have been quite friendly. The Europeans were surprised by the many natives who came to see them on the beach, and by their unclad state. In Columbus' eyes, such nakedness was a sign of their great poverty. For their part, the

Indians were amazed by the arrival of these strangers, as well as by their beards, the whiteness of their complexions and their clothes.

While chiefly obsessed with finding gold, Columbus did observe with some care the inhabitants of these islands. He had rather expected to find black men, since, according to late medieval geographic theory, the farther south a climate lay, the darker its inhabitants were supposed to be. But these people that Columbus had found were no darker than the Canary Islanders; those he saw were mostly tall, generally handsome young males in their early thirties. Their thick, black and very straight hair, rather like a horse's mane he thought, was cut short except for a fringe over the eyebrows and several long locks behind. They painted their bodies and faces mainly in red, brown, and white. They wore no weapons, and having no knowledge of steel touched the Spaniards' drawn swords with their bare hands and

Taíno pottery, *Greater Antilles, Santo Domingo. Fifteenth century. [Musée de l'Homme, Paris]*

Taíno pottery, Greater Antilles, Santo Domingo. Fifteenth century. [Musée de l'Homme, Paris]

Right-hand page
A map of the American continent, 1546. *An extract from a map of the world, painted on parchment by Desceliers on the orders of King Henry II of France. [Bibliothèque nationale, Paris. Photo © Bibl. nat.-Arch. Photeb]*

cut themselves. They indicated to the Admiral that men from neighbouring islands raided and captured them: the first reference heard by Europeans to the Carib Islanders and to local inter-island communications.

At this very initial stage of the encounter, the natives gathered on the beaches to watch the Spaniards disembark. The Indians would even approach the ships riding at anchor in dugouts carved of single tree trunks. These dugouts varied in size, some designed to carry only a single man, others a crew of forty or more. They were propelled by paddling and bailed out with calabash gourds. At shipside, the Taínos offered yarns of spun cotton, parrots, fishing or hunting spears, and any small objects they made, to barter against the Spaniards' trinkets.

The Spaniards discovered their first villages amongst the verdant islands, and these proved a sore disappointment to a navigator expecting to discover the rich trading ports of the Great Khan. As he met more of these Indians, however, Columbus began to realize that they shared the same language and customs, although some appeared to him more 'civilized' than others. The Genoese navigator seems to have judged the degree of civilization according to the amount of clothing worn: he noted that the women of one group, for example, covered their private parts with a little cotton apron.

At one point between two islands, Columbus saw a solitary Indian in his canoe and to help him on his way had him pulled up on board with his craft, hoping to give a good impression of the Spanish. But communications were limited to sign-language. The Admiral had been very concerned with the problem of linguistic contact, even going so far as to take on his first journey a converted Spanish Jew, Luís de Torres, a man familiar not only with his ritual Hebrew but also with some Arabic which Columbus reasonably thought might come in useful in Asian waters. But on 2

November 1492, not even Luís de Torres could communicate with the natives of Cuba. Here Columbus decided to take six or seven local Taínos to train as future interpreters.

From then on the Indian attitude towards the Spaniards began to change, however much the Europeans tried to entice them with gifts: too many of their people had been retained on board as hostages and news of this spread from one island to another. Now, when the Spaniards disembarked to look for water or to meet with the natives, they more usually found temporarily abandoned villages of round lodges, made of perishable materials whose cleanliness the Europeans noted. The Spaniards were further very much surprised by the Indians' bedding, consisting of strung cotton nets: here the men from the Old World saw their first hammocks. They also discovered that each house sheltered several hearths, whence they deduced that a number of families shared them. In those villages whose inhabitants returned after their initial fright, the Spaniards observed some Indian men to wear feather head-dresses and the married women to cover themselves with a cotton loincloth, whereas unmarried girls went entirely unclad. There were domesticated dogs in the villages, but they did not bark. Columbus regarded these people as so simple that he could distinguish no religious belief or creed of any kind among them, and thought that they would be easy to bring to Christianity. In early December, as Columbus cruised along the island of Haiti/Santo Domingo, the crew saw so many watchfires that the Admiral concluded that the island was thickly inhabited indeed. On this island the Spaniards met their first chiefs and found evidence of some kind of hierarchical structure in the native society. During one landing on the Cuban coast on Monday 29 October, sailors sent to investigate a village found it abandoned but reported numerous little statues and sculptured heads, rather skilfully carved, they added. On one of the hills overlooking the village stood a sort of 'mound' which they thought looked much like a small mosque.

Of the various cheap European trade-goods the Spaniards had brought, the Indians were particularly interested in the hawk-bells; for they could string series of them into a resemblance of a rattle-like musical instrument they already used in their collective ritual dances. This association of ritual, dancing and rattles is found in many Amerindian cultures. It was also in Cuba that the

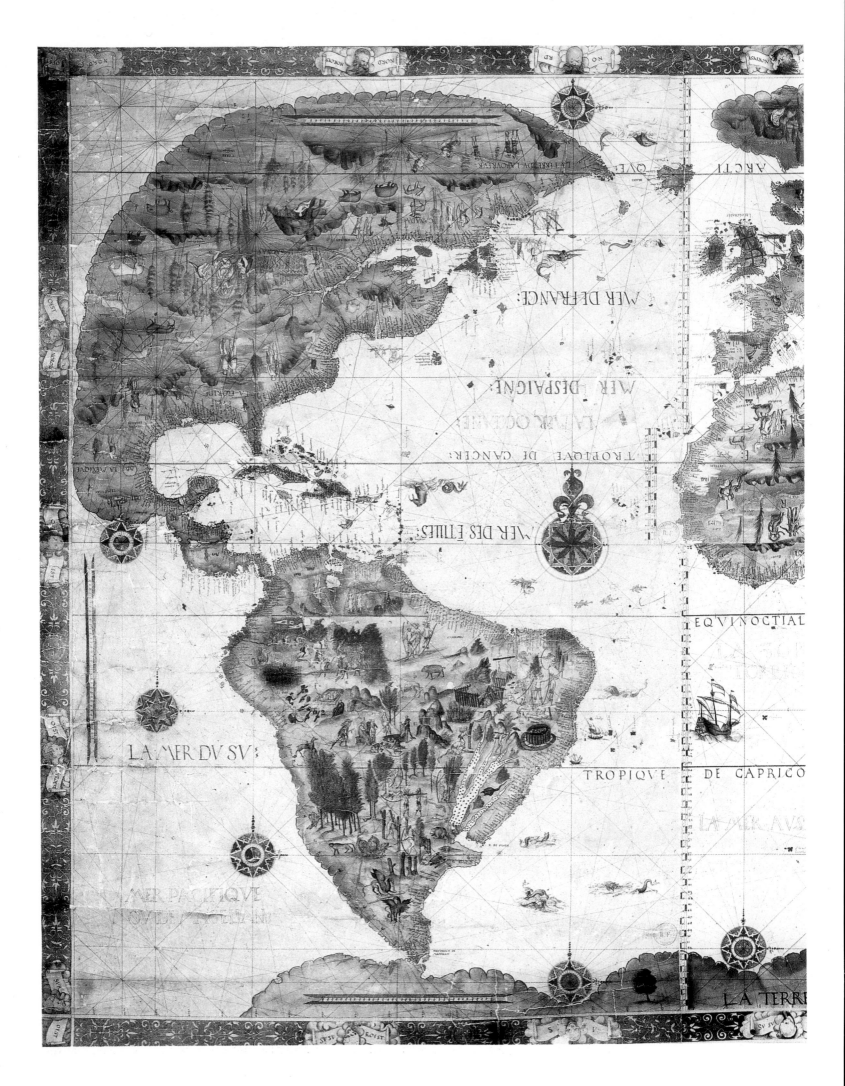

Spaniards first saw the Indians puffing smoke from a roll of leaves, and thus discovered the use of tobacco. Gifts of tobacco leaves were offered to Columbus as precious tokens in his very first meetings with these Indians.

On a Haitian beach, among a crowd of Indians come to meet the Spaniards, Columbus singled out a young chief who appeared to be deeply respected by his people. This chief was welcomed aboard the *Santa María* and the Admiral offered him clothes. For the Spaniards, clothing these naked creatures was equivalent to helping them along the first steps to civilization. Several days later the Spanish met a still more important chief, Guacanagarí. Once again the Europeans offered clothes (a shirt and gloves) to the Taíno chief, who gave in return some ornaments of gold: a belt and mask. The dignitaries or *caciques* around this Guacanagarí wore 'crowns' partially made of gold leaf combined with feathers and other elements, also golden earrings and noseplugs. On their return trip along the coast of Hispaniola, the Spaniards saw still another group of Indians (the Cigayos) who wore tremendous head-dresses of parrot feathers and something new: weapons – bows

and arrows. A party of seven Europeans disembarked and met some fifty of these Indians on the beach. Trade began in an atmosphere of mutual mistrust, the natives angrily refused to part with their bows and suddenly shot arrows at the Spaniards who hastily re-embarked for their homeward journey.

The indigenous peoples of the islands

From his initial observations of the islanders, Columbus at once distinguished between 'good Indians', the Taínos who had welcomed him, and 'bad Indians', the Carib cannibals of whom he had only heard but whom he immediately earmarked in his mind as a possibly profitable source of slaves. Not that this prevented him from estimating that the Taínos too, given the gentleness of their nature which he considered mere cowardice, could be turned into excellent servile labour.

Who were the first Amerindians encountered by the Spaniards, these Caribbean islanders whose very names would soon be erased from popular memory by the incomparably greater fame of the mainland civilizations?

In 1492, the native peoples of the Bahamas (called the Lucayos by the Spaniards) and the Greater Antilles, that is Cuba, Haiti/Santo Domingo, Puerto Rico and Jamaica, belonged to a relatively homogenous cultural group. The majority were ethnically Arawak (a more proper term than the popular 'Taíno', a name derived from one of their social classes).

The Greater Antilles were settled by the Arawak and the Lesser Antilles by the Caribs, both peoples who originally came from the South American mainland. These continental peoples canoed into the archipelago of the Antilles on currents caused by the flow of the Orinoco river into the Atlantic, and thanks to favourable prevalent south winds.

A hierarchical society

Arawak society was dominated by lords or *caciques*, whose titles were apparently transmitted matrilineally. Ranks were hierarchically organized. Every small village was ruled by its own *cacique*. The *cacique* of an important settlement extended his sway over the lesser *caciques* of smaller villages,

Christopher Columbus' first voyage.

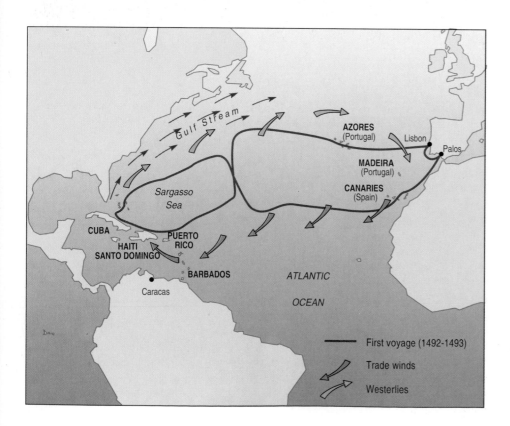

and he himself owed allegiance to a lord who might control a region or province. It is not impossible that the entire island of Hispaniola may have submitted to the authority of a single *cacique*, although the Spanish chronicles do not confirm this. The hierarchical degrees of *caciques*, however, did not escape the attention of the Spaniards who recorded such different titles of descending importance as *guaojeri*, *bahari*, *matunheri*, and *guamaheque* in Puerto Rico at the time of its conquest in 1508-09. That the concept of centralized power in the hands of one individual was not foreign to the Taíno way of thinking is shown by the title they bestowed on Columbus as the *guamiquina* or 'sole chief' of the Spaniards. After the *caciques* came the lesser dignitaries or *nitaíno-s*, the abridged form of which, *taíno*, yielded today's conventional term for the cultures of the Greater Antilles. Below the dignitaries came the common people, and the lowest class consisted of slaves, or *naboria-s*. According to the Spanish chronicles, social status was determined by birth.

Daily life and livelihood

Livelihood depended mainly on agriculture. Farmland was cleared and stumps burnt. Mounds of earth known as *conuco-s*, generally circular in shape, were raised as protection against erosion and flood. The *macana* was a sharpened machete carved out of wood, but used more as a farm tool than as a weapon. A common crop among the Taínos was *yuca* (the Hispanicized Haitian name for the foodplant which has become better known in English, through Brazilian Tupi-Portuguese *mandioca*, as *manioc*). Certain roots harvested once a year provided cassava, baked into tortilla-like flat cakes which were the mainstay of the islanders. The highly nutritional cassava tortillas kept for weeks on end. Columbus, who had once navigated along the African coast as a slaver in Portuguese service, was familiar with the use of roots for food and refers to the yuca in his diary under the African-sounding name of *niame* or *ñame*. Among other roots farmed for food was the *camote*, of which a sweet variety, the *batata*, was readily adopted by the Spaniards (the sweet potato). The Taínos also consumed maize, beans, a variety of peppers and gourds and such fruits as the pineapple which the Spaniards discovered on the islands of the Carib Indians. Besides foodplants, the Taínos

also farmed tobacco and cotton. The grains of the *bija* (heart-leaved arnotto) yielded vermilion dye. A balance in proteins and animal fat was ensured by fish and other seafood as well as by hunting (small mammals, sea birds, iguanas).

The chronicler Las Casas informs us that traditional farming in the islands produced substantial crops and was well organized, thanks to the system of the *conuco* embankments, but that the pigs introduced by the Spaniards devastated the fields and largely contributed to eliminating the Indians by destroying their food base. Moreover, unchecked by any local predator, European swine proliferated rapidly. But Spanish pigs were not the only factor to blame: massacres, harsh treatment, forced labour, murderous epidemics caused by European-imported diseases, and slavery, all combined to provoke the disappearance of the indigenous population of the islands within a matter of decades.

Taíno stone pestle, Greater Antilles, Santo Domingo. Fifteenth century. [Musée de l'Homme, Paris]

The natives used tools of stone, wood and shell. Aside from copper, the only metal they knew was gold, worked unheated. Small or middle-size nuggets were hammered with stone implements into gold leaf then cut with stone chisels into various objects (head-dresses, nosesplugs, earrings, belts, masks, figurines, ornaments for ceremonial seats). Because they did not practise smelting, the Taínos had no use for gold dust or nuggets too large to hammer into leaves. While calabash gourds generally served as containers, the Taínos did make clay pottery, left unpainted but incised with geometric patterns; the rims of some bear the designs of two complete figures, one human-shaped, the other animal-shaped.

The island nature of the Caribbean world did not prevent contact and trade between its various peoples: thanks to various sized dugouts carved of single tree trunks – the *canoas* or 'canoes'.

The first Spaniards to see the *canoa* considered it a fast, manoeuvrable and seaworthy craft; although easily capsized, it was easily righted again and the crew bailed out with calabash gourds. Some *canoas* were highly decorated, and sheltered under palm awnings. Columbus noted that each *cacique* owned his own canoe, elaborately painted on prow and stern.

Dwellings

According to Columbus and the Spanish chroniclers, Taíno villages averaged between one or two thousand souls distributed among some twenty to fifty multi-family homes. Dwellings were built of wood, roofed with palm leaves and usually circular with one doorway. The houses seen by Columbus in Cuba had two opposing doorways. The space beneath the roof served to stock goods and also held the remains of the ancestors. According to Las Casas, walls were constructed of crossed slats of wood between thicker upright stakes bound to one another with white- and black-coloured plant fibres: their intertwining also provided a decorative effect. Furniture mentioned by the Spanish consisted of hammocks – of which the chronicler Oviedo has provided us with the first European drawings. Such native bedding was quickly adopted by the Spaniards.

The dwellings of *caciques* were similar if larger. They also housed the ceremony known to Taínos as the *caney*. Peter Martyr transcribes with some awe the description of the great house of a *cacique* in the area near Cap Haitien, roofed with intertwined reeds and rushes of different colours. The houses of *caciques* opened onto courts, normally rectangular, reserved for social and religious ceremonies such as the *batey* or game of ball. Such a court might be surrounded by stone benches, but *caciques* and other important dignitaries sat on wooden stools known as *duhos*.

Large villages boasted as many as three ball courts. While the chronicles provide us here with

little information, we may surmise from the shape of these courts and other objects associated with them that Taíno contests resembled the games of ball practised in pre-Hispanic Mesoamerica. Just as in the art of indigenous Mexico and especially along the Gulf coast, in the Antilles too there have been found large sculpted stone collars resembling 'yokes'. The main difference is that the Mexican 'yokes' are open and U-shaped, whereas those of the Antilles are oval-shaped and closed. In both cultural areas, however, these carved objects associated with the game appear to have been representations in stone of the kind of protective belts of wood and leather worn by players to shield their bodies from the blows of the ball. One such stone 'yoke' from Puerto Rico preserved by the Musée de l'Homme might confirm this theory, for the carving distinctly appears to depict a belt-fastening. The ball itself was solid rubber. The first one ever seen by Europeans was brought back by Columbus in 1493 and shown in Seville to the young Las Casas, who describes it as bouncing twice as high and long as European air-filled balls.

The *duhos* were ritually important ceremonial seats, of carved and polished wood, indicating high social rank not only among the island Taínos but also on the nearby southern mainland. When Columbus on his third voyage landed on the Venezuelan coast in the Gulf of Paria, he and his crew were taken to a village where the Spaniards were invited to sit with Indian dignitaries on similar seats carved of dark wood and adorned with sculpted figures. On the island of Hispaniola, the

Duho, the ceremonial wooden seat of Taíno dignitaries. *A number of these seats were brought back to Europe by Christopher Columbus, probably including this one. Fifteenth century. [Musée de l'Homme, Paris]*

Left-hand page

Zemi adorning a duho, *the ceremonial wooden seat of Taíno dignitaries, Greater Antilles, Haiti. Fifteenth century. [Musée de l'Homme, Paris]*

cacique Anacaona presented Bartholomeo Columbus, younger brother to the Admiral, with fourteen *duhos*, of which several were sent to Spain. Some of the seats were encrusted with gold.

The Taínos also offered the Spaniards other prestige objects, all of which were closely associated with power. *Caciques* wore a golden disc as a pendant, which Columbus calls a 'mirror' in his journal. Other external signs of a *cacique*'s rank included cotton belts hung with shells, or with beads of coloured stone, or small carved wooden masks each covered in goldleaf. A dozen such belts were presented to Columbus by the *cacique* Guacanagarí in Hispaniola. They were much more than mere gifts. These elaborate belts corresponded to North American *wampum*, which means that they served the purpose of official documents, attesting to the sealing of a treaty between two partners in an alliance.

Religious beliefs

What little information we have on the religious beliefs of the Taínos derives from the sixteenth-century Spanish chronicles. The Taíno creed appears to have centred around figurines collectively designated as *zemi* (or *cemi*). These statuettes of stone, wood or cotton normally represented human beings, but also animals and plants and occasionally took purely geometrical forms. Some *zemi* of wood or cotton contained the remains of family ancestors and served to intercede between mankind and the divine. Columbus' friend, the Italian cleric Alessandro Geraldini who was ultimately appointed bishop of Hispaniola in 1520, sent to Pope Leo X several of these *zemi*, asking that they be displayed in St Peter's by way of symbolizing the triumph of Christianity over paganism; of these, some were cotton dolls with the skulls of caciques inserted directly into their headpieces.

Indeed quite a number of the surviving *zemi* represent only the human head, often under the aspect of a skull, involving ancestor-worship which played a major although by no means the only rôle in Taíno religion. The spirits of the ancestors were believed to act as oracles and also thought to intervene with the divine powers on behalf of mankind: hence the *zemi* which embodied them were no mere sculptures – they were animated with the ancestor's life.

Added to the profusion of these figurines were male and female *zemi*, family and individual *zemi*, and *zemi* associated with farming myths or natural elements such as rain, earth, water and wind. Those *zemi* which belonged to a *cacique* were venerated by his entire group. Moreover each individual owned his personal *zemi*.

Individual and family *zemi* were kept in homes whereas those associated with farming and the nature myths were placed in caves. *Zemi* most closely involved with the life of the whole community were set up in temples. Columbus describes one such house of worship wherein were to be found sculptures of wood or 'gold' (in the latter case, actually only wood covered in gold leaf). The building Columbus saw was a large well-built wooden lodge, with four doorways opening out onto the four directions of the winds. Within, the *zemi* wrapped in fine cotton multi-coloured embroidery stood upon the framework upholding the roof, and was considered by the Indians to be the god of Thunder. This *zemi* was surrounded by other wooden figures, gilded or left plain. In the centre of the temple stood a square altar covered with cotton weavings and draped with a banner-like cloth. A hammock, for the god's repose, was suspended from two carved wooden pillars set on either side of the altar. Above the hammock, a blue drape symbolized the sky, embroidered with cotton clouds and goldleaf stars. The doorway which opened onto the *cacique*'s house was reserved for his own use and for that of his family and fellow *caciques*. A second doorway allowed access to lesser dignitaries, the third was for the general population and the fourth set aside for the dead.

Triangular-shaped *zemi* referred to as 'three-pointed stones' were covered with carvings depicting human features, or adorned on either extremity of their base with a human and an animal head. These three-pointed stones were fraught with symbolism associated with fertility (the chronicler Friar Ramón Pané records that such *zemi* were supposed to 'cause the *yuca* to be born'). These stones were buried within the *conuco* embankments. *Zemi* also appeared as personal adornment in the form of diminutive masks hung from belts or set in head-dresses; a small *zemi* was bound to the forehead when leaving for war. *Zemi* also displayed the power of *caciques*. In a letter written in 1496 on his second voyage, Columbus relates how, upon penetrating the sanctuary of a *zemi*, the Spaniards heard the idol speak. The

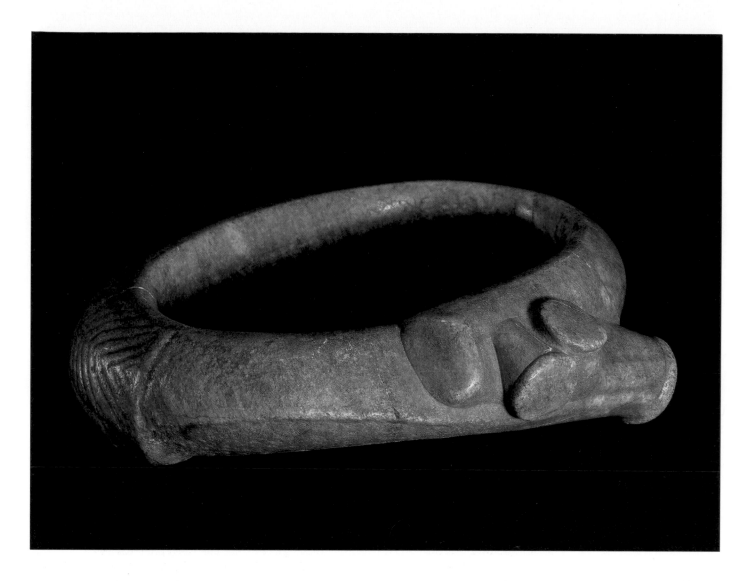

Stone 'yoke', *probably depicting the leather and wooden protective belt worn by players of ball, Greater Antilles, Puerto Rico. Fifteenth century. [Musée de l'Homme, Paris]*

Europeans sought and discovered the trick: the hollow *zemi* was connected by a wooden tube – ending in a darkened corner of the room – to a mouthpiece through which a man hidden under a bundle of grass projected his voice. The local *cacique* begged the Spaniards not to reveal this sleight-of-hand so that his vassals should continue to revere him.

The Taínos further believed in a supreme Being, immortal and invisible who dwelt in the sky, and whose name, *Yucahu Bagua Maorocoti* (recorded by Friar Ramón Pané who lived among the Taínos), evokes *yuca*, the basic food of the Antilles natives.

Our knowledge of Taíno beliefs unfortunately remains superficial: our sole informants are very early sixteenth-century European chroniclers who were not yet intellectually prepared to deal with all the refinements of utterly alien ways of thought in a totally unexpected world. Then the rapid disappearance of the enslaved and over-exploited indigenous population of the Antilles hardly allowed time for missionaries of the more learned sort, such as the Franciscans and Dominicans, to carry out the kind of admirably thorough ethnographical investigation which they were able to accomplish in Mexico only a few decades later.

Ritual and ceremony

To gain access to the divine and communicate with the godly *zemi*, men needed the intercession of one of their own kind, the specialized human being who became the shaman or *behique*. Through long and difficult initiation, the *behique* learned the art of dialogue with the invisible world. The *behique* held one of the most exalted positions in Taíno society and presided over all important ceremonies by the side of the *cacique*.

Two key tasks devolved upon the *behique*: to communicate with spirits, and to heal the sick.

To enter into communication with the *zemi* gods, the *behique* necessarily passed through two stages of self-purification and ecstasy. The entire ritual process leading to ecstasy was itself known as the *cohoba*.

Since dialogue with the divine required initial self-purification, the *behique* ritually forced himself to vomit by sticking down his throat a small spatula of bone or wood, often carved. Once physically purified, the *behique* inhaled a powder offered upon a small, highly polished dark wooden dish. The powder was a hallucinogen affording the *behique* direct contact with the *zemi*. The priest sniffed the powder on the dish through two wooden tubes inserted into his nostrils and when intoxicated heard the messages of the *zemi*. Las Casas, who witnessed the whole *cohoba* ritual several times, saw *caciques* and *behiques* sitting on their *duho* stools, arms around their knees, shaking their heads from side to side and lifting their eyes to the sky as they spoke. When they emerged from their trance, they communicated to the people what the *zemi* had said concerning crops, war or other matters.

Behiques were also responsible for carving the *zemi*. The material in which *zemi* were fashioned or carved depended upon the circumstances and natural environment of a given spirit's first manifestation on earth. For example, if a spirit first made itself known among trees, then its *zemi* would be carved in wood; if it manifested itself among rocks, then its resulting sculptural representation would be of stone. Las Casas describes how an Indian, walking by a tree that appeared more rustled than others by the wind, addressed this tree and asked what its spirit was. But the spirit would only vouchsafe its answer to a *behique*. The required shaman performed the *cohoba*, communicated with the spirit and then reported the shape it should be given and the rites it should be rendered.

Like all other Taínos, the *behiques* possessed their own *zemi*. But theirs were given the form of serpents. Shamans who communicated with the invisible world – including the shades of the dead or *opia-s* – needed powerful spirits to protect them.

In Taíno society, the *behiques* were also, primarily, healers. In Antilles culture, all disease was ascribed to some irritated spirit, believed to have introduced a foreign element – the sickness – into the body of the stricken human being. Treatment therefore consisted in extracting this foreign element which caused the disease. Only *behiques* were entitled to perform the extraction, in an operation which was more sleight-of-hand than surgery. Friar Ramón Pané describes the healing process which always took place inside the home, with the patient lying in the centre of his lodge. The *behique* sat by the patient, and since healing also required self-purification, induced himself to vomit. Once purified, the *behique* chanted, took some rest, then approached the patient. Twice the *behique* circled the patient, then he massaged him. The priest's hands were then suffered to tremble. Finally the *behique* applied his lips to the patient's limbs or torso, made sucking noises, and at last produced between his teeth a pebble, a sliver of bone or even a piece of meat which he gave to appear as if extracted from the sick body. After the suction the *behique* again had to undergo ritual purification, consisting of a rigorous fast.

Obviously such therapy did not always result in a cure. If the patient died, we learn from Friar Ramón Pané, the family questioned the corpse through magic as to whether there had been a failure to observe proper rites either on the part of the deceased or on that of the *behique*. The corpse might be laid on a bed of hot coals and then covered with earth, whereupon the deceased was asked ten times the reason for his death. According to Friar Ramón Pané, more often than not the deceased was understood to reply that he did not know. The earth was then removed and the smoke allowed to rise to the sky with burning cinders which, it was believed, would rain back down into the lodge of the *behique*. After an interval, the shaman's skin was examined: if found to be peeled and covered with blisters, the *behique* was judged guilty of not having observed a rigorous enough fast. A second method of questioning the deceased consisted in pouring down the corpse's throat a potion of juices from various plants mixed with clippings from the dead patient's own hair and fingernails, ground into a powder. The corpse was then asked the cause of death. Again, if the deceased was understood to reply that the fault was his own, he was simply taken to be buried then and there. But if the answer implied that the *behique* was guilty, the patient's family beat the priest, making sure to break all his limbs, then left him for dead. If the *behique* survived this beating, then he could claim that his own serpent-shaped *zemi* had protected him. Friar Ramón Pané's chronicle adds that when a family wanted to make sure a guilty *behique* died, they not only broke his arms and legs in the course of the beating, but castrated him.

Not that the Taínos considered their *behiques* to be quacks, however harshly they might treat them in some cases of failure: they only insisted on rigorous observance of the proper rites, and especially fasting. The shaman's art and the patient's trust, in other words psychosomatic suggestion, were at issue here.

The *behiques*' appearance was different from that of other Taínos. They wore not only a loincloth but also a very long cotton cape dyed black, tied around their neck, draped over their hair (twisted into many little braids), then left trailing down behind them to the ground. Over their bare chest hung a protective *zemi*.

Taíno ritual included great village gatherings with much music, singing and dance. Music was produced with conches, wooden rattles, flutes carved in bones and great drums, to the rasping rhythm of the strings of small shells worn by dancers around their necks, arms and ankles. Collective dancing lasted hours. The official chronicler at the court of Ferdinand and Isabella in Spain, the Milanese humanist Peter Martyr of

Anghiera, has transcribed descriptions of these ceremonies where dancing preceded worship of the *cacique*'s *zemi*. Dancers made obeisance to the *cacique* seated before the threshold of his lodge; before entering his dwelling to deposit their offerings at the feet of the *zemi*, they also had to purify themselves by inducing vomiting with the little carved spatula that hung from their persons; then the cleansed performers might enter and sit in a half-circle before the *cacique*'s *zemi* surrounded by the *behique* priests draped with garlands of flowers, who set before the statue finely-worked baskets filled with tortilla cakes and themselves began to sing and dance. The performers in turn rose and sang not only the praises of the *zemi* but also the exploits of the *cacique*'s ancestors. After thanksgiving was chanted to the *zemi* for past benefits, prayers were offered for the future. At the close of the ceremony, the kneeling participants, men and women, proffered tortillas to the *zemi*, which the priests blessed and then shared out among the male worshippers. The pieces of consecrated tortilla were preserved by the participants all year long.

The Taínos and death

Communication with the world of the divine also necessarily required the intercession of the spirits of the dead, the *opia-s*. The Taínos of Hispaniola considered the Land of the Dead, *coay bay*, to lie to one side of their own island. They believed that the dead returned to wander at night under the appearance of the living: only one detail distinguished them they had no navel. Ghosts could also take the shape of bats – often represented in Taíno art, especially on pottery – whereupon they fed on guava like the animals whose form they borrowed.

The Spanish chroniclers give us a little information about the funeral procedures that surrounded the death of at least the leading members of Taíno society, but we are at a loss to explain what motivated the differences in the rites simultaneously described. In some cases a *cacique*'s body was opened and dried over a fire for mummification. In others, only his head was preserved for relic-like incorporation into a *zemi*. The corpses of some *caciques* were burnt in the lodges where they died, while others were buried in caves with offerings of tortillas and a calabash gourd of water disposed around their heads.

When death took too long to come, the Taínos intervened. *Caciques* were consulted as to whether some gravely ill individuals should be strangled. In turn, *caciques* considered too aged or ill were also strangled, or left to die lying in a hammock outside their lodges while tortillas and gourds were disposed, as if they were already dead, below their heads.

The first Europeans in the West Indies were surprised by the density of the local population.

While in Mexico or Peru, *conquistadores* and missionaries tended to inflate population figures to add lustre to their own exploits, they hardly needed to do so in the islands. Based on the censuses taken by the late fifteenth- and early sixteenth-century Spanish, first to raise tribute from the Taínos, and then to parcel out the enslaved inhabitants and their lands among the conquerors, the number of approximately one million natives for the island of Hispaniola consistently appears with very few variations in the major chroniclers: Oviedo, López de Gomara and López de Velasco.

Their texts remain our principal source of knowledge regarding Taíno civilization; while the Spanish writers mostly concentrated their attention on Hispaniola, which was their principal base in the New World for further conquest on the mainland, it is also possible to integrate the more sparsely described native conditions found in Cuba or Puerto Rico, given the cultural homogeneity

Bone spatula for self-purification, to induce vomiting, *adorned with a zemi in the shape of a skull, Lesser Antilles, Martinique. Probably fifteenth century.* [Musée de l'Homme, Paris]

43

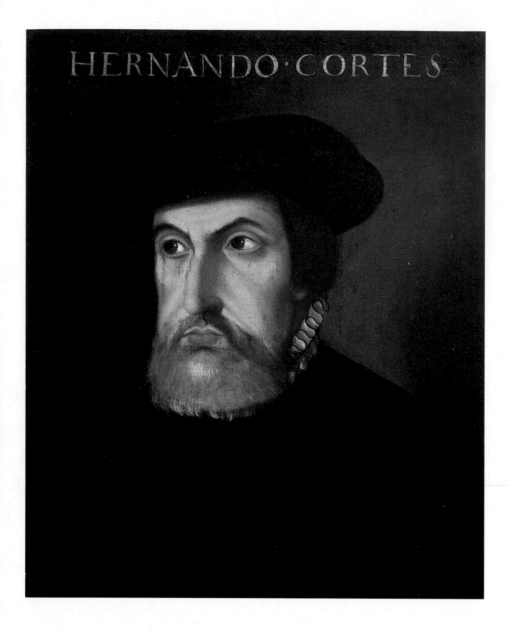

HERNANDO·CORTES

Portrait of Hernán Cortés, *in oil, anonymous. Sixteenth century. [Museo de Santa Cruz, Toledo, Spain. Photo J. Martin, © Arch. Photeb]*

CORSAIRS OF FRANCE
In 1522, a French corsair, Jean Fleury, captured the Spanish caravel bearing part of Moctezuma's treasure sent by Cortés to Charles V. The population of the French sea-port of Dieppe gaped at the New World treasures, the finely wrought gold jewellery, the gold vessels, the gold statuettes of animals, the head-dresses and mantles woven of *quetzal* plumes, and the precious stones including a pyramid-shaped emerald. Another French corsair, Guillaume Le Testu, seized some of the very first Spanish galleons returning with the plunder of Peru.

which clearly prevailed throughout the Greater Antilles in 1492.

Not only were the Greater Antilles the theatre where the initial encounter took place, they also witnessed the most traumatic effect of Conquest. Not at all prepared for what they were to meet with, the first Europeans in the New World provoked the wholesale destruction of the Indian societies of the Antilles, which indeed had almost disappeared by 1519. Among the reasons for this ravage might be listed: mental shock consequent upon the death of the gods and the disintegration of the Taíno social hierarchy; the collapse of the traditional way of life (the Spanish fed their Taíno slaves only on cassava tortillas without the complement of proteins and animal fat which they had formerly derived from fishing and hunting); death in combat against the Spaniards, although Taíno resistance cannot be compared to that offered on the mainland by the Aztecs and Incas; the forced labour of the enslaved Indians who were literally worked by their Spanish masters to death; and finally, sheer biological disaster with the introduction of European and African diseases to

which the Indians were not immunized (the first epidemic of smallpox hit Cuba in 1515 and spread in 1519 with Cortés' troops to Mexico where it claimed victims in the thousands).

Columbus had dangled the prospects of fabulous gold finds in the islands, but what yellow metal they held was quickly exhausted and the Spaniards had to make do with a substitute source of wealth: slave labour. The natives were 'parcelled out' into *repartimientos* among the colonists, some of whom were of very humble stock at home but passed themselves off as gentry in the West Indies. As the Taíno Indians died off the Spaniards were forced to look to alternative sources for bonded labour, and carried out armed slave raids among the Lesser Antilles and on the South American mainland to capture the man-eating Indians. The Spanish Crown officially authorized the enslavement of cannibal populations considered as 'warlike', permission consistent with fifteenth- and sixteenth-century Christian European legal practice, which specifically provided for bondage in the case of captive 'infidels' (Muslims or pagan Africans).

As of 1501, Spain's rulers permitted the import of African bondmen to the New World after Spanish slave-raids had significantly contributed to destroying the native populations of both the Greater and Lesser Antilles. While the institution of slavery had certainly existed among the peoples of pre-Hispanic America, bondmen were at least recognized as human beings and entitled to certain rights, and slave-trade had never reached the staggering proportions introduced by the men from the Old World. In the Antilles, the African slave-trade soon became immensely profitable to the Spanish: to begin with, the Blacks were as immune as the Europeans themselves to the Old World diseases which felled the Indians.

First steps on the continent

The conquered Antilles provided the European beachhead for the conquest of the mainland which reconnaissance expeditions reached very early. Columbus in the course of his third voyage was the first to touch the South American continent in 1498 by exploring the Gulf of Paria on the coast of Venezuela. On his fourth voyage between 1502 and 1504, he saw the eastern shore of Central America from Honduras to Panamá. The close of the fifteenth century and the opening years of the sixteenth saw the Spanish further reconnoitre the eastern coastline of the isthmus of Panamá and the beaches of Venezuela, while Brazil, with Cabral's landfall in 1500, fell to the Portuguese sphere of influence in the South Atlantic, recognized by the Treaty of Tordesillas since 1494.

By the end of the first decade of the sixteenth century, the Spanish were durably encamped on the continent at Darién, the area to the south of the isthmus of Panamá. Vasco Núñez de Balboa and his men set up a fort among the Panamá Indians in 1508. Hearing from the Indian woman who served as his interpreter of the existence of a great body of water to the south, Balboa led his troops on a ghastly march through the isthmus jungles until, on 25 September 1513, he discovered the Pacific Ocean which he called 'the great sea of the South'. The Spaniards had now seen the western face of the American continent and consolidated their base in Panamá, which they christened 'Golden Castile'. From Panamá they moved southwards in probes which eventually culminated in the conquest of Peru.

The conquest of 'Golden Castile' was completed in 1516 by Don Pedro Arias de Avila. The new forts on the isthmus meant that Panamá would become the new staging-ground for conquest in the South, somewhat to the detriment of Hispaniola and Cuba, which were now partly reduced to the status of supply stations on the return voyage to Spain.

The shock of the very first encounter with the New World had hardly faded when the Spaniards suddenly came to grips with the two great Native American Empires. The stupefaction of the *conquistadores* before what they saw in Mexico and Peru forced some of them to become writers in order to account for the reality which they had faced. The two Empires posed a military challenge while mentally almost reassuring the conquerors with evidence of mighty hierarchical social structures comparable to Old World standards. The underlying workings of the materially primitive Taíno culture on the islands

Spanish conquistadores, *from a colonial Mexican manuscript. Sixteenth century. [Bibliothèque nationale, Paris. Photo © Bibl. nat.-Arch.Photeb]*

THE MAGIC OF FAR HORIZONS

The first Spaniard to land in Florida was the governor of Puerto Rico, Ponce de León, in 1512, on Palm Sunday, called in Spanish Pascua Florida or 'Flower Sunday', whence the name.

In 1527, the adelantado, Panfilo de Narváez, took a large Spanish force to conquer Florida. The survivors of this force, shipwrecked and starving, wandered for eight years into the region of the Río Grande and thence down to Mexico. One survivor, Alvar Nuñez Cabeza de Vaca, wrote down his story in his Naufragios ('Shipwrecks'), evoking the rumours he believed he heard concerning the Seven Cities of Cíbola abounding in precious metals.

In 1539, Hernando de Soto, a veteran of Peru, again attempted the conquest of Florida. His guide was another survivor of the Narváez force. This expedition wandered for three years throughout what is now the United States' Deep South as far as Arkansas and discovered the Mississippi, in whose waters De Soto was buried. The survivors reached the Mexican port of Panuco, north of Veracruz, in September 1543.

From still another direction, in 1538, the Viceroy of Mexico, Don Antonio de Mendoza, sent a further expedition, again guided by a survivor of the Narváez adventure, the African slave Estevánico, accompanied by the priest Marcos de Niza, to try to find the Seven Cities of Cíbola in what is now the Southwest of the United States. Estevánico was killed by Indians; the friar returned to Mexico in 1539 and believed he could confirm that the Seven Cities of Cíbola existed and were crammed with gold and other wealth. In late 1539, Don Antonio de Mendoza sent a large force under the officer Don Francisco Vásquez de Coronado to find and conquer the Seven Cities of Cíbola at long last. All the Spaniards found, in the deserts of what is now New Mexico and Arizona, were the Pueblo Indians dwelling in adobe houses under cliff-faces or on the high tablelands, and the only treasures they brought back to the Viceroy were a handful of turquoise stones.

Just as they had begun to do with Columbus, the Indians never ceased hoodwinking the conquistadores with tales of gold to be found only 'a little farther beyond' their own territory.

Conquest of Mexico. *This episode shows the Spanish army on the march with its native porters. Hernán Cortés leads, accompanied by the Lady Malinche; colonial Mexican manuscript, Codex Azcatitlán. Sixteenth century.* [Bibliothèque nationale, Paris. Photo © Bibl. nat.-Arch. Photeb]

Right-hand page
The city of Cuzco, *capital of the Inca Empire, from a sixteenth-century engraving.* [Bibliothèque nationale, Paris. Photo M. Didier, © Bibl. nat.-Arch. Photeb]

had often baffled and usually escaped the Spaniards; but the power, wealth and glory of the Aztec and Inca Empires were something they thought they could understand.

The Mexican adventure

Even before the first Spanish landings on the Mexican coast, rumours of what was happening in the Islands seem to have reached the Maya of Yucatán and the Aztec rulers of Mexico-Tenochtitlán, where omens of ill tidings to come suddenly appear to have abounded during the two decades which preceded Cortés' attack.

The first Spaniards landed on the coast of Yucatán by accident in 1511, after the shipwreck of a caravel on its way back from Darién in Panamá to Santo Domingo. Most of the survivors who made their way in the ship's longboat to the eastern shore of Yucatán were sacrificed by the Maya, except for two, the priest Jerónimo de Aguilar who would one day be found by Cortés in 1519, and the lay soldier Gonzalo Guerrero who married a daughter of the *cacique* of Chetumal and elected to live out his life among a new people.

In 1517, Francisco Hernández de Córdoba was blown off course to the coast of Yucatán. On the western shore, at Champotón, his landing party was violently repulsed by the Maya. But the Spaniards had time to see monumental stone architecture, temples and palaces, such as they had never before witnessed in America. Shortly after

his return to Cuba, Hernández de Córdoba died of the wounds he had sustained in his clash with the Maya. But he had told his story.

In 1518, Juan de Grijalva, nephew to the Governor of Cuba, Diego de Velásquez, sailed to Yucatán to explore. He reconnoitred the eastern shoreline and saw more evidence of important settlements and buildings. Then, turning north, he rounded the tip of the peninsula and followed the western coast, bartering trinkets along the way for a considerable quantity of gold and finally reaching the mouth of the Río Panuco, where the Spaniards for the first time met with chieftains tributary to the Aztec Empire. On the return voyage, Grijalva stopped at Champotón and again the Spaniards were attacked by the Maya. In Cuba, Grijalva's report and treasure fed beliefs that here at last were new lands where gold was to be found in abundance.

Cuba's Governor, Diego de Velásquez, was quick to outfit a major expedition under the officer Hernán Cortés, a young hidalgo from Estremadura who had come to the West Indies in 1504 at the age of nineteen. The fleet weighed anchor in February 1519. Cortés' eleven ships carried five hundred men, ten cannons, and last but by no means least, sixteen horses. In the very first clashes, the Spaniards' command of thunder, and their armoured knights on horseback, would dismay the Indians initially convinced that charger and rider formed a single creature, like a centaur.

On the Yucatán coast, Cortés was informed by local Indians that two Spaniards dwelt among

CVSCO. REGNI PERV
IN NOVO ORBE CAPVT.

year *Ce Acatl*, 'One-Reed', corresponding in the Aztec calendar to the year 1519.

The Aztec ruler, Moctezuma, was told of the landing of the strangers and sent Cortés an embassy bearing rich gifts. The Aztec envoys were to report more fully on the strangers and diplomatically prevent them from penetrating as far as Mexico-Tenochtitlán, while the painter-scribes who accompanied the embassy were to depict the white men, their ships, their horses and cannons. To impress the Aztec envoys, Cortés and his knights duly gave a display of horsemanship while his artillerymen fired their pieces. Diplomatic exchanges dragged on for another few weeks between the capital and the Spaniards on the coast, until the impatient Cortés, spurred by his vision of so much wealth, decided to march on Mexico-Tenochtitlán. Perfectly aware that his few troops would hardly be a match for the Aztec Empire, the Spanish commander persuaded the Totonacs to throw off the Mexican yoke and join him, and bound his own soldiers to himself while cutting off all possibility of desertion and retreat by boldly burning his ships.

When the Spaniards and their Totonac allies reached the high plateaux, sixty-five miles from the capital, they were attacked by the warriors of the independent state of Tlaxcala, sworn enemies of the Aztecs. The defeated Tlaxcalans chose to offer fealty to the Spaniards and would remain loyal to them even through the most demanding trials. The conquest of Mexico-Tenochtitlán became a combined Spanish and Tlaxcalan adventure while the foundations of Aztec power began to totter. When this disquieting turn in events was reported to Moctezuma, the ruler still had not made up his mind whether the invaders were men or gods and remained irresolute as to whether he should meet them with armed force. Meanwhile the Spaniards with their new allies entered the holy city of Cholula, subject to the Aztecs. Claiming that the Aztec ruler had plotted with the people of Cholula to trap and destroy the Spaniards in the town, Cortés ordered the slaughter of its lords and dignitaries. The road to Mexico now lay open and, in early November 1519, Cortés discovered, from a pass between twin volcanoes, the Valley of Anahuac, a vast plateau dotted with lakes among which rose the glittering Aztec capital towering above lesser cities. The awed Spaniards moved down the range with their allies towards Mexico-Tenochtitlán. To enter the great city set in the middle of a lake, the Spaniards stepped onto one of the great stone causeways connecting the capital to the mainland. In the midst of the causeway, Cortés was met by Moctezuma, borne in a richly adorned litter and surrounded by high dignitaries, including the lord of the allied city of Texcoco. When the Spanish commander wished to embrace Moctezuma, the lords restrained him, for no human being could thus touch the Aztec ruler.

In the city, the Spaniards were lodged in the spacious palace of Axayacatl, a former Aztec ruler

CRVDELITATES HISPANORVM

92 CRVDELITATES HISPANORVM
nator, quod ille, qui nouo Granatæ regno deprædabatur, eum deprædationum, & cædium focium admittere nollet, inquifiti-ones & probationes, multis teftibus confirmatas confecit, qui-bus probat cædes, & homicidia, quæ ille commifit, & in quibus committendis vfq; in præfentem diem perfeuerat, quæ in Con-filio Indiæ lectæ funt, & hodie adhuc afferuantur.

In dicta inquifitione teftes deponunt, cum omnia hæc re-

Tortures inflicted on Indians by the Spanish and denounced by Father Las Casas. From an engraving dated 1598. [Bibliothèque nationale, Paris. Photo © Bibl. nat.-Arch. Photeb]

them. These were the survivors of the shipwreck of 1511. Only the priest, Jerónimo de Aguilar, willingly joined Cortés, and proved an invaluable interpreter through his knowledge of the Maya language. Sailing along the Gulf coast toward central Mexico, the Spaniards dropped anchor on the shore of Tabasco where the natives offered Cortés precious gifts, including the choicest of all: a young captive Mexican woman, Malintzin, who became Cortés' interpreter (she knew not only her native Nahuatl but also the Maya, which Aguilar spoke, and later learned Spanish), his adviser, and finally his mistress. The Spaniards mispronounced her name as 'Malinche', while the Aztecs in turn came to call Cortés himself Malintzin or 'Malinche', since he 'owned' her.

On 22 April 1519, the ships dropped anchor near present-day Veracruz, on the coast of the territory of the Totonacs of Cempoala, a people tributary to the Aztecs who welcomed the Spaniards peacefully. With Malinche interpreting, Cortés learned of the fatal weakness of the Aztec Empire, and of the discontent of the peoples ruled by the Mexicans and forced to pay heavy tribute to the capital Mexico-Tenochtitlán. At the same time, Cortés was also informed of the myth of Quetzalcoatl, a god white and bearded like the Spaniards, whose return was expected in this very and Moctezuma's father, while their Indian allies camped in the courtyard. Cortés and his men admired the splendour of the Mexican capital, a New World Venice in the midst of its lake and canals with majestic buildings and harmoniously laid-out streets; but the Spanish commander kept an eye on what could change the city into a trap: if the wooden footbridges set at regular intervals along the causeways were removed, his army would have no means of reaching the mainland again. To ensure the security of his men, Cortés carried out his boldest stroke of all: he seized and held hostage the Aztec ruler in his own father's palace.

While Cortés thus skilfully gained control of the Aztec capital with the ruler as his prisoner, the Spanish Governor in Cuba, Diego de Velásquez, sent a second fleet to the Mexican coast to recall his far too ambitious subordinate. Again Cortés was up to the situation. Leaving his lieutenant Pedro de Alvarado in the capital, he rode to the coast where he managed to convince the Spaniards sent to arrest him to join his standards instead, thus providing himself with fresh reinforcements.

Events in Mexico-Tenochtitlán, meanwhile, took a dramatic turn that precipitated the actual conquest. Fearing treachery, Pedro de Alvarado suddenly ordered his men to fall upon and kill some Aztec priests and nobles dancing at the base of the great temple. The population rose against the Spaniards and besieged them in their quarters. Cortés fought his way back into the capital while the surrounded Spaniards and their allies attempted bloody sorties from the palace they held.

On the rooftop of the palace, the captive Moctezuma tried to harangue his subjects and restore his own control, but the crowd of warriors pelted him with stones and arrows and the former ruler fell back mortally wounded among the Spaniards. Cortés realized that the position was no longer defensible and ordered evacuation on the night of 30 June 1520.

This night came to be known to the Spaniards as the *Noche triste*, the Sad Night: many Spaniards died retreating along the causeways, some of them slipping and drowning in the lake under the weight of booty which they had refused to part with, others captured by the Aztecs and sacrificed on their altars to the gods. A new ruler, Cuitlahuac, brother to Moctezuma, took responsibility for organizing Aztec resistance.

Once safely back on the mainland, Cortés ordered retreat as far as Tlaxcala, which remained loyal to its Spanish alliance despite the rout of the strangers from Mexico-Tenochtitlán. While fighting their way clear to Tlaxcala, the allied Spaniards and Tlaxcalans managed to defeat an intercepting Aztec force at Otumba, which revived their will to carry on with the struggle to a finish.

In Tlaxcala, Cortés drew the tactical conclusions forced by the *Noche triste*. Taking Mexico-Tenochtitlán, he realized, meant gaining control of its lake. He ordered the construction of brigantines on which he placed his artillery,

launched them on the lake and besieged the Aztec capital both on water and land. Meanwhile an epidemic of smallpox, a disease hitherto unknown to mainland America and apparently carried to Mexico by an African slave of Cortés, caused thousands of deaths throughout the country and especially within the beleaguered city, felling the ruler Cuitlahuac himself. A nephew of Moctezuma, Cuauhtémoc, now assumed leadership of what was left of Aztec resistance.

Weakened by disease and lack of food, the last defenders of the Mexican capital fought stubbornly, house by house, against the final Spanish assault buttressed by thousands of Tlaxcalan warriors. On 13 August 1521, quitting the ruined city in a canoe in an attempt to gain the mainland, the last ruler of Anahuac, Cuauhtémoc, was captured by the Spaniards. The Aztec Empire disintegrated. In a matter of years, metropolitan Spaniards flocked to Mexico to exploit the resources and enslave the inhabitants of a land henceforth christened 'New Spain'.

But Cortés' lieutenants pursued the Conquest southwards. Between 1523 and 1524, Pedro de Alvarado, known to the Indians as Tonatiuh ('the Sun') because of his flaming red hair, conquered the territory of Guatemala. Between 1524 and 1526, Cortés sent his lieutenant Cristóbal de Olid into Honduras, then himself had to intervene when this disloyal officer tried to throw off allegiance to his commander. In the course of this Honduran expedition, Cortés, on grounds of a suspected plot, ordered the execution by hanging of the last Aztec ruler, Cuauhtémoc, who had been forced to accompany the Spanish army as a hostage to keep the Indians in check. The Maya lands were officially annexed to New Spain in 1548 after the quelling of a serious revolt, although sporadic uprisings – always ruthlessly crushed – never entirely died down in the southern borderlands.

The Peruvian adventure

With Mexico conquered, the Spaniards concentrated on closing the gap between their colony of New Spain and the territory of Golden Castile (Panamá); this link was completed in 1530, and the Spanish empire was ready now to expand even farther southwards.

Only eleven years after the fall of the Aztec capital, the second great native State of the

Francisco Pizarro, *an anonymous portrait of the conqueror. [Museo de América, Madrid. Photo Oronoz, © Arch. Photeb]*

Americas, the Inca, crumbled in turn under Spanish assault. The history of the conquest of Peru shows marked resemblance to that of Mexico. In both cases, initial Spanish reconnaissance expeditions amassed evidence of immense wealth; native myths announced the return of white and bearded divine culture-heroes (Quetzalcoatl in Mexico, Viracocha in Peru); subject peoples betrayed discontent against a single imperial ruling ethnic group (the Inca Empire was even more extensive and also more centralized than the Aztec); finally, in both Mexico and Peru, the *conquistadores* were able to exploit both native mythology and internal political discord.

In 1513, Balboa had crossed the isthmus of Panamá and discovered the Pacific. Among his followers was an illiterate soldier from Trujillo in Estremadura, Francisco Pizarro. This Pizarro was given an estate and Indian serfs in Golden Castile, but soon struck up a partnership with another veteran, Diego de Almagro, to plan for further conquests: the Panamá colony was alive with rumours of a southern land of abundant gold and Pizarro and Almagro had heard them too. In 1523, Pascual de Andagoya had taken ship from Panamá and followed the shoreline down to the latitude of Colombia. Here he saw Indian boatmen who indicated that they came from a rich distant country to the south known as '*Biru*'. The Spaniards, who heard this name for the first time, mispronounced it as 'Perú'.

Andagoya's story spurred Pizarro and Almagro to sink their capital into a 'Peruvian' venture, in partnership with a priest in the Panamá colony, one Hernando de Luque, who represented the interests of a magistrate of Golden Castile, Gaspar de Espinosa. In 1524, the three partners armed two vessels and explored the jungle-lined coast of Colombia. For a second trip in 1526-1527, the partners hired one hundred Spaniards with Indian auxiliaries. Pizarro, camping on the Colombian coast to raid, sent his pilot Bartolomé Ruiz to reconnoitre even farther south. Off the shore of present-day Ecuador, Ruiz saw a great balsa raft with mast and sail – the Spaniards had never yet encountered such a native craft – carrying richly dressed Indians who gave to understand that they came from a port called Tumbes, on the present-day northernmost frontier of Peru. These Indians, who were coastal merchants, managed to confirm that there was much gold in their land which belonged to the Inca, Huayna Capac. Ruiz,

according to usual Spanish practice, took prisoners so that they might learn Castilian and become interpreters, and reported to Pizarro who, on this intelligence, decided to go see Tumbes for himself. The Spaniards received a courteous welcome in Tumbes and glimpsed something of the glory of the Inca Empire at its zenith. The expedition returned to Panamá and, in the spring of 1528, Pizarro took ship for Spain to solicit an interview with the King. Charles V was impressed with Pizarro's story and by the artefacts which he had brought from Tumbes, and granted him a charter as governor and captain-general of the lands that he might conquer. Almagro was appointed Governor of Tumbes, and the priest Luque was named its bishop. Before returning to Golden Castile, Pizarro paid a visit to his home town of Trujillo, to recruit his brothers and also to collect, throughout Estremadura, about one hundred tough veterans of Spain's Italian campaigns.

In January 1531, Francisco Pizarro left Panamá with three ships, twenty-seven horses and about two hundred men. At Tumbes, the captain-general learned through his native interpreter, Felipillo, that the Inca Empire was distracted by domestic conflict. The Inca, Huayna Capac, had been in the north putting down a rebellion, when he had been felled by a hitherto unknown disease which was killing his people by the hundreds: smallpox, the sickness which the Spanish had introduced into the hemisphere and which now preceded them. A war of succession had broken out between Huascar, the legitimate son of Huayna Capac, and Huascar's half-brother Atahualpa, son of a favourite concubine of the Inca. Atahualpa had been proclaimed Inca in the city of Quito, in present-day Ecuador, and was marching on the capital, Cuzco, at the head of a mighty army, against his rival. Pizarro used these Peruvian fissions as skilfully as Cortés had exploited those of Mexico. When the Spaniards disembarked, Atahualpa's headquarters were in the highlands at Cajamarca. Pizarro purposefully struck due east into the Andes to meet him there. Along his way, the Spanish commander took careful note of those native peoples exasperated by Inca oppression.

Before he left the coast, Pizarro had been seen by envoys of the other contending Inca prince, Huascar. Huascar certainly had no love for these meddling strangers, but thought they might serve as useful allies against Atahualpa since they already camped on territory controlled by his half-brother. In the meantime, the priests at Cuzco were reviving the pan-Andean myth of Viracocha, a divine bearded culture-hero believed to have departed upon the Ocean after completing the task of bringing civilization to mankind, and due to return. This myth accounts for the name '*Viracocha*' which designates the Spaniards in some of the chronicles.

For his part, the other rival prince, Atahualpa, did not fear the strangers either but regarded them more as nuisances. He also sent

Franciscus Pizarrus läßt den König Atabaliba wider verheissene trew vnd glauben auffhencken.

them envoys, but essentially to spy and report on them. On their return, the envoys reassured their royal master: the horses of the Spaniards, for example, lost their power at night when their bridles and saddles were removed to allow them to sleep. Atahualpa resolved to accept a meeting with the Spaniards at Cajamarca, probably planning to capture and neutralize them there.

On 15 November 1532, Pizarro rode at the head of his troops into the deserted streets of the city of Cajamarca. Fearing a trap, the captain-general deployed his men in defensive positions around the main square and in various strategic spots throughout the town. The Inca and his army remained encamped outside Cajamarca, near its famous hot springs.

Confident now in his position, Pizarro sent some of his mounted officers with his interpreter Felipillo to invite the Inca to an interview in Cajamarca. Noting the interest aroused by his

horse, one of the captains displayed his equestrian skill, hoping to awe the Inca: but the ruler remained impassive. The interview was set for the next day, in the great square of the city. Deeply impressed by the number and discipline of the Inca's warriors, the Spanish envoys rode back to Cajamarca and Pizarro sharply drew conclusions: he convinced his officers that their only means of securing their own safety lay in seizing the person of the Inca. Horsemen, and foot-soldiers with matchlocks and the expedition's two 'falcons' or light cannon, were hidden in the houses around the square, ready to rush upon the Inca at a given signal.

On the next day, the long royal procession wound into the city with the Inca upon his sumptuous litter borne by dignitaries of the highest rank. The mass of his warriors remained outside the city, but six thousand men (according to the chronicles) escorted their ruler into Cajamarca.

Execution of Atahualpa. *The last Inca ruler converted to Christianity out of fear that, if he were burned at the stake, the destruction of his bodily frame would cause the annihilation of his immortal soul; instead he was garrotted and buried, and so escaped the fate he most feared. From an engraving illustrating the Grands Voyages, by Théodore de Bry (1590-1620). [Bibliothèque nationale, Paris. Photo © Bibl. nat.-Arch. Photeb]*

51

BELALCÁZAR AND
WHAT IS NOW COLOMBIA

In 1533, Pizarro sent his officer, Sebastián de Belalcázar, to conquer the area around Quito which had remained loyal to the Inca Atahualpa. Meanwhile, from the north, Cortés' lieutenant Pedro de Alvarado, the conqueror of Guatemala, had reached Ecuador in turn after many adventures such as meeting with the Jívaro Indians who worshipped an immense emerald in a temple built in the middle of the jungle. But when he learned of Belalcázar's approach, Alvarado turned back and left the field to Pizarro's officer. Belalcázar conquered Quito and marched as far as the Chibcha country in present-day Colombia. In 1536, he founded the city of Popayán near a previous Indian site. In 1538 he reached the Indian settlement of Bogotá only to find that another *conquistador* had preceded him there, the Andalusian knight Gonzalo Jiménez de Quesada. Quesada christened the Chibcha territories 'New Granada' and founded still another Spanish city, on the site of the Indian town, Santa Fe de Bogotá.

Here, according to the questionable but celebrated account by López de Gomara, the Dominican friar Vicente de Valverde tried to convince Atahualpa through the interpreter Felipillo to submit to Charles V, renounce his heresies and embrace the True Faith, presenting his breviary to the Inca who examined it contemptuously, then threw it to the ground. Pizarro gave the signal, horsemen and foot-soldiers emerged suddenly from hiding and cut down the Indians who surrounded the litter of their sovereign like a human wall. To secure the life of Atahualpa himself, Pizarro plunged into the fray and dragged the Inca to safety inside one of the houses on the square. Outside Cajamarca, the native army made no move: perhaps they dared not imperil the sacred person of their ruler.

While Atahualpa was held by the Spaniards, his supporters defeated his rival Huascar in Cuzco. To avoid death, Atahualpa calculated that it would be better for him to remain as the sole Inca and thus be far too precious a hostage for the Spaniards to kill. From his prison, he ordered the execution of Huascar; and to recover his freedom, he offered to pay a ransom to Pizarro that would fill to the top one of the rooms in Cajamarca.

From the four corners of the Empire, caravans of llamas bearing gold, silver and precious stones, converged on Cajamarca. When the room was filled with treasure, Pizarro ordered the gold and silver to be melted into ingots, except for a few pieces of such marvellous workmanship that he had them sent intact to Seville, where they were displayed before the crowds until they in turn were pitilessly melted down by order of Charles V. Setting aside the 'royal fifth' and his own share, Pizarro distributed the booty among his soldiers, with horsemen receiving twice the amount that infantrymen did. His ransom paid, the Inca demanded his freedom. But the Spaniards hesitated: should they free a potential opponent of such importance, especially when a native army was rumoured to be fast approaching to help its ruler? Instead, the Spaniards set up a mock trial, accused the Inca of political treason, of murdering his brother, of incestuous marriage with his sister, of polygamy and idol-worship, and sentenced him to be burned alive. Atahualpa accepted conversion to Christianity, not out of fear of the pyre, but to prevent the destruction of his body by flames, in accordance with ancient Peruvian belief which held that disintegration of the bodily frame ended the immortality of the soul. Atahualpa was garrotted, thus escaping the annihilation he feared.

Huascar's murder brought to the Spanish side those Indians who had hitherto remained loyal to the legitimate successor of Huayna Capac, or who had thought until then that they could retain a measure of independence. As the invaders imposed their power throughout the country, numerous natives offered fealty.

On 15 November 1533, after four months of hard marching through the Andes, marked by ambushes set by one of Atahualpa's former generals, the Spaniards and their Indian vassals finally reached Cuzco. Pizarro recognized Manco, a half-brother of Huascar who made submission to the *conquistadores*, as new Inca. Leaving Cuzco to the care of this puppet ruler, Pizarro then left for the coast, where he founded the capital of 'New Castile', *Lima de los Reyes*, 'of the Kings', in honour of the Epiphany and of the Three Magi whose day it was. The foundation of Lima gave the newly conquered territories an important direct sea link to Panamá.

PEDRO DE VALDÍVIA AND CHILE

The Spaniards repeatedly attempted the conquest of Chile, a lengthy stretch of territory, the fringes of which the last Inca rulers themselves had only just begun to subdue, and that only imperfectly.

Pizarro's lieutenant, Almagro, left Cuzco in 1535 accompanied by several hundred Spaniards and thousands of Indian auxiliaries, but proved unable to push beyond the Bio-Bio river in the face of determined resistance from the Araucanian Indians.

In 1542, and for the next thirteen years, another of Pizarro's officers, Pedro de Valdívia, tried to conquer Chile with an army that now included mestizos or half-breeds, recruited for their knowledge of Indian languages. Valdívia crossed the Bio-Bio river, but the stalwart Araucanian Indians of the Chile highlands captured and learned how to ride horses, and now successfully checked the Spanish cavalry with their own.

Valdívia fought on, because the country of 'New Estremadura' was rich in gold and copper mines. He founded such fortified cities as Valparaíso and Santiago de Chile to attract colonists while hoping to push his conquests as far as the Strait of Magellan. But the Araucanian Indians proved formidable foes, rose again in 1553 under their war-chief Lautaro (a former servant of Valdívia) and in 1554 captured the Spanish captain-general himself with his father confessor. According to the chronicle of Garcilaso de la Vega, Lautaro had the two high-ranking Spaniards tortured to death. This was only the beginning of the Araucanian Wars, the toughest Indian fighting that Spanish colonists anywhere ever had to face, which lasted down to the end of the nineteenth century.

The Araucanian Wars were the stuff of frontier epic, and the rising of 1553 inspired a Spanish knight on the scene to write one: Alonso de Ercilla y Zúñiga's La Araucana became in fact the finest verse epic of the entire Spanish Renaissance, and deals fairly and movingly with the courage and nobility of Spain's staunchest Native American opponents.

The first years of the new colony were shaken by the last convulsive acts of resistance on the part of diehard Inca princes, and by civil wars between the conquerors themselves.

The Spaniards' technological edge and the superiority of their weaponry do not alone explain the success of mere handfuls of adventurers in conquering the New World and especially in overthrowing the two great native states of Mexico and Peru. In both cases, the Spaniards benefited from exceptionally favourable circumstances. Both Aztecs and Incas were affected by myths that predicted the return, from beyond the Ocean, of divine, bearded culture-heroes; the invaders exploited such myths which of course gained widespread currency as soon as they landed. The myths, however, prophesied the return of native deities and the restoration of the old order, not the imposition by force of a new religion spelling death for the traditional gods.

Yet Christianity did not entirely replace the old cults which clandestinely endured in urban centres, and were even more openly practised in the countryside and remote districts. Moreover, after the Conquest, elements of pre-Hispanic ritual were incorporated or absorbed by the Church. Nevertheless, the Indians were shocked by the intransigence and exclusive character of Christianity, which contrasted so strangely with the syncretizing religious approach of the Aztecs or Incas. Both imperial 'peoples of the Sun' had undoubtedly imposed the worship of their own tribal deities, but had never suppressed the cults of older gods. Quite the contrary, the Aztecs just like the Incas had assimilated a great many of the deities worshipped by the peoples whom they subjected. One of the most remarkable examples of such religious syncretism is offered by the great temple of Mexico-Tenochtitlán, remains of which were found in 1978. Before its destruction, this edifice was crowned with twin sanctuaries, one dedicated to Huitzilopochtli, the tribal war-god of the Aztecs, and the other to Tlaloc, the agrarian deity worshipped by the newly subjugated peoples of the central plateau since the early centuries AD. Setting them both at the very highest level and in the same rank, the Aztecs thus associated, in their worship, Huitzilopochtli the war-god of the imperial masters, and Tlaloc the supreme god of the subject peoples, who were thereby symbolically allowed to participate in the power of the ruling hierarchy of the Empire.

The impact of the Spaniards was not only psychological, however. Social and political factors also played a key role in provoking the collapse of both native Empires. The Aztecs and the Incas attempted to maintain a centralized sway over a mosaic of different vanquished peoples upon whom weighed heavily the tribute they imposed. Cortés and Pizarro quickly took skilful advantage of the deep grudges nursed by the subjugated peoples. At the outset of each of the two great Conquests, thousands of Indian auxiliaries swelled the ranks of

the few Spanish soldiers, creating large armies. Many of these native troops loyally observed their alliance with the Spaniards even when the latter suffered reverses. Cortés would probably not have carried his expedition to success, after his forced evacuation of the Aztec capital during the *Noche triste*, without the support of the Tlaxcalans. In Peru, the alliance of several coastal peoples, such as the Cañaris, contributed in large measure to Pizarro's own success. While not all the peoples tributary to the Aztecs or Incas gave active military assistance to the invaders, at least many of them observed a passive and trusting role and readily acknowledged the Spaniards as their new masters. Just as forced Christianization loosened the grip of the old gods, so Spanish military power destroyed the framework holding the indigenous society together; the Native American was no longer in harmony with his own explanation of the workings of the world, and became an uprooted exile upon his own soil.

But the Spanish Conquest was greatly speeded by the shattering biological trauma provoked by the appearance of hitherto unknown diseases. Old World microbes devastated native populations utterly devoid of immunity to smallpox and measles. During the fighting as in Mexico, or shortly before the Spanish landing as in Peru, epidemics mowed down thousands of Indians and wrought a demographic catastrophe.

It is now estimated that about 80 per cent of the Native American population, on average, disappeared in the course of the Conquest and during the immediately following years. The magnitude of these statistics has led a number of

Cutting and loading brazilwood: *a red dye, extracted from this wood, was an important object of trade with Europe. From an engraving illustrating the* Cosmographie universelle, *by Thévet, 1575. [Bibliothèque de l'Arsenal, Paris. Photo Jeanbor, © Arch. Photeb]*

ORELLANA
AND THE AMAZON
In the year 1541, the *conquistador*, Francisco de Orellana, descended from the Andes in Ecuador and reached the Atlantic Ocean after eight months of river-navigation along the Amazon. Orellana's men took their brigantine down the Río Napo, then the Río Marañón, and finally into the Amazon which Orellana called thus on account of the armed native women he saw and likened to the legendary warrior-women of Classical mythology.

ORIGIN
OF THE NAME BRAZIL
Brazil was originally a word designating a precious wood whence was derived red dye, in keen demand in sixteenth-century Europe's textile industry – especially in the peak years of 1525–1530. European crews of many nations established trade links with the coastal natives of the land of 'Brazil' to procure this wood. As early as 1504, the French navigator Paulnier de Gonneville, of Honfleur, made regular trading voyages in 'brazilwood' based on understandings with the coastal Tupinamba Indians.

authors to speak of a 'genocide of the Conquest'. But biology here was the worst culprit.

While military operations were attended by bloody fighting and enslavement certainly entailed great cruelty, it should be stressed that the Spaniards never planned the systematic extermination of the conquered peoples. Quite the opposite: some of the conquerors – notably Cortés in Mexico, or in Peru the knight Don García Lasso de la Vega who wedded an Inca princess and sired the famous chronicler *El Inca* Garcilaso de la Vega – even thought in terms of miscegenation between the ruling classes and the bringing to light of a new composite race.

The brutality of Castile's knights in the New World was very much that of their age and civilization.

Although the great native cities fell beneath the storm of the Conquest, new cities arose from their still warm ashes, and the vitality of the colonial settlements bore witness to the mutual enrichment of their varied populations. Outside the urban centres, traditional ways of life unnoticed by the chroniclers endured in the rural districts down to our own day. South of the Río Grande, the survival of many pre-Hispanic cultural traits was ensured by the very immensity of the Latin American lands, whose remoter stretches were, ultimately, occupied only very recently by Europeans or their descendants.

Overcoming the trial of Conquest, the traditional native cultures have held firm through the centuries as a final expression of the resistance of a people.

THE AZTECS

EDUARDO MATOS MOCTEZUMA

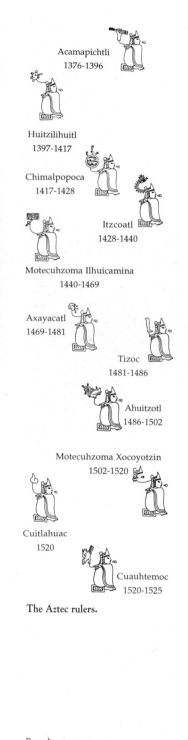

Acamapichtli
1376-1396

Huitzilihuitl
1397-1417

Chimalpopoca
1417-1428

Itzcoatl
1428-1440

Motecuhzoma Ilhuicamina
1440-1469

Axayacatl
1469-1481

Tizoc
1481-1486

Ahuitzotl
1486-1502

Motecuhzoma Xocoyotzin
1502-1520

Cuitlahuac
1520

Cuauhtemoc
1520-1525

The Aztec rulers.

Preceding page
Xipe Totec, *'our lord of the flayed skin',*
a pendentive mask, made of rhydite
representing the god of goldsmiths and the
divinity of renewed flora. The god's face
is represented as covered with skin flayed
from the body of a sacrificial victim.
Mexico, State of Oaxaca, Aztec period,
fifteenth–sixteenth century. [Musée de
l'Homme, Paris]

It is not possible to say precisely where the Aztecs originated. History and mythology are interwoven to such an extent that it is difficult to know whether they came from northern country beyond the valley of Mexico or whether, as certain researchers think, they were already settled there. The majority of sixteenth-century chronicles which talk about these people share the northerly origin theory. They refer to a place called Aztlan, a difficult term to translate from the Nahuatl language, but which, depending on the interpretation, might mean the 'place of the egrets' or simply 'whiteness'.

It would seem that in about 1000 AD, the Aztecs inhabited those countries which were at that time perhaps subjugated and controlled by the Toltecs, a people who had extended their ascendancy over several regions beyond their capital, Tula. So it is possible that the Aztecs might have been a tribute people of the Toltecs. From historical sources, we know that before its final destruction, about 1165 AD, the Toltec empire experienced different crises which gradually weakened it. In the same way as other tributary groups, the Aztecs were able to profit from this disintegration in order to begin to free themselves from Tula.

It would seem that from the beginning of the settlement at Aztlan, Aztec society was hierarchical, organized around agriculture and familiar with the exploitation of lakeside sites. It also possessed astronomical knowledge linked to the counting of time (calendar) and associated with various complex rituals.

There was a surprising similarity between the ancient city of Aztlan and the town of Mexico-Tenochtitlán, which the Aztecs founded much later, so much so that certain authors believe the first might have been the prototype for the second. Both cities were in the centre of a lake. Each had a neighbouring city: Cohualtepec for Aztlan and Tlatelolco for Tenochtitlán. They were both divided into districts and exploited *chinampas*, a system of cultivation which resulted in high levels of production.

However, mythology tells us that at Aztlan, Huitzilopochtli, the principal god of the Aztecs, told his priests that the people should make a journey southwards. Who, in fact, was Huitzilopochtli? Probably, as happened in many societies, he was an important governor or ruler who was deified after his death.

Cristobal del Castillo, a sixteenth-century chronicler, explains how the god was originally a man called Huitzil, priest of the god Tetzauhteotl (the 'prodigious god'), who commanded the departure from Aztlan. After some time Huitzilto explained to his people that he was close to death, and that the gods would reincarnate him as Tetzauhteotl, with whom he would henceforth form one and the same god. From this comes his name Huitzilopochtli Tetzauhteotl.

So began the journey which was destined to lead the Aztecs to a place designated by their god. This migration was marked by numerous incidents. On leaving Aztlan, they first passed through a place called Cohualtepec, then through another called Chicomoztoc, the 'Seven Grottos'; they also settled in a number of places. This is important, since groups which existed before the Aztecs had already mentioned these places and this therefore means that the Aztecs incorporated into their own myths those of more ancient peoples.

The settlement at Coatepec

One stage of the migration was very important for the different tribes which made up the Aztec nation. This was when they decided to settle in the *cerro* of Coatepec (the 'snake mountain'). Thanks to their knowledge of irrigation, they were able to build a dam and start to cultivate prawns, fish, different kinds of water plant life, water birds and so on. As the place prospered, the people of Huitznahua, who were part of the most important group right from the beginning of the journey, decided that Coatepec was the place intended to be the definitive settlement.

Huitzilopochtli was not of this opinion: the god became very angry with the people of Huitznahua and destroyed them. According to the priest, Diego Durán's account, a loud noise was heard at midnight and, at dawn, the Huitznahuas, along with a woman called Coyolxauhqui who led them, were discovered dead, their chests cut open and their hearts torn out.

This act, which permitted the god (or his people) to reinforce his power and to control the majority group, played an important role. This was emphasized by the proximity of the site of Coatepec to Tula, the Toltec city. There is no doubt that an important event took place here and that it might have been linked to an act of aggression.

It could well have been a conflict in which the Aztecs, with the help of other subjugated and

tributary peoples, opposed the Toltec oppressor – a conflict which might have culminated in the destruction of Tula. Alternatively, there might have been internal differences between the Huitnahua and Huitzilopochtli groups, at the end of which the latter perhaps succeeded in asserting itself and assuring its supremacy.

Whichever is the case, the conflict was elevated to the status of a myth, and a war between men was transformed into a war of the gods. There was another important event: mythology tells of the birth of the god Huitzilopochtli although, as we have seen, he was already in existence. From this moment onwards, the destiny of the Aztec people would be accompanied by their principal divinity, their god of the sun and of war, Huitzilopochtli.

The myth which arose out of this story became the theological means of justifying and sanctifying war as a means of economic control over the enemy. It is also possible to see in this the daily victory of the sun god over the powers of the night, represented by the moon, Coyolxauhuqui, and the southern stars, the Centzohuiztnahua. In the end, it is not surprising that an agrarian and sun-worshipping people might have seen the succession of days and the cycles of life and death reproduced on a much grander scale by the succession of wet and dry seasons. Once more the observation of the universe and of its cyclical processes generated a conception of the universe.

The founding of the city of Tenochtitlán

After the events which occurred at Coatepec, the Aztecs continued their march southwards. According to the chroniclers, they passed over the sites of Tula-Coatepec, Atitalaquia, Atotonilco and others until, having reached the shores of the lake of Texcoc, they settled at Chapultepec, 'the mountain of the cricket', where they stayed for many years. But because of problems with neighbouring peoples who picked quarrels with them, they were forced to move away towards lands in the domain of Culhuacan, where other difficulties awaited them.

They decided then to go back to the territories controlled by Tezozomoc, the lord of the Tepanecs of Azcapotzalco, who was very powerful in the valley and who held sway over numerous important cities. Tezozomoc accepted the allegiance of the Aztecs and gave them some little islands in the middle of the lake where they were to

The Great Temple, Mexico City, showing the different stages of construction. Each time the temple was extended, the structure was first covered with an important 'backfill' of stones and earth, on top of which the new, larger building was founded. Note the sculpture of Coyolxauhqui, the moon goddess, in place (above). Several small shrines have been discovered on the north and south sides of the Great Temple, two of which were decorated with a series of predominantly red frescos, hence the name 'the Red Temple' (opposite). [Museo del Templo Mayor, Mexico]

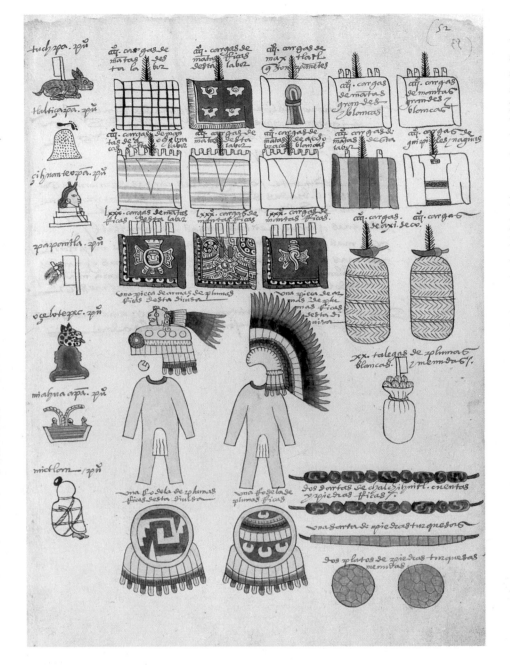

'Firstly they saw a tall tree, totally white and very beautiful, at the foot of which there was a spring. Then, they saw that all the willows which surrounded the spring were white in colour, stripped of all green leaves. All the reeds in the place were white, as well as all the rushes growing nearby. Then out of the water came white frogs, white fish and some very beautiful white water snakes. The water itself came from between two large rocks, flowing so clear and limpid that it induced a feeling of supreme contentment. The priests and the old people, remembering what the god had told them, began to weep with joy and happiness and made great gestures of pleasure and rejoicing. They said: "We have finally found the place which was promised to us; we have seen the relief and the rest granted to this people from Mexico who are so tired; there is nothing more to desire. Be at ease, sons and brothers: that which your god promised you, we have discovered and found. Because he told us that we would see marvellous things between the rushes and the reeds of this place, and so it has come to pass. Nevertheless, brothers, let us keep silent and go back to the place where we were and await the orders of our god. He will give us a sign as to what we should do." '

The following day, they came back to the same place and continued just as before until they encountered the symbol of the eagle. The story continues thus:

'Realizing that all this was still shrouded in mystery, they went further, seeking the sign of the eagle. Moving from one side to another, they saw the cactus. On top of it was perched an eagle, its wings spread out towards the heat of the sun's rays and the freshness of the morning. In its talons, it held a bird with precious and splendid plumage. When they saw it, they bent down and bowed as if before a divine phenomenon. When it saw them, the eagle acknowledged them by nodding to them on every side. On seeing the eagle's greetings and realizing that it knew what they wanted, they wept and cried: "How have we deserved such goodness? Who has judged us to be worthy of so much grace, grandeur and magnificence? We have finally seen what we desire, we have reached what we were looking for and we have found our city, our place: let us give thanks to the lord of creation and to our god Huitzilopochtli." '

At this point in the story, it is necessary to appreciate the important aspect of these two days linked with different symbols.

On the first day, everything they meet is connected with whiteness, a colour referring to Toltec myths, that is to say to more ancient people, themselves a symbol of greatness for the Aztecs. It is also a question here of legitimizing the place. On the following day they discover the eagle on the prickly pear, the symbol of their sun god Huitzilopochtli. And so they make sacred the place where they are to build their city.

The following part is just as interesting, because a sacred area is separate from profane ones.

The Codex Mendoza, *page listing cities subject to the Aztec capital and the tributes they were obliged to offer regularly (lengths of cloth, warriors' costumes, shields and so forth). [The Bodleian Library, Oxford. Photo © of the library]*

settle and found their city. In exchange they were forced to pay tribute, in the form of various types of produce from the lake, and they accepted that they would participate in the lord of Azcapotzalco's military campaigns.

The historical explanation is that the Aztecs were constrained to settle in a place especially advantageous for their Tepanec oppressors. This was as much from a strategic point of view, since the newcomers were given territory neighbouring the domain of Culhuacan, as from an economic one, since the produce from the lake (prawns, fish, reptiles, birds and so on) was necessary to the people of Azcapotzalco.

The explanation given by the Aztecs themselves is completely different, at least if we are to believe the sixteenth-century chronicler, Brother Diego Durán, who narrates the historical event which by then had already been elevated to the status of myth:

Right-hand page
Sculpted effigy of Tlaloc, *supreme god of water and rain, to whom a shrine was dedicated on the summit of the Great Temple alongside that of Huitzilopchtli. Aztec civlization (1325–1521), Mexico City. [Musée de l'Homme, Paris]*

An iron pyrite mirror. *The reverse is decorated with a representation of the god of wind, Quetzalcoatl-Ehecatl. Aztec civilization. [Musée de l'Homme, Paris]*

Right-hand page
The Codex Mendoza, *page recording the tribute that cities under Aztec rule were obliged to pay regularly to Mexico-Tenochtitlán (precious feathers, jaguar skins and so forth). This manuscript was prepared for the Emperor Charles V on the order of the Viceroy of Mexico, Don Antonio de Mendoza. The first part is dedicated to the history of the Aztecs, the second is an inventory of the tributes, and the last part traces the life of an Aztec from cradle to grave. [The Bodleian Library, Oxford. Photo © of the library]*

Right at the heart of the former will be found the ceremonial space with the great Temple – the spot where the encounter with the eagle took place. The area thus defined will be separated from the profane area, on which they will build their houses. The first page of the *Codex Mendoza* shows the division of the city with its four large districts (whose number will be increased afterwards as the population rises). Thus, in the course of the year 1325, emerged the Aztec city of Tenochtitlán, whose sacred area, the ceremonial enclosure comprising the Great Temple at the centre, appears as the navel of the Aztec concept of the universe.

The war against Azcapotzalco

Once they were settled in their city, the Aztecs dedicated themselves to agriculture and to the exploitation of the lake. The control which

Azcapotzalco exercised over them led them to seek certain allegiances to relieve the pressure to which they were subjected. For example, they took the decision to marry their sovereign Acampichtli (1375–95) to a Tepanec princess. From this union was born Chimalpopoca (1417–27), grandson of Tezozomoc, the sovereign of Azcapotzalco.

This kinship link was used profitably to lighten the tribute of Tenochtitlán. However Maxtla, son of Tezozomoc, lord of the city of Coyoacan and enemy of the Aztecs, ordered the assassination of Chimalpopoca. The situation worsened when Maxtla inherited the governorship of Azcapotzalco on the death of his father. War was declared and, under the leadership of their ruler Itzcoatl, 'obsidian snake', the Aztecs secured the allegiance of the city of Texcoco and were victorious over Azcapotzalco in 1428. From this date, Azcapotzalco passed into the control of the Aztecs and had to pay them tribute. A triple alliance was

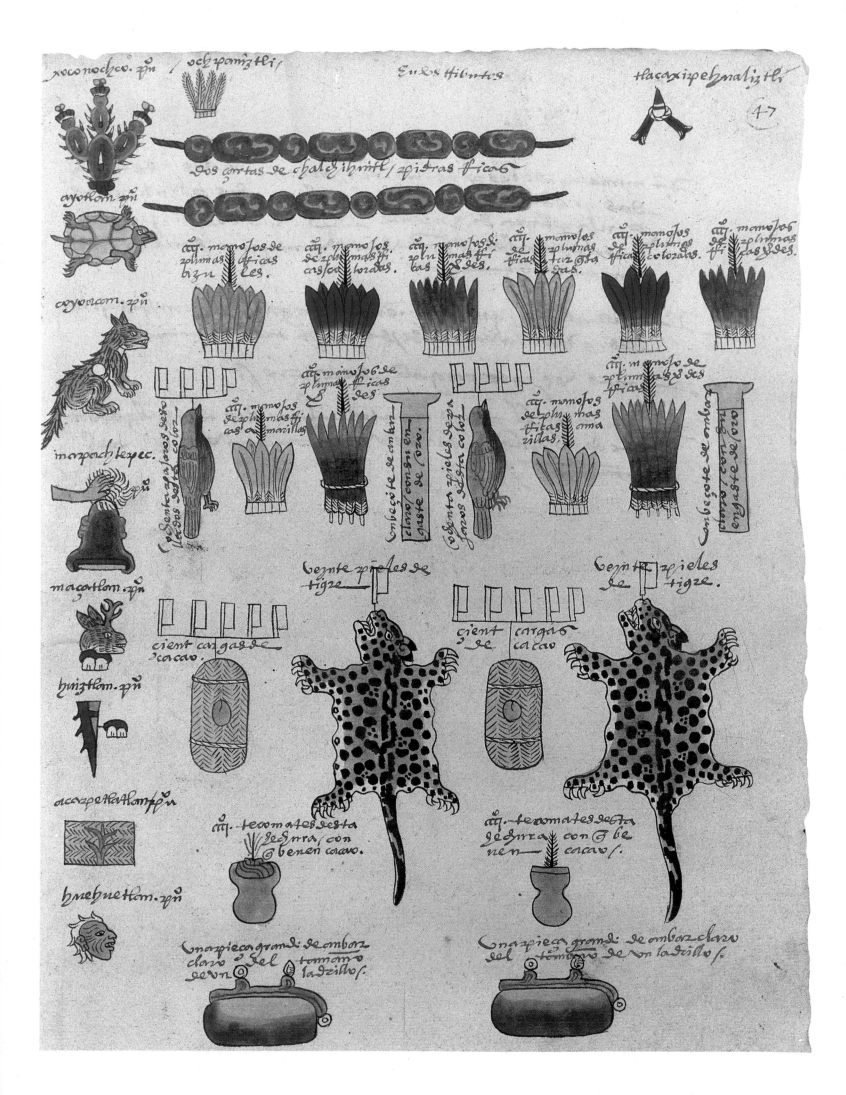

61

An Aztec ceramic, *Aztec civilization, Mexico City. [Musée de l'Homme, Paris]*

Coatlicue, *drawings of the large sculpted effigy of the goddess. According to Aztec myth, she was the deity of the earth and also the mother of both the moon-goddess Coyolxauhqi and the Aztec war-god Huitzilopochtli, who was believed to have been born in Coatepec. Beneath the statue's feet is engraved the image of the god of the earth, Tlaltecuhtli. This was not meant to be seen, since it was supposed to lie in contact with the god's elemental realm, namely the earth itself.*

Right-hand page
The face of a dead Mexican warrior, *earthenware mask with horizontal paint markings. Fifteenth–sixteenth century, region of Mexico City. [Musée de l'Homme, Paris]*

created between the cities of Tenochtitlán, Texcoco and Tacuba.

This event was the beginning of Aztec expansion, first in the valley of Mexico and then beyond. The second Tepanec city which was conquered was Coyoacan, which in turn was subject to Tenochtitlán. Then the Aztecs launched an assault on Xochimilco, which controlled intensively cultivated regions of *chinampas*, looked after by the people who occupied the southern part of the lake. The strategic importance of this agricultural production made the city of Xochimilco a highly prized capture for the victorious Aztec armies.

Itzcoatl, who governed from 1427 to 1440, ensured Aztec control of the lake shore and began expansion into other regions. On his death, he was replaced on the throne by Moctezuma I (1440–69) at a moment when the Aztecs and their allies were about to launch into the conquest of distant lands in Mesoamerica.

More than one hundred years had passed between the foundation of Tenochtitlán in 1325 and the moment of freedom in 1428, a century of Aztec indecision as regards Azcapotzalco. Another one hundred year period was needed, from 1428 to 1521, before Tenochtitlán reached its peak and extended its domination over a large part of Mesoamerica. Thus, in only two centuries, the people of Huitzilopochtli had lived through their destiny of misfortune and glory.

Social and economic organization

Aztec society was divided into two large groups, the *pipiltin* and the *macehualtin*. The former were the ruling class of nobles who, by occupying the main civil and religious posts, controlled society. The ideological domain (religion and control of knowledge) and the military domain (the army) were both in the hands of the Aztec élite. The sovereign,

the *tlatoami*, whose post was not hereditary, was elected from among the nobles.

The choice of *tlatoami* was based on several criteria, including a thorough knowledge of religion and distinction in the wars of expansion, because it was necessary for him to be ready to take on the functions of high priest and of commander-in-chief of the armies. The word '*tlatoami*' signifies 'he who has the word' or 'he who has the power to speak'. Besides the government of the people, there were two other tasks to be accomplished: enlarging the temple of Huitzilopochtli and extending the power of the empire.

An imposing administrative apparatus was at the service of the *tlatoami*. In each conquered region, there was a *calpixque*, or local administrator, controlling the tribute which the subject peoples had to send regularly to Tenochtitlán. The Aztec capital was organized in *calpulli*, divisions corresponding to 'districts', to which lands were attributed. These furnished the men for the public works in the city as well as contingents of soldiers for the military campaigns.

The rulers of each district, the *calpulleque*, belonged to the nobility, as did the *tetecuhtin*, those who had distinguished themselves in war and thus became owners of land and of the people who worked it. As a general rule, it could be said that the nobles (*pipiltin*) benefited from a series of specific privileges such as, for example, the ownership of land, high public office, exemption from agricultural labour and payment of tribute. Special tribunals were reserved for them; they could possess several spouses; they had the right to signs of distinction and they also studied in a special school, called a *calmecac* .

On the other hand, the lower classes, the *macehualtin*, formed the majority of the population. They were spread around the different *calpulli*, or districts, and they comprised farm workers, potters, gold and silversmiths, masons, carpenters, weavers, fishermen, gem-carvers, craftsmen of all kinds and specialized practitioners living from the exchange of their produce.

They were different from the nobles in that the *macehual* had to render to the *tlatoami* a tribute which took two forms: the payment of a part of their produce, and participation in communal work in the district. These tasks were undertaken by teams of twenty to one hundred people under the direction of a foreman.

The *macehualtin* also had to be prepared to go to war, and within their *calpulli* they made up the troops of the Aztec army. Thus the district was the base unit of the city. In each one of them there was a school for the *macehualtin*, called a *telpochcalli*. These establishments taught the arts and various crafts, as well as military skills.

There was another social category called *mayeque*, who worked lands belonging to other people and paid tribute to their landowner. Slavery existed, but not in the sense in which the ancient Romans understood it. An individual who did not

Teponaztli: *this was a horizontal drum, with two thick strips of wood left above the hollowed-out body of the instrument. The player hammered these and caused them to vibrate. The Aztecs also used an upright drum stretched with an animal skin (usually deer) similar to our own, known as* huehuetl. *Along with such percussion instruments, conches, whistles and flutes, and also rattles, provided the background rhythm for dances, songs and the reciting of poetry. Music was an integral part of cultural and religious life.* [Musée de l'Homme, Paris]

pay his debts, or who lost having bet on a ball game, became a slave. Theft and murder were also reasons for making someone a slave, to the profit of the injured person or his family.

A person who had financial difficulties could resort to selling himself as a slave; nevertheless, a slave could recover his freedom if he managed to settle his debt, or if he took refuge in a temple. A woman slave also became free if her master chose to marry her. Slavery was not hereditary, and as a general rule slaves did not play a significant role in the Aztec economy.

The merchants, or *pochtecas*, formed another important class in Aztec society. They had secured their own social status and had to pay tribute to the *tlatoani*. As well as commerce, they provided the information service of the empire. This role was highly important: using trade as a pretext, they penetrated the provinces which had not been conquered and informed Tenochtitlán of everything they had observed there.

The merchants benefited from certain privileges, notably the right to be accompanied by their own militia during their journeys. In the markets, they had their own magistrates, who passed judgement in cases of litigation over exchanged produce and the like.

As far as the markets were concerned, the most important one was established at Tlatelolco, the neighbouring city to Tenochtitlán. This was founded in about 1377, a few years after the Aztec capital, on a little islet to the north. Tlatelolco had always acted independently of the Aztec city. It was already giving importance to commercial activities when in 1473, under the government of Axayacatl (1469–81), the two towns entered into conflict. When it was conquered, Tlatelolco was incorporated into Tenochtitlán. The competition between the two cities was perhaps due to the economic supremacy of Tlatelolco, which functioned as a centre of trade for numerous products.

The Aztec economy was based on two main elements: agricultural production and war, as a means of imposing tribute on conquered peoples. As far as agriculture was concerned, certain techniques brought about high productivity. Among these, the system of *chinampas* was based on the use of very wet areas traversed by canals. Mud dredged from the excavations was piled up in mounds. The constant humidity ensured the fertile conditions necessary for cultivation. These *chinampas* stretched over the whole southern part of the lake.

Planting was by traditional tools such as the *coa*, or wooden digging stick. The commonest crops were maize, beans, tomatoes, marrows, peppers and so on. All these plants had been known in Mesoamerica for several thousand years.

As far as war and tribute were concerned, right up to the arrival of the Spaniards in 1519, Tenochtitlán received tribute from 371 cities spread over 33 provinces of the different cultural areas of Mesoamerica. Two principal sources list the conquered cities: the list of tributes (*Matricula de los tributos*) and the *Codex Mendoza*. From these documents, it can be seen how each town regularly paid tribute to the Aztecs according to the specific

produce of the particular region. Thus charges were settled in maize, in beans or other food products, in raw materials like semi-precious stones, chalk and all sorts of products. The tribute could equally be paid in bird feathers, in warriors' costumes or in animal pelts.

Thus, in the Aztec city, the public funds of the *tlatoami* grew, thanks to the produce of the various conquered regions. Some experts who have studied this society think that the majority of the goods accumulated in the royal warehouses of Mexico were probably tribute from conquered provinces. This shows the critical importance of war as a means of supporting or widening the economic base of the main political centres.

These two fundamental features of the Aztec nation, agriculture and war, were duly represented in the main temple: Tlaloc, the god of water and of everything associated with fertility and the growth of plants, sits enthroned at the side of Huizilopochtli, god of war and supremacy over other peoples. Thus the Aztecs had established parity between their gods on the same lines as their economic structure.

The structure of the universe

Every people has its own concept of the universe. In central Mexico the Aztecs inherited a concept going back to a distant past, to the time of cities such as Teotihuacán, the growth of which covers the first seven centuries of our era. One key to

understanding the process of thought over the millennia is the notion of duality.

Pre-Hispanic man was a constant observer of nature. The movement of the stars, the succession of day and night, the annual passage from rainy seasons to dry seasons, the birth and death of plants and men were so many well observed cyclical phenomena. In this way, all the dualities gave a structure to the concept of the universe and appeared in certain primordial myths.

Some of the Aztec myths speak of the couple Tonacetecuhtli and Tonacacihualt who created the universe, a divine duality who inhabited the highest level, and also of Omecihuatl and Ometecuhtli, the lords of duality. This couple created four gods (the three Tezcatlipocas and Quetzalcoatl), whose succession and subsequent struggles are the origin of the four ages, or 'suns', and of the successive re-creations of a human race which improved each time, and each associated with a particular foodstuff. An ancient myth relates these facts:

'Then, they (the gods) created the days and they divided them into months each of twenty days; thus there were eighteen months and three hundred and sixty days in the year. The gods then created Mictlantecuhtli and Mictecacihualt, husband and wife, divinities of the kingdom of the dead, where they were placed. Then the gods created the heavens, all thirteen of them, and water, and in the water they placed a great fish called Cipactli, who is like a cayman, and from this fish, they made the earth.'

Jade pendant *in the form of a vulture, Aztec civilization of the fifteenth–sixteenth century, Valley of Mexico City. [Musée de l'Homme, Paris]*

The Aztec Universe. *At the centre of the terrestial plane lies the Great Temple, the navel of the world. Above are the thirteen heavens, in the highest of which live the gods of creation, Tonacatecuhtli and Tonacacihuatl. Below are the nine subterranean worlds, in the lowest of which, known as the Mictlan, reside Mictlantecuhtli and Mictecacihuatl, lords of the kingdom of the dead.*

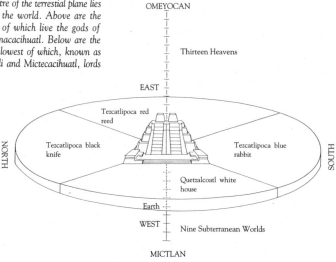

The structure of the universe was equally the work of the gods. There was an underworld which the missionary monks confused with hell, heavenly planes, and the earth which occupied an intermediary position.

The earth, created from the *cipactli*, a kind of cayman, was the dwelling place of men. It had a centre, or navel, which communicated with the celestial level above, where the stars were, and with the level below, the dwelling place of the dead. The centre of the whole edifice was situated in the Great Temple, from which radiated the four directions of the universe. This *Templo Mayor* was the main building of the ceremonial enclosure of Tenochtitlán, at the heart of which, according to the descriptions of Bernardino de Sahagún, there were some seventy-eight buildings. From this enclosure four causeways started, each aiming towards a cardinal point: the Tacuba causeway pointed towards the setting sun (west), Tepeyac towards the north and Iztapalapa towards the south; and certain texts mention a fourth roadway pointing east. In this way the city itself was a reflection of the concept of the universe.

The celestial plane stretched from the earth upwards. The *Mexica* (Aztecs) applied their knowledge of the movement of stars and phenomena such as rain, comets and lightning to the organization of the thirteen heavens of their cosmology.

In the *Codex Vaticanus* 3738 the first of these heavens is that of the moon and the clouds. The second is that of the stars, known as 'Citlalco'. The third heaven is that which the sun crosses daily from the east to the west. In the fourth Venus is found. Another version also exists, according to which this level might be that of Uixtocihuatl, goddess of salt waters. The fifth heaven is traversed by comets. It is equally that of motion. The sixth and the seventh are marked by colours. The eighth, in which storms are created, was decorated at its angles with slabs of obsidian. In the ninth heaven, and in the others that followed, the gods resided, the last two being the Omeyocan, the place of duality. In this way, there was an obvious relationship between certain heavens or 'levels' and the movement and observation of both natural and astronomical phenomena.

The subterranean level started with the earth and continued underground; it was the dwelling place of the dead (Mictlampa), itself associated with the north. It is interesting to note that in order to arrive at Mictlan, the ninth subterranean level, eight places had to be traversed, full of pitfalls and dangers. Both Sahagún and the *Codex Vaticanus* make reference to these places.

The first obstacle was two mountains which were forever colliding with one another, while it seems that the first test was the crossing of a river. Then came the encounter with a snake which guarded the way ahead. After that, the traveller had to go through the territory of the green lizard, followed by eight desert areas; he had to cross eight summits and the place of the cold wind as sharp as

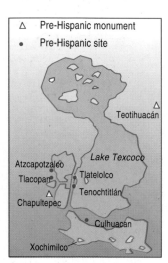

The Valley of Mexico in 1520.

This action of the gods resulted in the creation of the calendar of 360 days, plus five days of bad luck, so important to an agrarian people such as the Aztecs. The calendar was based on two main cycles: the dry season and the rainy season, separated by festivities in honour of the god of fire, Xiuhteuhtli. The calendar derived from observation of the movements of the sun: equinoxes and solstices in relation to the rainy season when everything is born, and to the dry season when everything dies.

There also existed a ritual calendar of 260 days which is assumed to have had some connection with the length of a human pregnancy and with the lunar months. It could be said that the solar calendar has a masculine connotation, while the second one has a feminine connotation.

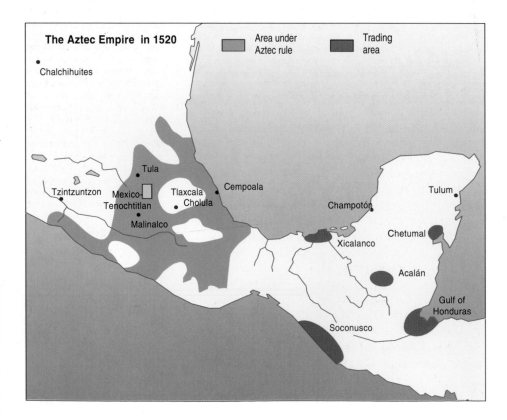

Date from the 'four red' calendar, carved on a stone medallion, Aztec civilization (1325–1521), Mexico. [Musée de l'Homme, Paris]

THE AZTEC CALENDAR

The chronological system of the ancient Mexicans is based on the imbrication of a solar computation of 365 days and a ritual calendar of 260 days. The solar year comprises eighteen months of twenty days, plus five intercalary days without rites. The ritual calendar, known as *tonalpoualli*, rests on the combination of a figure from one to thirteen and a sign taken from a series of twenty. In Mexico, this series is as follows: crocodile, wind, house, lizard, snake, death, deer, rabbit, water, dog, monkey, dead grass, reed, jaguar, eagle, vulture, movement, flint knife, rain, and flower. The numbers and the signs succeed one another without interruption in parallel series and in an immutable order. Thus there exist 260 original combinations arranged in twenty thirteens, starting from day one crocodile and finishing on day thirteen flower. Traditionally each day of the solar calendar was called by the name of the day in the *tonalpoualli*. The two calendars operated continuously and in parallel. The same day-name was used for example on the first and on the 261st day of the first year, the 156th day of the second, the 51st and the 311th day of the third, and so on. The solar years were designated by the name of their first day; they thus had a name taken from the ritual calendar. We have seen that in the *tonalpoualli* the same sign reappears every twenty days. If the solar year lasts 360 days, which is a multiple of twenty, all the years will start in perpetuity with the same sign. But the Mexican year is still a year of 365 days; each year is therefore five signs out from the year before; after four years the difference is twenty and we come back to the initial sign. There are thus only four signs which should start a year. These four signs each combine with the thirteen figures to offer fifty-two possible starts to the year. According to the Aztecs, these four 'year-bearing' signs were *acatl* (reed), *tecpatl* (sacrificial knife), *calli* (house), and *tochtli* (rabbit). In Mexico, the cycle starts with the year two-*acatl*, followed by the years three-*tecpatl*, four-*calli*, five-*tochtli* and so on. The local cycle is therefore a cycle of fifty-two years. Each date carries a strong symbolic charge.

obsidian; then he had to cross the Chiconahuapan River in order finally to arrive at Mictlan. Another version involved passing through the land where lay the corpse which Tlatecultli was to eat. In this case the journey started by first crossing a river (crossing water), then continued through the mountainous area, past the obsidian mountain, through the place of unfurled banners, followed by that place where the people had been pierced by arrows. There was also the place where the hearts were devoured, that of the obsidian of the dead and a place which was without exits, from which smoke could not escape.

According to Aztec thought, the form of death determined access to the underworld, where an individual would go after death. The conditions of access were very important for an agricultural and warlike society because the forms of after-life proposed were closely linked to the two economic aspects that underlay the *Mexica* social structure.

Corresponding to their vertical concept of the universe was a horizontal concept ordered by the four directions of space. Each was ruled by a god, a colour, a sign of the calendar and a tree. The representations provided, notably by the *Codex Fejervary-Mayer*, show this division in the form of a flower with four petals. As a general rule, the south side of the universe was under the protection of Tezcatlipoca, blue, who was in reality Huitzilopochtli. His sign was the rabbit (*tochtli* in Nahuatl). The east corresponded to another Tezcatlipoca, identified at Xipe Totec. His colour was red and his sign was *acatl*, the reed. The north was ruled by the black Tezcatlipoca whose sign was *tecpatl*, the knife of sacrifice. The north was connected with death and designated the Mictlampa. The west corresponded to Quetzalcoatl, whose colour was white and whose sign was *calli*, the house. This was the direction of women, the Cihuatlampa.

Coyolxauhqui, monolith representing the goddess of the moon, sister to the tribal god of the Aztecs, Huitzilopochtli. This sculpture was discovered at the foot of the Great Temple of Mexico. Vanquished by Huitzilopochtli at Coatepec, the goddess lies decapitated, with her body dismembered at the foot of the temple to Huitzilopochtli, in confirmation of the supremacy of the Aztec people. The presence of this sculpture near the Great Temple allows the mythical Coatepec to be given a real geographical location while, at the same time, recreating by means of the sacrifice, the myth of the birth of Huitzilopochtli. [Museo del Templo Mayor, Mexico]

Right-hand page, top
Chac-Mool, *Toltec god, probably connected with fertility, discovered on the second level of construction of the Great Temple of Mexico-Tenochtitlán. This was one of the most ancient structures atop the Great Temple; raised at the beginning of Aztec settlement, at a time when the tribe was attempting to legitimize its presence in central Mexico by connecting its origins to the city of Tula. [Museo del Templo Mayor, Mexico]*

The centre, where the thirteen upper levels and the nine lower levels bisected and from which the four directions of the universe stretched out, was the Great Temple of Tenochtitlán, the most holy of places, where all the levels met. There, the two mountains were represented, Coatepec and Tonacatepetl. The first was dedicated to Huitzilopochtli, as a reminder of the combat survived at Coatepec, and the second was dedicated to Tlaloc. It is on the latter mountain that, according to another myth, maize was preserved, the original food of mankind.

So this cosmogony rested upon a real base, centre of centres located in the Great Temple. And as the centre of this base there was Ometeotl, the principle of duality, in the person of the old god of fire, Xiuhtecuhtli-Huchueteotl. This god, guardian of universal equilibrium, inhabitant of both the celestial and the subterranean worlds, was in his rightful place only at the centre of the centres, that is to say in the Great Temple.

An ancient song explains the central position of this god at the heart of the universe: 'Father of the gods, father of the gods, ancient god stretched out over the navel of the earth, fixed in a shrine of turquoise. He who is found in the waters the colour of a blue bird, prisoner of the clouds, ancient god, he who inhabits the darkness of the dead world, lord of fire and of the year.'

As we have just seen, the entire Aztec concept of the universe was based on the observation of nature. Pre-Hispanic man experienced with great intensity a changing world, and his myths sprang from a perception of cycles which revealed themselves in struggles between the gods. The Great Temple was the expression of this constant, basic duality – between Tlaloc, that is fertility, water, the growth of plants, in a word everything which had to do with life, and Huitzilopochtli, linked to sacrifice, war and death. Thus life and death were present simultaneously in the main temple of the Aztecs.

Art and literature

The symbolic character of Aztec art in particular and Mesoamerican art in general is the first thing which strikes the observer, whether it is the sculpture, painting, architecture, dance or poetry. In fact, in order to come to terms with pre-Hispanic art, one really needs to understand the society which produced it and the strength of the symbolism that existed within it.

Some experts have stated that this pre-Hispanic art starts and ends with mythology; others have claimed that it has two fundamental aspects: the terrible and the sublime. Both these interpretations required the exploration of realms which would take us some distance away from the presentation of the different forms of artistic expression which flourished in central Mexico five hundred years ago.

As a matter of fact, we enjoy access to a wide range of major and minor carved material created by these people, made available to us through excavations beginning in 1790, when the two monumental sculptures of Coatlicue and the Sun Stone were discovered in the main square of Mexico, down to the morning of 21 February 1978, when the statue of Coyolxauhqui was dug up, yielding the first clues that led to the subsequent discoveries in the Great Temple project.

There were no limits to what could be created in sculpture. At the same time as the statue of Coatlicue was created, expressing in stone the entire abstraction of the cosmogonic thought of the Aztecs, a figure such as that of Coyolxauhqui, brilliantly successful in its realism and sense of movement, was also being worked on. All this was achieved using only stone tools.

It is the same with the eagle discovered in 1985 in front of the Great Temple; its anonymous artist has paid particular attention to representing in stone the minutest details of the bird. At the same time the enormous head of *xahuatl*, the fire serpent, was created – a form passing the limits of realism to approach a level of abstraction which is almost fantasy. This is typical of Aztec art in particular and Mesoamerican art in general: the artist may create obscure syntheses or depict reality in the smallest detail. The two approaches exist simultaneously and are offered to the onlooker together.

In certain aspects Aztec sculpture does not follow the same principles as Western art, where everything which is carved is meant to be looked at. For the Aztecs, the concept was different: in some works of Aztec art the surface on which they rest is sculpted. Coatlicue offers a good example. Under the feet of the goddess is engraved the representation of the god of the earth Tlatecuhtli – the precise spot on the stone where he should be depicted, of course, but it was not meant to be seen. When first Antonio León y Gama, then Alexander von

Humboldt in the late eighteenth and the early nineteenth centuries, studied the goddess, they thought she should have been placed high up so that the engraving on the bottom part could be seen. They had not realized that the engraved figure was that of telluric divinity – the master of the earth – which consequently should be in direct contact with its element. This error was due to the fact that, for Western man, everything which is sculpted should be visible – an aesthetic concept based on the idea of a dialogue between men. The concept of the Aztec of ancient Mexico was quite different: their dialogue was with the gods.

The subjects of Aztec statues are widely varied. Among the animals are found statues representing coiled snakes, birds of different species, jaguars, coyotes, tortoises – all the way down to insects, which are accomplished brilliantly. The red stone crickets are a good example, attaining a unique quality. So are the representations of fleas, where the observational skills of the artist reach impressive heights. To this list one should add spiders, centipedes, scorpions and other kinds of animals, each one with its particular symbolism.

Representations of the gods are very numerous; they include Ehecatl, god of the wind, Xilonen, divinity of maize, Xiuhteuhtli, god of fire, Mictlantecuhtli, lord of the world of the dead and the *cihuateteo* – women who have died in childbirth. The statues also represent the common man, the *macehual*, the warrior or death. All these figures were carved from different types of stone. Finally there was minor sculpture consisting of masks, snakes, and other figures worked in alabaster, jade, obsidian and similar materials.

There are few traces of wall painting. The excavations of the Great Temple have been the main source of what there is, such as the two pilasters of the sanctuary of the god Tlaloc from the second stage of construction corresponding to the year 1390. On the outside face of the pilasters, painted circles evoke the eyes of Tlaloc. Below them runs a blue band decorated with black motifs. From this band extend vertical lines – alternating white and black – which could well represent rain. On the other face of the pilaster, facing the interior of the sanctuary, is painted a human figure with yellow skin and the decorations (bracelets) in blue or black. The figure is in profile and holds in its hands what appears to be a lance or a stick. It is walking along a watercourse. Its general aspect reminds one of certain pictographic figures in manuscripts. These vestiges of frescos are the oldest discovered in the Great Temple.

Other wall paintings have come to light near this principal temple of the Aztecs, notably in the east-facing red temples to the north and south of the Great Temple. The dominant colour in the two buildings is red, enhanced by motifs in ochre, blue, white and black. One of the principal decorative elements is a knot with two hanging fringes, a motif which has been interpreted as the symbolic representation of the god Huitzilopochtli. Another

Shrine to Tlaloc, *painted façade of the entrance, corresponding to the second stage of construction of the Great Temple. Aztec civilization, circa 1390. [Museo del Templo Mayor, Mexico]*

'Eagle Knight', *a ceramic sculpture standing 190cm high, made of several interlocking sections. An identical warrior was also found at the Great Temple. These two statues were housed in a single building found to the north of the Great Temple, where the eagle warriors, members of one of the two high orders of knights of the Aztec army, congregated. The style is reminiscent of the art of tribes around the Gulf of Mexico. [Museo del Templo Mayor, Mexico]*

Right-hand page
Tezcatlipoca, *a jade statuette representing the god of creation, protector of sorcerers, defender of slaves and young warriors. Aztec era, fifteenth–sixteenth century, Mexico City. [Musée de l'Homme, Paris]*

drawing, a semi-circle or half-eye, evokes the eye motifs associated with the watercourse which are found at Teotihuacán – as much as in the architecture itself as in the elements associated with it. The figure of the god Huehucteotl, discovered a very short distance away from the Red Temple on the north side, is a sculpture in the Aztec style which quite clearly imitates the statues of the same god that were created at Teotihuacán about a thousand years before.

In 1964 an oratory was discovered whose walls were decorated with masks painted as an effigy of the god Tlaloc. The face was represented with three white teeth and the characteristic 'moustache' of the divinity. The colours were quite magnificent: blue, orange, white and black – all contributing to an abstract idea of the god of water. So, painting and sculpture are alike: the forms of expression could be either the most sombre realism or magnificent abstraction.

In the sixties, during the excavations at Tlatelolco, another Aztec city, various wall paintings, mostly executed on clay, were brought to light. Unfortunately, they were not studied. However, the 1989 excavations on the oratory of the Calendar started with the discovery of a very important wall painting. It shows two old people, a man and a woman, and is reminiscent of the representation of Cipactonal and Oxomoco as they appear in the *Codex Borbonicus*. In the upper part of the oratory, glyphs represent the cycle of the Calendar, carved all around the building. This was an important discovery, partly because it enabled better understanding of the building itself.

Malinalco is another Aztec centre on which vestiges of wall paintings have been found. Situated fifty miles from Mexico-Tenochtitlán, it is unique in its architecture: the temples were carved out of the rock. In one of them, the remains of frescos show a procession of warriors; this theme is not

Opening page of the Codex Mendoza, *recounting the foundation of Mexico-Tenochtitlán by the Aztecs in 1325. They halted their migration when they saw, on an islet in the Texcoco lagoon, an eagle (a symbol of the sun) perched upon and pecking at a prickly pear (the fruit or 'tuna' representing the human heart). Beneath this scene, in the middle of the page, the Aztec glyph for war is inscribed (arrows and shield). The highly symbolic treatment of this account establishes human sacrifice (by pulling out the heart) as a warlike deed which is one of the founding principles of Aztec society. [The Bodleian Library, Oxford. Photo © of the library]*

Right-hand page
Nezahualpilli, tenth king of Texcoco (1472–1516), *dressed in a blue Xiuhtilmatli (royal cloak). In his right hand, he holds flowers and in his left, a fly-whisk. His hair is arranged in a Tzotzocolli (a style worn by warriors as a sign of bravery). Codex painting attributed to Don Fernando de Alva Ixtlilxochitl, sixteenth century. [Bibliothèque Nationale, Paris. Photo © Bibl. nat.-Photeb]*

inappropriate, for we know that initiation rites for the Eagle and Jaguar warriors took place here.

Pottery is a traditional material in Mesoamerica. The Aztec potters knew how to fashion clay not only into pottery, statuettes of gods or other figures, but also into large pieces which bear witness to their mastery of this material. One example is the superb figures of Eagle warriors discovered in the north of the Great Temple through which the artist managed to convey the dignity and pride of the warriors of Huitzilopochtli.

Very little information has come down to us about dance and music – we have only the descriptions of the chroniclers concerning certain ceremonies. The *Codex Borbonicus* contains some paintings, but the rhythm and important details are now lost in time. And, if some poetry has managed to survive, it is because it has been possible to transcribe Nahuatl into Roman script. This art, which has produced both warrior songs and prayers to the gods, is also able to express infinite anguish in the face of death:

'Weep: I am a poet
In my hands, I see flowers
Which embellish my heart: I am a poet
Where you will my heart, my spirit
To which handful of turquoises like a
    brilliant emerald
Have I compared my poem and my beautiful
    flowers
Rejoice, my friends: no one will remain on
    earth
For this reason, I weep and I strew my flowers
By chance will you come with me to the
    region of mystery?
I will not take my flowers with me, although
    I am a poet
Rejoice, we are still alive: you are listening to
    my song

neçaSual pilçontli

208

neça Sual pilçontli

Huehueteotl, stone sculpture of the old god of Fire. This deity was one of the most ancient gods worshipped by the populations of the Valley of Mexico – a region surrounded by volcanoes. [Museo del Templo Mayor, Mexico]

This is why I weep, I the poet:
The poem has not reached the house of the
    sun,
The pretty flowers cannot descend from the
    kingdom of the dead
Here, and only here, beautiful poems take
    shape
It is your majesty and your splendour, oh
    captains of war
The song and the pretty flower will not go as
    far as his house
The pretty flowers do not go down to the
    kingdom of the dead
Here and only here do pretty flowers
    intertwine.'

Poetry also tackles the topics of death in combat or in sacrifice:

'Emerald, gold
Thy flowers, oh god
Only thy riches
Oh thou who givest life
Death by the obsidian arrow
Death in combat
You will make yourself known
At the start of war, around the brazier
You make yourself known.'

The poem of Axayacatzin to Itzcoatl, sovereign of Mexico-Tenochtitlán, depicts the sadness and affliction caused by the death of Itzcoatl and other princes. The reply to the questions which the poet poses is always the same: everything disappears, no one comes back; only this sad poem is left:

'Flowery death has descended
It has arrived on the earth
Those who live with us create it at Tlapalla
Tears rise
But there everyone is already at his post
In the heavens.'

In this way, Aztec man managed, thanks to his art, to leave us his vision of the world. This art expresses the cult of the gods and sings about life and death. It was through mythology engraved in stone and expressed in colour that man was able to talk to his own heart.

In 1519, the Spaniards arrived on the Mesoamerican coast. Two years later, on 13 August 1521, after three months of siege, the cities of Mexico-Tenochtitlán and Tlatelolco fell. They were razed to the ground by the Spanish forces and their local allies, enemies and tributaries of the Aztecs. Today, at Tlatelolco, the final point of resistance, this inscription can be read:

'On 13 August 1521, heroically defended by Cuauhtémoc, Tlatelolco fell into the hands of Hernán Cortés. This was neither a triumph nor a rout, but rather the painful birth of the Mexican people, and of a land which constitutes the Mexico of today.'

THE INCAS

Jean-François Bouchard

Preceding page
Machu Picchu: Intihuatana. *Atop an isolated, rocky hill overhanging the ruined city, the Intihuatana may well have been connected to sun worship in some way: the great sculpted rock found at the summit is sometimes considered to be the rock to which the sun was attached, or as a gnomon (a kind of primitive sundial). This interpretation finds support in various first-hand accounts of the Spanish chroniclers. At Machu Picchu, the Intihuatana is particularly well-preserved, having escaped destruction at the hands of Spanish idol thieves, who attacked all huacas associated with the cults and rites of the Andean peoples. [Photo J.-F. Bouchard]*

Right-hand page
Ceremonial Inca knife, tumi. *The blade at a right angle to the handle (in the shape of a llama's head) is characteristic of Andean tools. [Musée de l'Homme, Paris]*

QUECHUA was not a written language to begin with, so there are different ways of spelling vernacular names. This book follows the version most frequently used in reference works. For example, we write Viracocha and not Wiraqocha; Tahuantinsuyu and not Tahuantinsuyo or Tzwantinsuyu, which are typical of a more purist approach based on the phonetic transcriptions of linguisticians. The Quechua names in the text (apart from proper names) are in italics.

For many people, the Incas and Pizarro still symbolize the Spanish conquest of Andean America. While it is important not to forget that other *conquistadores* set out to conquer regions lying beyond the Inca empire, it is no less true that the expeditions of Pizarro and Almagro from Panamá, in search of a vast rich empire, push these other ventures into the background.

The Incas at that time represented a powerful state with a perfect structure, comparable in many respects with contemporary nations of the Old World or the great powers of antiquity and the Middle Ages. Having imposed their rule on the major part of the Andean world, they had proclaimed themselves the civilizers of the Andes. In the opinion of the Spaniards, dazzled by this ascendancy, the other contemporary cultures seemed negligible. Nor were the *conquistadores* able to measure the significance of any Andean civilizations of preceding centuries since memories of them faded fast – not least because of the Inca policy of playing down their importance.

Thus the Inca empire exercised an intense fascination upon the Spaniards. Even today, some people consider this civilization to be a social and economic model in which man had adapted perfectly to the specific nature of his environment.

The abundant literature on this topic proves the point. However, it does bring together scientific works which are the fruits of long investigations in archives or on the ground as well as some much less reliable publications which are based more on fabrications than on serious study. The research of the past few decades enables an up-to-date picture to be presented of the greatest state of pre-Hispanic Andean America.

When Francisco Pizarro reached the north of Peru in 1532, the Inca empire stretched from the shores of the Pacific in the west to the edge of the Amazon jungle in the east, and from the present frontier between Colombia and Ecuador in the north and the Río Maule, in Chile to the south (see map). Across this enormous tract, one landscape succeeded another in incredible variety, each occupied by a native population dominated by the Incas. In fact, the generic term 'Incas' should really designate only that ethnic group which settled originally in the Cuzco basin and succeeded, during the century before the Spanish conquest, in bringing together peoples as diverse as the Chimus of the north Peruvian coast and the Kollas of the high plains near Lake Titicaca.

The Inca (or, more accurately, the Sapa Inca) was the sovereign of this empire; in the Quechua language he was known as the Tahuantinsuyu. The empire itself was divided into four quarters (Cuntisuyu, Antisuyu, Chinchasuyu and Kollasuyu), with the capital, Cuzco, at the centre.

Unlike other Andean cultures of greater antiquity, known to the modern world only through a few archaeological fragments, a lot is known about Inca civilization because of the accounts of the *conquistadores*. They noted the traditions and history, which had not previously been written down, thus preserving oral accounts given shortly after the conquest. A number of these accounts came from the descendants of the American Indians, some of whom were of mixed blood and more or less assimilated. These people carefully gathered together everything that could be remembered of their own past.

All these documents and the archives of the colonial era have enabled present-day researchers to build up a more accurate picture of the Inca civilization. Archaeological work has contributed to this through the study both of remains discovered during excavations and of the architecture of the urban centres constructed by the Incas. In the same way, museum collections, which were often put together at a time when scientific knowledge did not always permit complex analysis, can now throw new light on the technologies used by the Incas.

The origins of the Incas

Official history, such as was memorized by the Incas themselves and then written down by the chroniclers, is still somewhat enigmatic about the origin of the Inca people. One important myth which is repeated by the chroniclers refers to the journey of four brothers, accompanied by their sisters, from a cave in the Andes to Cuzco. One of the brothers, endowed with awesome magical powers, is supposed to have been quickly eliminated by the others. Then two other brothers were turned to stone and transformed into *huacas*, divinities worshipped in Andean religion. Only the final survivor, Ayar Manco, managed to settle in Cuzco and then became, under the name of Manco Capac, the mythical founder of the empire. Most researchers consider that this myth refers, in a cryptic manner, to the elimination by the Inca

tribe of other groups who also occupied the Cuzco basin during the fourteenth century, forming with them a confederation which the Incas succeeded in controlling.

The Inca hegemony: wars and alliances

After Manco Capac, the official history of the Incas lists several kings succeeding one another; but it is not possible to be sure either of their existence or of the facts attributed to them by certain chroniclers. However, starting with the reign of the Inca Viracocha at the beginning of the fifteenth century, it is possible to pinpoint the first conquests of the Incas outside the Cuzco basin. This monarch is believed to have annexed the nearest part of the

valley of the Río Urubamba and so begun an expansionist phase which marks the passage to the truly historic period of the empire. However, only towards the end of the reign of Viracocha does the first reliable date in Inca history occur. In 1438 the Chancas, a warrior tribe from north of Cuzco, invaded the territory of the Quechuas and threatened the young Inca state. As a result King Viracocha, now elderly and weak, fled his capital. With his son Urco, whom he wished to succeed him as head of state, he took refuge in a palace safe from the Chanca threat. Another son, Cusi Yupanqui, rallied those who wanted to resist the invaders and, against all expectation, defeated the Chancas before they took the Inca capital.

Strengthened by this victory, which fully established him as a war leader, Cusi Yupanqui did

Machu Picchu: the Torreón. *This curved-plane building has as its foundation a massive block of granite, which rises up to form part of the upper storey. At the winter solstice of the southern hemisphere, in June, the sun's rays at dawn lit up a ridge carved into the rock, thereby allowing the date of the Inca festival Inti Raimi to be determined.*

Overall plan of the site at Machu Picchu. *This site, discovered in 1911 by Hiram Bingham, was abandoned by the Incas after the Spanish conquest. The conquistadores were unaware of its existence and during the period of resistance which followed the conquest, Machu Picchu and the surrounding areas offered places of refuge for Incas opposed to Spanish rule. Situated in the Andean foothills, on the fringes of the Amazon jungle, Machu Picchu illustrates the ability of Inca architecture to adapt to natural environments very different from that of the high sierra. [Photo J.-F. Bouchard]*

not allow his father to return to the throne which he had fled. This victory also brought about a rallying to the Incas of those tribes who had prudently decided to await the outcome of the invasion. Pursuing the last invaders to the very heart of their own territories, the new sovereign was thus able to annex a major part of the central Andes. He then reigned under the name of Pachacuti Inca Yupanqui.

The defeat of the Chanca invasion transformed at a stroke the course of the history of the Andes. Urco, the heir designated by Viracocha but now made destitute, died shortly afterwards while trying to regain power. More importantly, however, the local tribes over a vast area around Cuzco became the subjects of the Incas, willingly or by force. From this desperate resistance which had

A complex astronomical observatory, *the Torreón must rank among the most beautiful architectural creations of the Inca empire on the strength of the perfection of the granite blocks, fitted with such precision, and of the boldness of its conception, set upon an oblique outcrop supported in turn by walls. [Photo J.-F. Bouchard]*

Machu Picchu: the temple of the three windows. *This 'temple' derives its name from the three large openings which pierce the rear wall, looking out onto the main site. It is a remarkable example of Inca megalithic architecture, in which vast blocks were fitted together without mortar. [Photo J.-F. Bouchard]*

transformed apparently certain defeat into victory, the empire was born.

The victory, undoubtedly glorified by the Incas, is reported by all the Spanish chroniclers. Pachacuti appears in it not only as a king endowed with unquestionable talents as a warrior but also as a skilful politician. To him is also attributed responsibility for the major reforms which enabled the Inca state to manage its conquests in a better manner, as well as redesigning Cuzco on lines more appropriate to its role as a powerful capital city.

Pachacuti planned to halt the ambitions of another of his brothers, Capac Yupanqui, by entrusting him with the pacification of the Chanca territories. He himself wanted to devote his energies to reforming the power structure. But Capac, far from stopping at the predefined limits, kept pushing the Inca troops further north, probably in the hope of attaining a position whereby he could claim supreme power because of

his abilities as a conqueror. Eventually Pachacuti managed to eliminate his rival and transferred command of the troops to his son, Tupac Yupanqui, who continued the conquests until in the end he took from the rear the great coastal kingdom built up by the Chimus in the north of Peru. Threatened with losing the water essential for the irrigation of the desert, the Chimus did not even enter into battle, but simply joined the empire.

At the end of Pachacuti's reign, Tupac Yupanqui claimed his right to succession by stressing his competence in military strategy. Although there was no statute to this effect, a claimant to the title of Inca had to be a *sinchi* – either a warlord capable of leading troops to victory, of defending the empire against aggression, or of crushing the rebellions which always threatened to break out.

Once he attained power, Tupac Yupanqui pursued his conquests, annexing more coastal lands in the south of Peru. He also ventured, without great success, into the warm lands of the Amazonian foothills. He constantly had to suppress rebellions, particularly in the high plains to the south where the subjugated tribes tried to free themselves from the Incas so as to pursue their own expansionist policies.

When Tupac Yupanqui died in 1493, Huayna Capac, his son, succeeded him and pushed back the boundaries of the Empire. After conquering the southern Andes, Huayna Capac consolidated and extended Inca acquisitions in the equatorial Andes, which were particularly fertile. In order to control his campaigns in the north, the Inca established himself in Tumibamba, in Ecuador. Cuzco remained the official capital, but the monarch did not take up permanent residence there. The transfer of the real seat of power was justified in terms of being closer to the battle-front, but there seem to have been other motives. Huayna Capac had himself been born in the north of the empire, which perhaps explains his choice of Ecuador to the detriment of Cuzco.

Towards the end of his reign, various diseases which had been brought to America by the *conquistadores* began to spread and affect the Andean population: in fact, they ravaged the people before the Spaniards even reached the Inca empire. Huayna Capac himself probably died from one of these illnesses in 1528.

As was almost always the case in the empire, the problem of succession caused a power crisis. History records particularly the names of the two main claimants, Huascar and Atahualpa, both sons of the Inca but each born of a different mother. Huascar seems to have more claim to being regarded as the legitimate heir since he had been the governor of Cuzco for a long time. Atahualpa, on the other hand, seems to have been a last-minute claimant who succeeded in profiting from Huascar's misjudgements in asserting his rights to the throne.

The succession crisis erupted into a struggle which tore the unity of the empire apart. For several years the two factions supporting each pretender fought a war, which eventually ended in favour of Atahualpa. His victory was, however, short-lived, for this was the moment when, at Tumbez in the north of Peru, Pizarro and his men reached the boundary of the empire and set about planning the seizure of its fabulous riches. Atahualpa was captured by Pizarro at Cajamarca in November 1532, and executed in June the following year.

This version of the history of the empire, transmitted by the Incas to the chroniclers, naturally gives them a leading role: the Inca hegemony appears to have been imposed on the Andes without great difficulty. The expansionism was not intended merely to annex tribes but – or so it was claimed – to bring them the benefits of a better civilization, sometimes against their will and by armed force.

Machu Picchu: terraces in the farming sector. *These terraces were designed to stabilize the slopes and safeguard them from erosion, while at the same time shaping the land to form a greater surface area for farming plots. Like other sites in the region, Machu Picchu's terraces, known as* andenes, *extend over a considerable area, taking advantage of slopes which would otherwise be too steep or vulnerable to erosion to be farmed. These vast agricultural expanses, created by the Incas, allow us to see these sites as part of a systematic colonization of warm lands at medium altitude in order to grow crops which were not adaptable to the climate of the sierra. [Photo J.-F. Bouchard]*

Machu Picchu: the 'great cavern', or Temple of the Moon. *This edifice was built below the rest of the site, near the course of the Urubamba River, which it slightly overhangs. The name 'Temple of the Moon' is certainly not an indication of its true function which remains unknown. It is built in the ample shelter of a large granite outcrop. As with the lower section of the Torreón, the natural rock walls of the shelter have been used by the Incas as the basis for higher walls, which they decorated with the trapezoid niches typical of their architectural style. [Photo J.-F. Bouchard]*

Huchuy Cuzco: overall plan of the site. *Not far from Cuzco, in the sacred valley of the Incas, this site overlooks the Vilcanota river. According to P. Cieza de León, Viracocha ordered a residence to be built for him in this region, to which he would come and rest. Some archaeologists believe that this was the retreat – known as Huchuy Cuzco, or Xaqui Xahuana – where the Inca Viracocha fled with his son, Urco, to escape from threatened invasion by the Chancas.* [Photo J.-F. Bouchard]

Cuzco's streets *show an architectural mix of both Inca and colonial styles; Spanish walls crown Inca foundations. In the centre of the old capital, modern roads often follow original Inca paths, and lead the visitor past many traces of imperial architecture which have survived both the destructive zeal of the conquistadores and the violent earthquakes which have damaged so many buildings built after the conquest.* [Photo J.-F. Bouchard]

The empire: a synthesis in organization

The socio-economic and political structures of these prehistoric Andean cultures explain to some extent the mechanisms leading to the acceptance of Inca hegemony. Generally speaking, the tribes conquered by the Incas had been settled for a long time in regions where they grew crops and reared stock. These lands had been made profitable only through major irrigation, or terracing of the mountain slopes.

While a small group of people might certainly be able to do a limited amount of such work, only a powerful state was capable of undertaking the major projects that were necessary in order to improve the land. A so-called 'vertical' economy enabled them to exploit flat stretches of land at different altitudes, sometimes running from the coasts as far as the high plateaux. The natural limitations of the terrain led to a quest for complementary political alliances, which were essential for ensuring an adequate and varied agricultural production.

These alliances did not, however, prevent local conflicts, which were frequent in the period before the Inca empire. Raids for pillage and plunder were common. Some powerful groups had conquered and annexed lands before the Incas came. To mention but one example, in the north of Peru the coastal kingdom of the Chimus had occupied much of the low valley area bordering the Pacific and had also formed an alliance with the powerful confederation of Cajamarca in the Andes in the north of Peru.

When the Incas established themselves in the Andes as an expansionist power, their policy was to exploit both conflicts and alliances. Their victory over the invading Chancas enabled them to appropriate the territory of the defeated army, but they also annexed the land of the Quechuas, which was located between the Cuzco region and the high valleys of the Chancas. After the victory, the neighbouring tribes to the south became allies of the Incas and they thus affirmed their allegiance to the empire.

The terms of these alliances might vary according to the tribe concerned, but all involved total integration into the Tahuantinsuyu. In return, the Incas offered the local chieftains (*curacas*) continuation of their rule and gifts of items which were highly prized among the people of the Andes, such as textiles and herds. As for the populations thus integrated into the state, the 'Inca peace' protected them against local warfare and also assured them of aid from the empire in the event of hardship or poor crops.

For the groups which accepted without resistance, this alliance was preferable to subjugation. In the latter situation the irresistible Inca armies would invade their territories, pillage their crops and storehouses, destroy traditional local power structures and wipe out their gods. Rebels were punished just as severely as any people which, at least initially, rejected integration. The history of the empire prefers to stress the civilizing role of the Incas, but some episodes reveal the cruelty of the fate reserved for those who resisted conquest and pacification, or who rebelled against the empire.

One of the more reliable sources, the chronicler Pedro Cieza de León, reports that the Inca Huayna Capac, after a long siege of the town of Guarco, executed all the high chiefs who had been opposed to his conquest. Similarly, in Ecuador in the northern Andes, the lake known as Yahuar Cocha, 'the lake of blood', acquired its new name following the massacre of the warriors captured after resisting Huayna Capac.

In order to eliminate all opposition, the Incas paid little attention to the finer feelings of the vanquished populations. Any group that proved too rebellious or too warlike was immediately split up, and one part was moved away to another region. Other groups who were more loyal were then installed in the subject territories in their place. The groups displaced from their original lands, the *mitimaes*, formed a separate class in Inca society; and those who had been deported as punishment had a different status from those who were moved to colonize new territories or to pacify conquered regions.

These practices did not, in reality, shock the Europeans of this period. However terrible these actions might seem to us today, we must assume that they were viewed in a different light by the people of the pre-Hispanic Andes. All that the Incas were actually doing was perpetuating customs which were not uncommon before their rise to power, as can be seen from the execution scenes portrayed on Mochican vases, for example. What distinguishes the various Inca conquests from the Spanish conquest is the way in which the Incas made their civilization coexist with the many cultural elements of the ethnic groups absorbed into the empire.

A dual organization

The socio-economic organization of the Incas was based on a dual imperial and regional structure. The local chiefs who submitted with good grace retained their power. In this way, traditional chiefs kept considerable autonomy in their internal affairs, and their subjects, who were also subjects of the Incas, still belonged to their original cultural group. The regional traditions and beliefs were maintained – conditional, of course, on their not being in any way opposed to the imperial culture. The traditional deities belonging to each ethnic group continued to be tolerated by the Inca state alongside the gods of the empire, in particular the sun god, Inti, of whom the Inca himself was the representative on earth.

None the less, integration into the Inca empire imposed a whole series of modifications on traditional ways of life. In addition to their own structures, non-Inca populations had to obey all the regulations governing the Tahuantinsuyu. Belonging to one of the four quarters, or *suyus*, they became part of the organizational plan of the Inca empire. This was based on an evaluation of each region, which involved making an inventory of the territories, their products and their inhabitants. This information was recorded using *quipus*, an accounting system based on the representation of numerical data by knotted cords; the colours and the position of the knots indicated values known to the book-keepers, who were called *quipukamayocs*. In this society which knew no system of writing, these *quipus* permitted very accurate and comprehensive inventories to be made, serving as accounts which could be used to manage the state by establishing targets. This system made it possible to calculate both the extent of agricultural land as well as its yields, the availability of stores and the number of livestock. The population was managed in the same way. Thus the Inca could find out, very accurately, the number of inhabitants in a region, as well as their age and how they were employed.

This duality of organization was also reflected in the geography of the empire. Archaeological research in various regions has shown in the majority of cases that alongside the traditional sites predating the Inca conquest lie the Incas' own constructions, recognizable because they were typically designed to further the smooth functioning of the administration. Located amid a great network of roads and tracks constructed by the empire are urban centres, often of considerable size, serving as regional capitals in which representatives of the Inca government resided. They also include buildings of the imperial religion, as well as warehouses and granaries. Between all these large centres were multitudes of small relay stations, *tambos*, where the garrisons controlling the roads were stationed. These tambos were also used as halts for the chaskis – runners who, operating in relays, transmitted from one end of the empire to the other government orders and

Ollantaytambo. *The site of Ollantaytambo in the Urubamba valley is made up of an Inca settlement (inhabited to this day) and a fortress looming over the conurbation. One of the side walls of the fort is built of megalithic rock of some religious significance to the Incas. In between each large block, a number of smaller blocks are inserted vertically, thus creating a flawlessly fitted wall. [Photo J.-F. Bouchard]*

Above
Sacsayhuaman. *The fortress of Sacsayhuaman surrounds the peak of a hill overlooking Cuzco. The three circles of walls are built from perfectly interlocking blocks of considerable size. [Photo J.-F. Bouchard]*

Left
The apse of Santo Domingo at Cuzco. *This church was built by the Spaniards on the still-visible base of the Sun Temple, the main place of worship for the Incas. [Photo J.-F. Bouchard]*

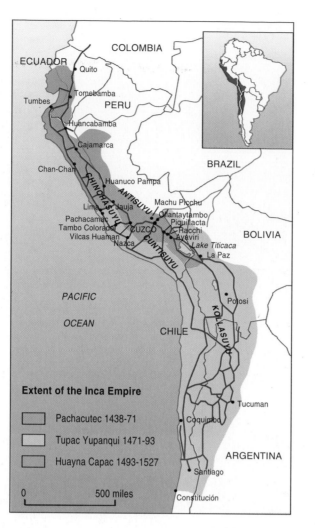

Development of the Inca empire.

Extent of the Inca Empire

Pachacutec 1438-71

Tupac Yupanqui 1471-93

Huayna Capac 1493-1527

0   500 miles

SACRIFICE OF A LLAMA
The Incas sacrificed animals on various occasions as offerings to the gods in their pantheon. The llama, the most commonly domesticated animal, was the preferred sacrificial victim in the Inca religion. Even today, in spite of their conversion to Christianity, the inhabitants of the Andes continue to make offerings and sacrifices in accordance with pre-Hispanic rituals: coca leaves, alcohol and various other objects are added to the foetuses of llamas – replacing the sacrifice of a living animal, which would be too costly nowadays.

information for the Inca or the imperial representatives.

Excavations have clearly shown the differences between Inca sites and traditional ones. In the latter, it is exceptional to discover any objects that are Inca in style, which seems to confirm the fact that regional cultures were maintained. In contrast, the administrative centres contain very few local objects among the vast quantities of Inca remains.

In the same way that they constructed their own sites alongside pre-existing ones, the Incas did not dispossess conquered tribes of their own lands. In each conquered region, some lands were indeed handed over by way of tribute to the Inca and to the sun, as reported by the chroniclers, but this was mainly land which had hitherto been under-exploited. Because of their skill in large-scale irrigation and conservation, the Incas were able to make use of this kind of land for the production of tributes without having any harmful effect on local production of crops. A proportion of the yield obtained was used to feed the imperial administration, but the remainder was distributed to other populations in the empire.

This state system of providing aid for contingencies was effective insurance against the constant risk in the Andes of poor crops and food shortages. It was also a means of sharing the riches of the empire, with the most prosperous regions helping the most deprived. By exploiting the agricultural technology of the pre-Hispanic era, the Inca empire achieved for the people of the Andes a balance between their everyday needs and the productive potential of their environment. This balance was destroyed after the Spanish conquest, when the Amerindian population was shorne of the major part of its riches in order to profit the colonizers who had come to settle in America or those who had stayed on the Iberian mainland.

The arts of the Incas

Compared with the long development span of the other Andean cultures, the very short life of the empire explains why examples of the Inca arts are often in relatively short supply. In contrast to the rich variety of styles which archaeologists have defined for pre-Inca cultures, a single style is found with hardly any signs of evolution – the imperial Inca style – alongside provincial styles which amalgamate regional artistic expression with the authentic Inca style. It is not possible to list here all these provincial styles, but it is important to stress some aspects of this fusion which illustrate further the achievement of the Incas in integrating other cultures with their own.

Inca jewellery is the most striking example. The treasures found by the *conquistadores* were almost all melted down, but we know from texts of the period and the few objects saved from pillage that the Incas possessed many objects made of gold and silver. To the various decorative objects should be added cult objects and figures of a religious nature. They also made more mundane items, such as tableware for banquets and instruments, all of precious metal. The chronicles tell of a sacred garden, in the temple of the sun, where life-size plants and animals were made of gold.

For the Incas, as well as for other Andean cultures, gold and silver did not represent a money supply, as perceived by the Western world. Their value was much more symbolic: associated with the sun and moon, they were considered to be a part of these divine astral bodies.

As the last civilization in the Andes, the Incas brought together the technologies known to their predecessors. Thus they used the very skilful Chimu goldsmiths to create many of the treasures

A pajcha ritual object, carved in wood and painted. *Inca 'pajchas' were used for ritual libations: the liquid flowed from the bowl-shaped vessel by means of a channel, hollowed out along the decoratively engraved 'appendix'.* [Musée de l'Homme, Paris]

A narrow-necked vessel, Inca. *These vessels, designated as Arybale in the scientific literature because of their resemblance to similar Greek vases, were used for storage. A human face in relief adorns the upper part of this exceptional piece from Bolivia.* [Musée de l'Homme, Paris]

of the empire. This does not mean that they themselves invented nothing: one only has to compare the two styles to see the differences and realize that the Incas integrated their own practices into an imported technology.

In addition to the production of gold and silver jewellery, they also worked in bronze. Mainly everyday objects, such as arms and various kinds of tools were fashioned from this alloy, but their functional purpose is combined with an elegance comparable to modern designer-ware.

Ceramics, which occupies an important place in Andean cultures, is represented in pottery shapes and motifs typical of the imperial Inca style. The Inca *arybales*, large jars decorated with various geometrical designs, are among the most remarkable of these. Other receptacles used the same designs, which cover almost the whole visible surface. Although this decoration is very standardized in itself, its variations add some diversity to what are otherwise rather monotonous shapes. Alongside this commonplace pottery, made in bulk to rationalize production and to satisfy the need for a large range of objects, there exist less uniform items. This pottery is more provincial than imperial, and integrates earlier regional styles. It is much more varied and attractive.

Related to the pictorial decoration of the pottery, the painting on wooden vases, known as *qeros*, is very typical of Inca art and continued into the colonial period. Originally these vases were decorated with engravings or geometrical designs. With the conquest came figurative representations, and this hybrid art has given us some rare and precious depictions of Inca individuals. Still within the art form of wood carvings are objects, like *pajchas*, which were used for ritual libations.

Inca sculpture in stone: *This man's head is an exceptional representation of an Inca, adorned with the trappings of Imperial power. The head and body were found at Cuzco in two different places. The head was first to be found and is now preserved at the Museo de America, Madrid.* [Photo Oronoz © Photeb]

The term 'Inca' has several definitions. In its most widely accepted connotation, it designates an ethnic group, the Incas, who settled in the region of Cuzco and, along with three other tribes, formed part of the confederation of Cuzco. The Incas founded the empire of Tahuantinsuyu, which brought about the final cultural and political unification of the central Andes before the arrival of the *conquistadores* in Peru. By extension – but incorrectly – the term is also applied to the various ethnic groups who were subjects of the empire, although in reality each non-Inca tribe had its own cultural identity before integration. Finally, the term 'Inca' designated the sovereign of Tahuantinsuyu. The correct and complete title is Sapa Inca (Great Inca), often followed by the title Intip Churin (son of the Sun). Chroniclers generally applied the simple title of Inca to designate the various sovereigns of the empire.

Stone sculptures play only a minor role: they exist mainly in the form of small objects used in religious rituals and known as *conopas*, which represent very stylized miniature llamas or alpacas. A depression carved in the back of these animal shapes was intended to hold some kind of offering. *Conopas* are characterized by a very simplified style, which often looks strangely modern to the twentieth-century eye.

Some zoomorphic stone vases and tools or arms, such as star-shaped clubs, complete this range of work. However, there is also one example, so far unique, of a large-scale sculpture; it may perhaps represent the Inca Viracocha. The head, decorated with insignia of imperial power (the *mascapaycha* and the *llanta*), has been handled with a realism far removed from the stylization normally associated with Inca sculpture.

Weaving is one of the major arts of the Andes. The cloths made from the wool of the mountain-dwelling members of the camel family – llamas, alpacas and vicunas – were of very special value in the Inca empire: among the precious goods held in stock by the authorities, textiles were of prime importance. They functioned as luxury items and were included in the gifts offered by the Inca to his allies. The cloths were also used in religious sacrifices. This range of products, intended for imperial worship and authority, was stored in vast warehouses, just like foodstuffs. When they discovered these warehouses the Spanish *conquistadores* were awestruck as they realized the scale of opulence existing in the empire.

Incontestably, however, the most accomplished of the Inca arts is architecture, which reveals remarkable expertise and technical mastery. This architecture is the very image of Inca power: the state was able to demonstrate its authority by erecting throughout the conquered territories the buildings necessary for administration and control. However, it is in Cuzco and its surrounding countryside that the greatest concentration of imperial architecture is found. The former Inca capital has now been transformed by urban growth, which has overflowed the boundaries of the old town. But the Inca heart has not been completely destroyed. Many streets still retain pre-Hispanic traces and the colonial buildings press against

strong Inca walls which formerly enclosed palaces and sacred places. Outside Cuzco, a multitude of Inca sites are scattered across the countryside: they are mostly found looking out over built-up areas which had been colonized, their purpose being to gather together and control the native populations. Pisac, Ollantaytambo in the sacred valley of Vicanota, and the fortress of Sacsayhuaman above Cuzco are among the best known.

Even though Machu Picchu was built at altitude in a hot and humid jungle, very different from the sierra of the Andes, this site is for many people the most evocative in all Inca architecture. The builders achieved the feat of remodelling the landscape by creating gigantic terraces to contain the mountain slopes, without the architecture ever disturbing the beauty of the natural site. To this perfect equilibrium must be added the quality of the constructions and the romance of this city buried for centuries by tropical forest.

Along the desert coast, the Incas succeeded in adapting to some very special conditions. Following the techniques of the pre-Inca coastal architecture, they used raw clay bricks (adobe) and terraced roofs.

This architecture, with its simplicity of design and unambitious elevations, reflects the methodical spirit of the Incas, who were more concerned with building solidly and durably than in throwing monuments high into the sky. For this reason they fit perfectly into the constraints imposed by the Andes. At night the thick walls release the heat stored during the day, so neutralizing the huge variations in temperature. These same walls, with their solid bonding, also demonstrate remarkable resistance to all kinds of damage, notably the earthquakes which are common in the Andes. While even very modern buildings are badly affected by seismic disturbances, it is rare for the Inca walls to be touched.

Admiration of these qualities becomes all the greater when one realizes that the Incas had only fairly primitive means at their disposal: hardstone tools, supplemented by some bronze instruments, were sufficient for the precise shaping of the enormous blocks of stone which they fitted together by polishing them with sand. Transportation from the quarries to the workshops

---

AN ASPECT OF THE INCA RELIGION

Inca funeral rite: parading of a mummy.
Like many of the preceding Andean cultures, the Incas mummified the corpses of the most important people. All the Inca sovereigns were mummified after death and formed the object of a complex funerary cult secured by their lineage, the panaca. *In November the mummies of the kings were paraded in procession in public. After the conquest, the Spaniards tried to stamp out all kinds of idolatry by destroying the sacred places and objects known as the* huacas. *If they succeeded in finding any of the mummiesof the kings these were immediately destroyed in order to eradicate the veneration shown by the people of the Andes.* [La nueva coronica y buen gobierno, F. Guaman Poma de Ayala]

Anthropomorphic and zoomorphic (llama) figures in gold. *The earlobes are distended by the wearing of ornaments, a common feature among the Incas. [Musée de l'Homme, Paris]*

Painted *quero*, Inca wooden bowl.
The inverted cone shape of the body is the most characteristic form of these bowls. It is decorated with ornate panels, featuring geometrical motifs typical of imperial art, representing the tropical flora of the sierra. [Musée de l'Homme, Paris]

empire at a time when it was tearing itself apart in the war of succession between the factions of Huascar and Atahualpa.

But underlying this crisis was an even more significant one, namely that the enormous empire was assimilating its conquests with ever-growing difficulty. The transfer of the capital to Tumibamba had relegated Cuzco to no more than a second-rank city, just as the integration of a new non-Inca nobility into the existing power structures was about to reduce the Cuzco lords to a minority grouping. And to the difficult conquests in the north were now added internal revolts among tribes which, although conquered, were inadequately pacified and so were always alert to the possibility of exploiting any weakness in Inca power in order that they might reclaim their independence.

The *conquistadores* arrived at just the right moment to launch their audacious enterprise: Atahualpa did not have time to reconcile the factions separated by the war of succession. Fresh from his triumph over the armies of Huascar, he thought he could easily crush this handful of foreigners. But he could not understand the strategy of the *conquistadores*: everyone stood in dread of him, yet Pizarro and his men dared to approach him without showing any fear. The first meeting with the Spaniards at Cajamarca brought these few cavalrymen face-to-face with thousands of Atahualpa's warriors. The Inca was flung off his throne and captured without a single warrior daring to intervene.

Subsequently, when Pizarro advanced with his men to take Cuzco, several non-Inca tribes collaborated with them so that they could throw off the Inca yoke. The Spaniards were no longer considered to be the Viracochas, but they were certainly still liberators.

After the conquest, some Incas thought there remained some possibility of negotiating: Pizarro had little difficulty in finding a puppet king to take over Atahualpa's throne. In this apparently neo-Inca state the final attempt at local resistance took place in 1572 with the capture and death of Tupac Amaru, the last Inca of the empire of Vilcabamba. By being beheaded in the main square of Cuzco, the vanquished king gave birth to the myth of Incari: the head of the Inca, separated from its body by execution, would one day rejoin it. Then, for the people of the Andes, the Tahuantinsuyu of the Incas will be reborn and return to them the liberty lost by conquest.

No doubt there is still a hope in the Andes that the real Viracochas will come, as will the Inca foretold in the myth of Incari, for he is still alive somewhere in today's Andes. But what is really needed today is a genuine coming together, like that expected for centuries, so that the Viracochas of the future will not once again be bearers of disillusion and misfortune. And when the old myth becomes reality the Andean people will obtain the benefits so eagerly awaited.

was effected by yoking dozens of workers to the stones, which were slid along beds of clay or gravel on logs. The blocks were moved into position using angled planes of soil which were destroyed when the work was complete.

There is no mystery attached to any of these techniques which are closely related to those used in ancient constructions in the Old World. There is therefore no need to impute to the Incas any knowledge that was more magical or esoteric than technological. Their technical mastery and the perfection of the architecture are sufficient in themselves to elicit our admiration.

These outstanding features of Inca civilization demonstrate quite adequately the power of the state which the *conquistadores* found in Peru. The Inca empire, with its high degree of organization, was able to provide its subjects with a standard of living which was often comparable and in many respects superior to that existing in the Old World.

Among the pre-Hispanic beliefs in the Andes, the return of the Viracochas – beings who were strange and very different from those then inhabiting the empire – was awaited and inscribed in the destiny of the world. When Pizarro and his men arrived, they were considered by some to be these very same Viracochas who were expected to return in order to save the Andes. This mistaken belief helped them to obtain a foothold in the Inca

CHRONICLE
OF AN ENCOUNTER
in the land of Canada

ANNE VITART

Tradition has it that, in about AD 1000, the fabled Viking Leif Eriksson left the Scandinavian colony in Greenland, apparently in search of wood, skirted the North American coast and discovered Newfoundland. Traces of the Vikings appear to have been found. A Canadian archaeological dig at the site of l'Anse-aux-Meadows, on the north-eastern tip of Newfoundland, has brought to light, remains of a Viking settlement from the early eleventh century – apparently occupied for about twenty years – including the foundations of eight houses and a forge. This site is at present the only one to attest to the Viking presence in North America.

Preceding page
Portrait of an Indian, *oil on canvas by George Catlin. [Musée de l'Homme, Paris]*

The voyages of Cartier and Champlain.

The earliest contacts between Europeans and North American Indians occurred so far back in the mists of protohistory that it is difficult to assess the effect of such encounters. The Vikings built settlements, of which some archaeological remains have been found, but their presence seems to have left no significant mark on local populations even though the men of the North continued to look for wood along the American coast down to 1347.

In 1497, John Cabot, five years after the 'discovery' by Christopher Columbus, took possession of Newfoundland in the name of the King of England. He seems to have encountered no Indians, unlike his successor, the Portuguese Gaspar Corte Real in 1501, who scouted part of the same coast and took fifty-seven local captives to ship back home. For the first time, the people along these shores became raw material for the European slave-trade. Although the traffic in North American Indians of course never reached anything like the scale of the African slave-trade, it did provide European cities and noblemen with some human 'curiosities', on a par with rattlesnakes or other exotic animals.

In these very same years at the outset of the sixteenth century, Basque, Breton and Norman fishermen (among other nationalities) began operating extensively along the north-eastern Canadian shore. Cod was important in European trade because the religious calendar imposed numerous fast-days. Fishing camps multiplied along the coast. But the sailors seem to have had no curiosity about the inhabitants in the interior and have left no eye-witness accounts, although evidence of growing European knowledge of the north-east American shore begins to appear in contemporary maps. Still, we have tantalizing hints as to the extent of early contact and trade between local Indians and European fishermen. Thus, when the French navigator Jacques Cartier, on his voyage of 1534, saw his first group of Indians in canoes off Miscou Island (near Percé Rock), these did not scatter in flight but on the contrary paddled around the ships and then pulled up on the beach offering furs: 'And there descended from the said boats a great host of men who made much noise and made several signs to us that we should land, showing us furs on sticks.' (Cartier, *First Relation*.)

A land of surprises

Significant contact between Europeans and Indians on the north-east coast had been on the increase since the early 1520s. Before Cartier, the Florentine navigator Giovanni da Verrazzano, sailing under a French flag in 1524, provided the first known sixteenth-century description of the north-east American shore and of the people he encountered there: depending on the stretch of coast, some of these Indians had welcomed him warmly and indeed had shown themselves as curious of him as he of them; others had been hostile and indeed betrayed fear stemming from previous unpleasant experience with Europeans. The Maine Indians, notably, were wary after their first dealings with Portuguese sailors.

But only as of Tuesday, 7 July 1534, did North American Indians truly enter into the mainstream of European historical awareness: mainly through the French influence. On that day, Cartier, having skirted the Newfoundland coast after an uneventful twenty-two day crossing of the Atlantic, took his plunge into the unknown, entered the Gulf of the St Lawrence and discovered the '*sauvaiges*' who dwelt there. 'Savage' was the word specifically used by sixteenth-century Frenchmen to describe foreign peoples whose civilization did not appear to them as developed as their own, just as ancient Greeks and Romans had called them 'barbarians'.

From Cartier onwards, the French in North America gradually discovered a land full of surprises, inhabited by human beings different from themselves yet obviously akin, alternatively friendly or hostile, whose historical existence appeared as intertwined with that of the landmass which was quickly coming to be known – to Europeans – as 'America'.

In Mexico, the encounter with Aztec civilization had provoked among other Europeans – the Spanish – both dismay and surprised admiration. Instead of the 'savages' expected after

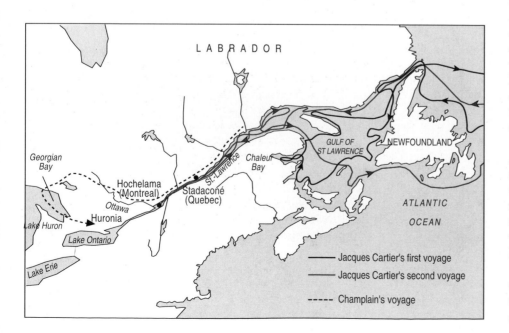

LABRADOR

GULF OF
ST LAWRENCE

NEWFOUNDLAND

Georgian Bay

Hochelama
(Montreal)

Ottawa

St-Lawrence

Chaleur Bay

Stadaconé
(Quebec)

Huronia

Lake Huron

Lake Ontario

Lake Erie

ATLANTIC
OCEAN

—— Jacques Cartier's first voyage

—— Jacques Cartier's second voyage

----- Champlain's voyage

Columbus' first landfall in the Bahamas, the Old World had confronted in Mesoamerica a New World of the kind which 'not even the Sibyl had predicted' (as Montaigne's *Essays* would put it). The Spaniards were initially taken aback because the Aztec social and intellectual framework, which found expression on the ground in elaborate architectural forms, was comparable in so many ways to European models: the evidence of Aztec power was forbidding to the conquerors, but also, in a way, understandable and hence even reassuring.

Nothing of the sort was to be found in North America, where social and intellectual structures seemed to show no analogy whatsoever with European standards. No firm features that Europeans could grasp appeared to stand out: there was no architecture in stone to point to the existence of a capital city or a mighty state, nor a chief or, at any rate, no paramount chief around whom people rallied. This apparent lack of any kind of centralized power was painfully unsettling to the European way of looking at things: without a leader there could be no order, no laws, only anarchy, a state of childhood, sheer hedonism. Throughout the entire history of relations between Indians and the French down to the eighteenth century, the latter constantly sought to identify the distinctive marks of chiefs, especially their amount of personal adornment: a European attribute of authority, no doubt, but certainly not an Indian one. Bewildered by what looked like a total absence of any fixed rules, the French failed to realize that they were dealing with societies which actually had their own way of organizing and of living on delimited territories, because they did not really want to know: these were savages, after all they went naked, had no chief.... Only slowly, as Indians became increasingly involved in the fur trade and as French exploration intensified, did Old World observers begin to acquire better knowledge of their local societies and to perceive their complexities and differences.

What struck Cartier at first, however, was not so much the oddness of the local population as the natural beauty of their hitherto unknown land. The admiration and indeed enthusiasm which he first felt – before the bay which he called 'des Chaleurs' ('of the heatwave') before proceeding to Gaspé Bay – never left him. 'We disembarked to see the trees which were wonderfully beautiful and fragrant.' (Cartier, *op. cit.*) Charmed by a natural setting which was 'the most temperate that could be', but also somewhat intrigued by the alien human beings to be found in it, Cartier tried to find the proper response to the warm welcome displayed by the handwaving 'savages' whose canoes he suddenly came upon after rounding a cape. However the French were worried by the number of them in 'more than forty or fifty craft' and refused to set foot on land. When the Indians 'paddled so furiously that they surrounded our vessel', Cartier's crew lost their nerve and put an abrupt end to their first meeting with the natives of the New World

Jacques Cartier. *Portrait by Théophile Hamel. Nineteenth century. [Library of the Canadian Parliament, Ottawa. Photo © Coll. Viollet-Arch. Photeb]*

with a warning shot from a small cannon on board. But the Indians renewed their approach the next day and trade finally took place. Two crewmen went ashore with knives and other trinkets, including a red cap, which they bartered for some furs which Cartier thought of poor quality. Yet this little exchange of paltry goods foreshadowed what would become the most profitable commercial activity in northern America: the fur trade. These Indians had obviously been used to trading with European fishermen for some time. They were the Micmacs. In the sixteenth century they lived in the area south and east of the Gulf of St Lawrence, a thickly wooded region dotted with lakes, subject to severe winters with only a relatively short summer. The harshness of the climate limited their agriculture to small tobacco crops.

The Micmacs were hunters and fishermen. They spoke an Algonquian language and organized their social life around two alternating phases: nomadic when rivers started freezing in October, settled between May and September. In winter the Micmacs scattered into small, autonomous bands and social relations were reduced to a minimum. With the return of spring, when the rivers began teeming again with shellfish and other life, groups of more than two hundred people each gathered anew to fish – each along their traditional stretch of bank. Water transport was by birch-bark canoe, a craft more than four metres long which carried 'all their dogs, sacks, pelts, kettles and other heavy baggage' (Jesuit *Relations*). The traditional dwelling was the *wigwam*, a conical tent covered in bark. Both sexes dressed in virtually the same way in

BASQUE FISHERMEN
We know of Basque fishing activity extending back to Roman times. Medieval Basques were considered the leading European hunters of whales. But by the beginning of the fourteenth century, whales were becoming scarce in the Bay of Biscay and the fishermen had to sail farther out into the North Atlantic. In these waters they discovered whales that were not only larger but also more placid and easier to hunt, making the chase profitable and leading to an increase in Basque fishing which reached its peak of activity in the sixteenth and seventeenth centuries. It was in the course of these whaling trips that the Basques made sporadic contact with the inhabitants of the coasts of Newfoundland and of the Gulf of the St Lawrence, basically to trade for fur but also to procure wood and supplies. Proof of these centuries-old and repeated contacts is furnished by Canadian topography: 'Isle aux Basques' (Basque Island), 'Port aux Basques' (Basque Port) ...

Mocock *of the Montagnais Indians. These receptacles, made from birch bark, are found over most of the sub-arctic zone of Canada, but those decorated with floral designs are typical of the region of Quebec and the province of Ontario. The seams are made from split roots of spruce and the edges reinforced by strips of wood and root. [Musée de l'Homme, Paris]*

CARTIER
Even before his first trip to Canada in 1534, Cartier knew of the inhabitants of the New World. It is known that he had previously visited Brazil, and that the merchants of his home port, St Malo, were much involved in the brazil-wood trade in the early six-teenth century. Cartier's wife, Catherine des Granches, was godmother at the christening of a little Brazilian Indian girl, perhaps brought back to France by her husband.

skins of elk or deer; they went bareheaded and wore their hair long.

Society was organized into the following units: the family, the local group, the band. A band brought together several hundred people and formed to make a camp in summer, or for war. Like most North American Indian societies, the Micmacs were egalitarian. Chiefs derived their status from the number of their wives, children and allies. However, it is probable that the arrival of the French and the growth of the fur trade strengthened the role of these chiefs, for the Jesuits in their *Relations* speak of local groups dependent upon a paramount leader whom the seventeenth-century French texts call the 'Sagamore' and who was 'the elder son of an important family and by consequence also the chief'. It is possible, however, that the Jesuits' description was suggested by the need to identify a hierarchical authority, indispensable to the European logical view of group

cohesion. Here again, a pattern was deciphered according to a European 'model': a chief's elder son, for example, simply had to be a chief in turn. Nonetheless, trade with the French probably did yield advantages to a few chiefs whose sons were thereby more readily enabled to command a measure of power and influence.

Be that as it may, Micmac society in the eyes of French observers was one 'where several chiefs without either order or hierarchy' decided about everything and nothing (Jesuit *Relations*) in a state of complete political disorganization, while their creed lay far beyond Old World comprehension. Convinced that these savages abided in total error in the grip of Satan, the Whites refused to see any coherence in the Micmac religious system structured around belief in a Creator identified with the Sun. Around this solar deity existed intermediary spiritual beings such as the culture-hero Gluskap, held to have taught wisdom, skills and crafts to mankind: in case of dire need, this beneficent warrior-god would one day return. The Micmacs believed that life was all-pervading, both visible and invisible on earth and beneath the waters; that all men were equal or ought to be; that no one should think himself superior to others and that leaders derived their authority only from their own merits. (P.K. Bock, *Handbook of North American Indians*, vol. 15, 1978.)

Early European observers failed to perceive these concepts among the Indians, because it was hard for sixteenth-century Frenchmen to accept that 'savages' might entertain ethical values identical to those of the 'civilized' world.

In any case, the brief period which Cartier spent among the Micmacs hardly allowed him an opportunity to gauge the richness of their culture. But he did see 'that they are people who come and go from one place to the next taking fish in the fishing season in order to live, and that their land is the most beautiful that it is possible to see'; moreover, noting their gentleness and the warmth of their welcome, he thought that they would be 'easy to convert'. But the real purpose of Cartier's mission on behalf of King Francis I of France was to search for a north-west sea passage to China (although he might claim lands discovered along the way in the name of his royal master). Hence Cartier could not tarry among the Micmacs. When satisfied that Chaleurs Bay was a dead end, yielding no passage west, he weighed anchor on 12 July 1534 and inched further north along the coast until forced by bad weather on 16 July to turn into what was the estuary of a great river: 'and there came to us many savages who were upon the same river to fish mackerel.' (Cartier, *op. cit.*)

This second encounter held even more surprises. These people did not resemble those previously seen in Chaleurs Bay. Cartier found them even poorer and more primitive than the Micmacs. On this day of 16 July 1534, Cartier opened the first chapter of the history of the French in Canada.

These Indians had travelled from far upstream into the great estuary of the St Lawrence to fish in the surroundings of Gaspé Bay. The strangers had no furs to barter, but they paddled close to the ships all the same and waved and shouted for joy in their canoes when the crew handed down to them knives, rosaries of glass beads, combs and other trinkets. Their appearance and the sound of their language were markedly different. They went almost naked and shaved their heads except for a scalp lock 'which they leave long like a horse's tail'. They seemed to own no other homes than their canoes, which they beached, overturned and slept under at night. They ate their meat and fish almost raw after only heating them a little over embers. They seemed so destitute to Cartier that he thought them utter savages, 'the poorest people that there could be in the world'. Their welcome was friendly enough, and when French crewmen disembarked they

danced and chanted merrily. But the Iroquois were also cautious; no doubt warned of what could happen from previous encounters with European fishermen, they had taken care to hide their womenfolk in the surrounding woods.

Strong headwinds kept the French in their sheltered cove for eleven days. Friendly relations were struck up between the two groups, each curious to find out more about the other. Cartier learned that these people came to fish from farther upstream and that in their own land, there grew a kind of 'millet' whose grain was 'as thick as a pea, as in Brazil'. With this grain they baked a tortilla-like flat cake which served them for bread and of which they had brought considerable supplies.

On the tenth day of his forced halt in Gaspé Bay, Cartier on the headland raised a thirty-foot high wooden cross with the royal coat of arms of France on a heraldic shield nailed to the crossbar. Thus Europeans had been taking possession of

Savages fishing. *Extract from the* Codex Canadiensis. *Seventeenth century. [Bibliothèque nationale, Paris. Photo. © Bibl. nat.-Arch. Photeb]*

Indian agriculture in Florida, *cultivation and sowing. From Brevis narratio Floridae by Theodore de Bry, 1591. [Historical Service of the Navy, Paris. Photo © Lauros-Giraudon]*

AGRICULTURE

One of the most stubborn clichés holds that North American Indians were nomads who practised little if any farming. The fact is that almost the sum total of native peoples who occupied the area between the Plains and the Atlantic coast lived in permanent villages and farmed. Among the numerous foodplants cultivated, in addition to maize which was basic, were beans, squash, sweet potato, pumpkins, sunflowers whose seeds were crushed and eaten, tobacco, and in the South, cotton. Fertilizers were known and Lescarbot noticed that some Indians in Virginia 'enrich their fields with shells and fish'. (*Histoire de la Nouvelle France, 1617.*) The first European explorers and colonists on American soil long depended on the foodplants of the Indians and learned from them how to farm, preserve and use them.

whole stretches of the New World since Columbus' first landfall in the Antilles. But the chief of the Iroquois party, Donnacona, was worried by this marker and suspicious. Wrapped in an old black bearskin, this chieftain with his three sons and his brother canoed close to Cartier's flagship and gestured to the effect that the land was theirs and that no cross could be planted there without their permission. Cartier suddenly had them seized by some of his armed crew in a longboat. On board, by further sign language, he tried to reassure the captive Iroquois that the cross was there only as a signpost marking the entrance to the bay. Then the French, after admittedly feeding and treating the Indians well, released Donnacona, his brother and one of his sons, but kept his other two sons as hostages. The Iroquois chieftain was forced to put up with the situation, sending some of his men in canoes with supplies of fish as parting gifts to the prisoners, and conveying to the French by sign-language that he would not cast down their cross.

For two weeks, the sailors cruised around the Gulf of the St Lawrence, meeting with more local Indian fishermen who astonished the crew by clambering aboard Cartier's ships with no more fear or hesitation 'than if they had been Frenchmen themselves'. (Cartier, *op.cit.*) Indeed, these Montagnais Indians of the St Lawrence estuary region, also an Algonquian-speaking people like the Micmacs, had been in contact with French fishermen for years. This group dealt with a certain Captain Thiennot, the Montagnais Indians gave Cartier to understand. This Thiennot, they indicated, normally anchored not far off and had

just set sail for his own country with a rich catch of fish. At this point, fearing the onset of the cold season with its attending storms, Cartier cut short his explorations and hence did not, on this voyage, reach the mouth proper of the St Lawrence itself. But he relied on his two hostages, Donnacona's sons, to be taught French over the winter and so serve him as interpreters and guides up the St Lawrence when he returned.

He was not disappointed. On his second voyage to Canada in 1535, the hostages took Cartier all the way up the Saint Lawrence to the village of Stadacona – site of the future Quebec – of which their father Donnacona was the headman. Then, despite the marked reluctance of his Stadacona guides, Cartier proceeded upriver to the island of Hochelaga, and he saw there a village surrounded by a palisade of stakes: the site of the future Montreal. Cartier had, as it were, reconnoitred the very heart of what would become New France.

The onset of the cold season held up Cartier at Stadacona and forced him to winter on the banks of the St Lawrence, an appalling experience with scurvy killing twenty-five out of his 110 men, while the natives of the area observed an attitude of sullen hostility. But throughout the long icy months, Cartier developed a fascination for what he had been hearing of a reported land of red copper, the wonderful Realm of Saguenay, which he understood the natives of Hochelaga and then here in Stadacona to describe glowingly as a distant region abounding in copper and gold with many cities and people dressed in good cloth of wool. By

Small bark box decorated with porcupine quills, Micmacs. *Almost all the Indian tribes in the north, east and centre of North America practised this decorative technique, but the Micmacs, whom Cartier met in Chaleurs Bay on his first voyage, were past masters in the art of applying quills to objects made from bark.*

It was the women who performed the decoration. From the dead porcupine they removed the quills, which were then sorted by thickness and length, the longest and thickest being on the back, the finest and shortest on the tail. The size of the quills chosen was determined by the design and the support to which they were to be applied. First they were flattened by chewing with the incisors, then they were dyed and applied by various techniques to the object to be decorated. During the eighteenth century, the demand for 'souvenirs' decorated with quills increased enormously, and the Micmac art was strongly orientated to the European market. [Musée de l'Homme, Paris]

CANADA

Cartier used the name 'Canada' to refer to the Laurentian region extending between Grosse-Ile in the east (to the north of Ile aux Couldres where the water in the St Lawrence estuary no longer appears as salty to the sailor coming in from the sea), to roughly half-way between Quebec and Trois Rivières in the west. Various explanations have been given of this name. In the vocabulary given in his second *Relation*, Cartier writes that the local word for a *ville* or 'settlement' was 'canada', and that the query, 'Where do you come from?' was pronounced, 'Canada undagneny?' In 1617, Lescarbot noted in his *Histoire de la Nouvelle France*: 'The people of Gachepé (Gaspé) and the Baie des Chaleurs call themselves Canadoquoa....'

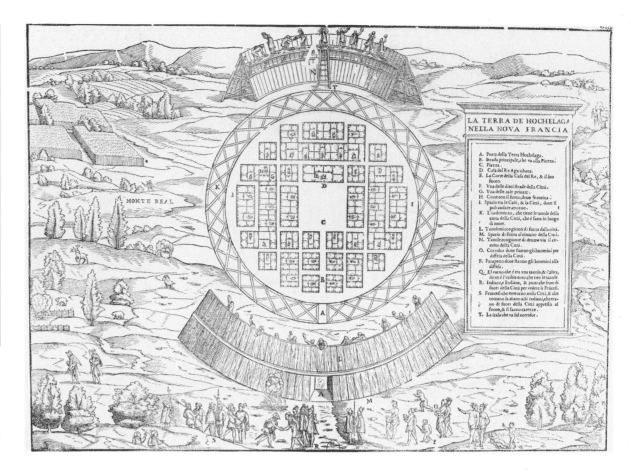

La Terra di Hochelaga, Nella nuova Francia. *Wood engraving, 1556. [Bibliothèque nationale, Paris. Photo © Bibl. nat.-Photeb]*

KIDNAPPINGS

The kidnapping of natives was standard European practice in the New World many years before 1534. The day after his first landfall, Columbus took seven Indians captive and sent them to Spain to learn the language, before returning as interpreters. Cartier kidnapped Donnacona's sons for the same reason. With the intensification of colonization, the need for interpreters led explorers to leave one of their own group with a native people to learn the required language, while in turn taking back hostages to teach them their own idiom, so that they should serve on their return as guides. This manoeuvre often backfired when interests diverged, as when Cartier's two hostage-interpreters took the side of their own people when returned to Stadacona, and interpreted accordingly.

In sixteenth- and seventeenth-century French colonial writing, the name normally used for an Indian 'interpreter' was 'truchement', a word derived from medieval Arabic.

the spring thaw, Cartier was determined that the King of France should hear of these marvels directly. When his ships weighed anchor, the crew seized Donnacona himself and nine of his men and took them back to France: not one of these Indians ever saw the New World again. Perhaps Donnacona's interviews with Francis I were what convinced the French King to dispatch a group of colonists under the Sieur de Roberval in 1541 to establish two forts upriver from the site of Quebec. But the kidnappings of their people had chilled any welcome for the French along the banks of the St Lawrence, and not only did Roberval abandon both outposts by 1542 and return with all his men to France, but Francis I lost all further interest in Canada as European wars engulfed his attention. Cartier had as it were knocked on Canada's door and the Indians had cordially opened it. Now the door of the 'new found land' slammed shut again on the French – or at least on *official* French explorers sailing under royal commission – for another sixty years. *Private* French fishermen from Brittany and Normandy, however, continued to haunt the North-eastern American coastline for the rest of the sixteenth century.

Even so, this historic gap – for fishermen unlike royal officers left no chronicles – explains our relative ignorance of the reasons why these Laurentian Iroquois of the Quebec/Montreal area had disappeared by the time official French contact with American Indians was resumed with Champlain at the outset of the seventeenth century. Among the answers suggested is that the Laurentian Iroquois may have aroused the hostility of their neighbours by attempting to keep a monopoly of what contact and trade remained with the private white sailors on the coast. Other tribes may then have tried to force their way into this trade, with the Mohawk Iroquois, in particular, intensifying their raids against these same Laurentians. Perpetual warfare with their rivals would then have resulted in the physical destruction of the Laurentians or their dispersal among other tribal groups.

Indeed, Cartier had been the first to come up against this stubborn insistence on a commercial monopoly among the Laurentian Iroquois at Stadacona (Quebec). The Stadacona Iroquois had tried every device – including recourse to magic and the intervention of their tutelary god – to discourage Cartier from pursuing his journey even so far as Hochelaga (Montreal). When Cartier's ships did sail upriver, Donnacona arranged for a canoe to glide by the French with three masked men on board 'appearing to be three devils with great horns on their heads', one of them haranguing the foreigners at length. When asked the meaning of this performance, Cartier's hostage-interpreters explained that these three men were messengers from the god Cudouagny, warning the Whites that if they pushed on to Hochelaga, the ice and snow would kill them all.

What we do know of these Iroquois of the Saint Lawrence stems essentially from what Cartier tells us of them himself. He notes that the peoples of Stadacona and Hochelaga were to be

Map of New France, *containing the account of Jacques Cartier in Canada in 1534-1536. From Delle navigationi et viaggi, by Giovanni Battista Ramusio, 1605. [Bibliothèque nationale, Paris, Photo Jeanbor © Arch.Photeb]*

distinguished from one another. They spoke the same language, Iroquois, but did not live off the same stretch of country and even their mode of subsistence differed; nor were they politically linked either to their Iroquois neighbours of the Five Nations confederation, nor yet to the Hurons, another people of Iroquoian speech.

The Stadacona Iroquois lived in some seven to ten unfortified villages around the site of the future Quebec. They cultivated maize but also relied on fishing in summer and hunting in winter. This economic dependence explained their semi-nomadic scattering into fishing parties throughout the summer such as the band which the French first encountered in Gaspé Bay. Cartier also noted with surprise the lengthy spells of absence of so many of Stadacona's hunters in the winter, in search of game. On the whole, however, Cartier's French were at a loss to detect the main social underpinnings of, and economic ties between, the various native peoples they saw. According to Cartier's writings, the headmen of the different groups and villages themselves seemed to be dealing with the Europeans independently of one another and in a rather haphazard manner. Even so this remark should be qualified with the proviso that such an observation may also merely reflect a sixteenth-century Frenchman's disapproval of a non-hierarchical society.

While Cartier says little concerning Stadacona, for Hochelaga he gives what might be termed the first 'anthropological' description of an 'Iroquois'-type settlement. Such a settlement, built in the middle of fields where 'grew the corn of their land', was circular and surrounded by a triple palisade of wood with only one gateway. Around the crowning parapet of this fortification ran a gallery, reached by ladders, in which stones were stockpiled for use as projectiles to be hurled in defence. The palisade protected about fifty wooden dwellings covered with sewn bark. Each dwelling sheltered several families: the model of the Longhouse which Champlain, three generations later, would find again among the Hurons and Iroquois. The inhabitants slept on bedding of birch-bark covered with furs which they wrapped about themselves as clothing during the day. As farmers, they cultivated maize which their womenfolk pounded in large wooden mortars; the resulting paste was baked over a bed of heated pebbles spread upon a larger heated flat stone. The product resembled a tortilla or flat cake. Cartier tasted this bread and observed that, like all their food, 'it had no taste of salt'. The people of Hochelaga tilled their fields and fished; they did not seasonally migrate like their neighbours of Stadacona, in relation to whom they seem to have enjoyed a somewhat superior status, almost as overlords. At any rate this degree of lord and vassal relationship was so perceived by the French and reassured them at long last as a comprehensible social pattern: in their eyes, nomads, by definition, could only be less civilized than sedentary folk, hence naturally the latter should be dominant. Still, the social workings of Hochelaga mostly escaped Cartier. He recognized that they had an

IROQUOIANS
The generic term 'Iroquoian' now conventionally designates the member of any group belonging to the general Iroquoian language family. The name 'Iroquois', strictly used, designates only those who were members of the confederation of the Five Nations, known to the English colonists as: Seneca, Cayuga, Oneida, Onondaga and Mohawk. The equivalent colonial French names were Tsonnontouans, Goyogouins, Onneiouts, Onnontagués and Agniers respectively.

Huron costumes. *From* Voyages and Discoveries made in New France, *by Master Champlain from 1603 to 1629. [Bibliothèque nationale, Paris. Photo Jeanbor © Arch. Photeb]*

Wampum of the Four Nations, *Huron Indians. The word wampum, Algonquin in origin, is a contraction of a more complex word meaning 'a string of white beads'. The beads used by the North American Indians were made from the shells of different kinds of marine molluscs, in particular a large bivalve* (Venus Mercanaria) *found in the Atlantic and whose internal nacre (mother of pearl) is white and purple. The wampum was considered by the Hurons and Iroquois to be the most appropriate gift in terms of serving as a letter of introduction and proof of authority. For this reason, ratification of treaties between Hurons, Iroquois and other Indian or European nations was accompanied by an exchange or gift of wampum. The colour of the beads was of significance, with white representing prosperity and peace, purple pain and war. In addition, the horizontal lines symbolized tracks or unions between nations (themselves represented by diamond shapes, squares or human outlines); the diagonal lines represented alliances or confirmation of messages. The wampums formed part of the public treasury of a tribe and were kept in a special place, often supervised by a woman, and they served also as archives. This example, known as the 'Four Huron Nations', was given in 1611 to Champlain by the Hurons seeking an alliance with France. At that time it might have been the 'voice' of Atironta, chief of the Arendaronons, one of the four groups comprising the Huron Confederation. [Musée de l'Homme, Paris]*

agouhanna – their chief, as he puts it – but he 'is no better attired than the others', only wearing around his head a sort of thong woven of hedgehog hairs and dyed red. Taken up a hill which he called the 'Mount Royal' or Mont Royal – whence the name of French Canada's future metropolis – Cartier discovered 'the finest land which it is possible to see, ready to be tilled, level and flat'. He also described some of the upper course of the St Lawrence, flowing from what he understood to be the Realm of Saguenay. At the same time he learned of the existence of hostile peoples there, armed 'to their fingertips' and constantly warring against each other. Perhaps these were Hurons from Georgian Bay, or other Iroquoian groups.

In the early seventeenth century, France finally emerged from the economic and social torment of its civil Wars of Religion and could turn its eyes once more towards Canada. Except for the few points along the coast reconnoitred by Cartier and his descriptions of the St Lawrence and the settlements of Stadacona and Hochelaga with their inhabitants, little was really known of this land. But the French realized by now that it was useless to look to Canada for the sort of dream-riches described by Marco Polo, while they were aware that the country enjoyed fertile land and rich forests with a welcoming population. In a devastated, famine-stricken France, even this was enough of a vision of an earthly Paradise to begin again to attract official attention.

Huronia

On 15 March 1603, Samuel de Champlain weighed anchor at Honfleur, bound for Canada on

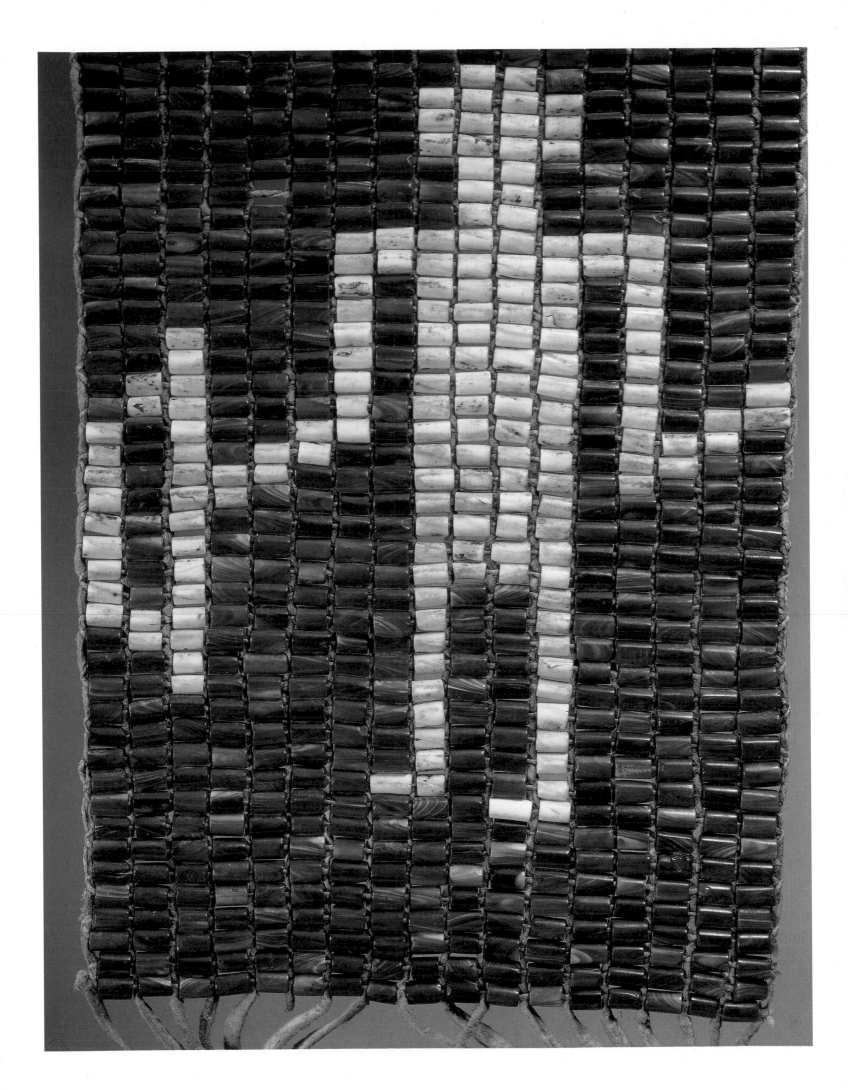

Samuel de Champlain. *Anonymous portrait. [Photo © Arch. Photeb]*

Defeat of the Iroquois at Lake Champlain. *Anonymous engraving. [Private collection. Photo H. Josse © Arch. Photeb]*

behalf of King Henry IV. This would be the first of Champlain's succession of rather short voyages, in the course of which the French and several Indian nations would forge enduring ties of trade and alliance while the political foundations of New France were laid. But between the last departure of Cartier and Roberval from Canada in 1542 and the official return of France with Champlain in 1603, both Indian and French perceptions and attitudes had somewhat changed.

Cartier had been looking for a passage to China, and the New World was basically an annoyance in his way. He had observed the inhabitants, but his journeys had been a failure in terms of what he wanted to do: sail through a north-west strait to Cathay.

The coastal and Laurentian Indians had observed and noted too: they had not been too surprised and worried by Cartier and his ships, because they had already dealt with European fishermen; and Cartier's crews had only amounted, after all, to a handful of men.

The early seventeenth century ushered in a different situation. Champlain knew where he was going and what to look for. He had read Cartier's *Relations*. Even when he pushed into *terra incognita*, he always travelled in the company of experienced Indian guides. The seventeenth-century Indians, in turn, now knew more of Europeans. Some of them would even go to France and return. Algonquins, Hurons and Iroquois were interested in commercial ties with the French. And France for her part was no longer searching for a hypothetical passageway to the Orient; rent by her civil strife between Catholics and Huguenots in the later sixteenth century, she wanted now to bind her wounds and invest in a land of hope, wealth and economic freedom: in short, in a colony. Both sides, French and Indian, had a stake in the issue and watched each other closely: two worlds met.

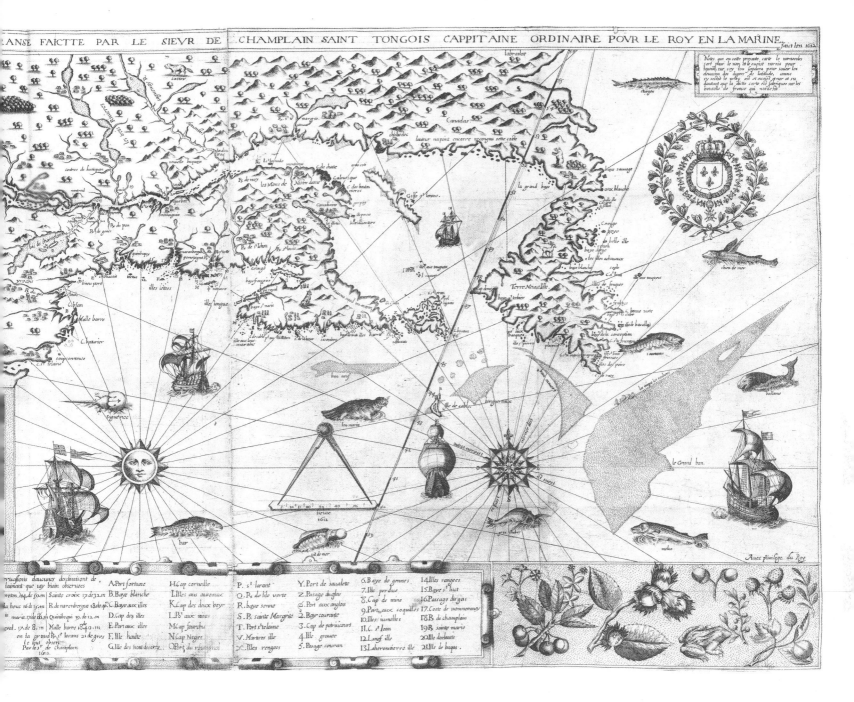

To establish his colony Champlain needed more information. Among the Algonquins of the St Lawrence estuary, Champlain noted, as had Cartier before him, that they seemed to have no law; but he was disquieted to learn that they believed in a single Creator. Travelling upriver he found that the St Lawrence flowed through wild, uninhabited territory, whereas Cartier had described it as peopled and settled with villages.

In 1608, in the course of a later voyage, Champlain built a fort which became the nucleus of the future city of Quebec, and met for the first time with representatives of the Huron nation. These had come from their distant homeland around Georgian Bay to seek alliance with the Algonquins of the St Lawrence estuary against their common foe, the Mohawk Iroquois, and wished to establish trading ties with the French.

In 1609, Champlain agreed to move with the Hurons against the Mohawks, whose raids sowed terror amongst the Algonquins. To reach Iroquois territory, Champlain and two French soldiers, all three armed with matchlocks, travelled up what would become known as the Richelieu river and discovered the great lake which now bears the explorer's name. Champlain's matchlocks carried the day against the Mohawks and their defeat sealed a close and enduring alliance between the Hurons and the French.

In 1611, on his return from a visit to France, Champlain travelled up the St Lawrence as far as the Lachine rapids, reputed among the Indians to be impassable by the French. Indeed three of Champlain's men were drowned. Undaunted, the explorer transported his canoes overland around the hurdle to Lake Saint Louis, 'the loveliest place upon this river', and found traces of previous farming along the banks but no sign of any substantial settlement comparable to what Cartier had described of Hochelaga.

Geographical map of New France, *drawn up by Champlain, 1613. Note the references to 'Montaignais' and 'Alnouchicois', as well as to fruits and vegetables cultivated on their lands. [Bibliothèque nationale, Paris. Photo © Bibl. nat.-Arch.Photeb]*

THE GEOGRAPHERS
Since European fishermen so often haunted the Strait of Belle-Isle between the northern tip of Newfoundland and the coast of Labrador, their reports may have fed the belief in a 'North-west Passage' which sixteenth-century geographers were convinced must exist in the North as a parallel to the passage to eastern waters and China found far in the South by Magellan.

Left
Wooden club. *The design of this fearsome weapon is ancient and typical of the Huron and Iroquois tribes. [Musée de l'Homme, Paris]*

Right
Mohawk warrior. *Watercolour drawing, English school, eighteenth century. [Museum of the New World, La Rochelle, Photo © the Museum]*

Right-hand page
Pouch made from cloth and decorated with beads from Europe, *Huron or Iroquois. Like Columbus upon landing in the Antilles, the first friendly act of Cartier towards the men he met in the Chaleurs Bay was to offer them a handful of small multi-coloured glass beads, made in Europe. These beads very quickly spread throughout the continent because they were handed out in profusion and bartered against furs. In North America they rapidly replaced traditional materials, such as moose hair or porcupine quills, which did not lend themselves at all, or only with difficulty, to curving or spiral designs. In addition, they saved considerable time by eliminating the whole preparatory phase. [Musée de l'Homme, Paris]*

Near Mount Royal (Montreal), the Hurons wished for further assurances of French military protection and invited Champlain to visit their huts at midnight, explaining that their custom was to deal with important matters after dark 'so as not be diverted by the aspect of anything'. The Indians guaranteed to the French officer that their friendship would ever remain unbroken and that since he had decided to visit their country, then they would risk their own lives to guide him. To seal the alliance, they produced fifty beaver pelts and four 'halters wrought of their porcelain', to wit, belts made of the mother-of-pearl derived from the seashell *Venus mercenara*. Such belts were known as *wampum*. It is possible that these gifts included the belt of *wampum* now preserved in the Musée de l'Homme in Paris and identified as 'the *wampum* of the Four Huron Nations'. If so, this object would be the earliest surviving token of diplomatic relations between France and North American Indians.

Only in 1615 did Champlain discover Huronia. On 9 July, accompanied by a party of nine 'savages' and a Récollet friar (the Récollets were a French branch of the Franciscan order), Champlain followed the course of the Ottawa upriver from the Montreal area as far as the Lake of the 'firesticks', crossing landscape which he described as disagreeable, desertic and sterile! Then, quitting the Ottawa river, the expedition portaged through territory spotted with swamps before reaching a fine great lake and discovering the inhabitants of its shores: the Nipissings. These Algonquian-speaking people enjoyed peaceful relations with their Huron neighbours and welcomed the French. They lived in settled summer villages by the lake but migrated to spend the winter in the neighbourhood of the Hurons. Champlain writes that they farmed only very little and much resembled the Montagnais at the estuary of the St Lawrence.

After two days' rest, the expedition canoed down the river which came to be known as Des Français ('of the French') and reached the shores of what a later age would call Georgian Bay. Champlain still thought the countryside forbidding, rocky and unfit for the plough.

The French party now met with a group of nearly three hundred warriors whom Champlain calls, on account of their hairstyle, the Cheveux Relevés, 'those of upright hair'. According to Champlain's *Voyages*, these men 'wear no leggings, cut a fine appearance and paint their faces in several colours; they pierce their nostrils and ears and adorn these with shells, stones and copper'. He established contact and presented a steel axe to their chief, who drew a rough map of his country with a piece of charcoal on a strip of bark. These people were the Algonquian-speaking Ottawas, who dwelt by the River des Français and occupied the peninsula between Lake Huron and Georgian Bay. The men wore their hair short, cut to a mere bristle over the forehead, and not only painted their faces but tattooed their bodies. The women clothed their bodies entirely and Champlain was struck by the intricacy of their braids.

At the time of this encounter, the Ottawas played a key role in the pattern of trade between groups to the north and west and the people in the area of Montreal. The permanent villages of the Ottawas were built along the river banks and their dwellings recalled the birch shelters of the Hurons and Iroquois. They farmed maize, squash and beans but relied mainly on fish. In many ways their social organization and customs resembled those of the Iroquois, notably in war: they took scalps, adopted captives into their own tribe as sons or tortured them to death: often enough practising cannibalism on them, eating the hearts and limbs of prisoners they chose to kill. They believed in the existence of a number of good and evil spirits, endowed with supernatural powers, over which reigned a supreme being: the Master of Life.

One day after meeting with the Ottawas, the French party paddled on to Lake Huron, reaching the shores of Huronia on 1 August. Here Champlain considered the landscape to change for the better, cleared by man, cultivated, with pleasant dells, crossed by numerous streams.

Champlain's arrival on Huron soil marked a decisive turn in the history of relations between these people and the French. The Hurons would remain staunch allies to the French and this tie would cause irreversible changes in their livelihood and society. A monopoly on the supply of furs to the French, and choice access to French trade goods, at first gave the Hurons a privileged role within the general commercial network between the allied native peoples. But this inevitably provoked the jealousy and irritation of other neighbours excluded from the network, especially the Iroquois. In 1640 the Iroquois picked up and intensified their raids against Huronia, smashing Huron resistance and destroying whole villages.

But European-borne epidemics did even more damage to the Hurons than did the Iroquois. By 1634 smallpox had wiped out roughly a third of a Huron population estimated at its height at about twenty thousand individuals. As a consequence of this double disaster, Huron society quickly disintegrated; conversions to Christianity multiplied; in 1649, only thirty-four years after Champlain's first visit to their villages, the last Hurons abandoned their original homeland. By 1672, when Marquette and Joliet opened the Mississippi to French penetration, Huronia no longer existed.

Wedged between the northern shore of Lake Ontario and the north-western tip of Lake Huron, along the shores of Georgian Bay, Huronia consisted of tillable soil emerging from water and swamps. Considered by the French as a kind of state, Huronia was described as comprising several provinces each commanded by a 'captain'; each province was said to include a number of towns and villages according to the Récollet friar Gabriel Sagard-Théodat.

Champlain and the missionaries who followed him spoke of Huronia as a Promised Land. Champlain writes that the country was 'very fine, maize grows well there, vines are abundant, also plums and walnuts'. The people who welcomed Champlain were 'dressed in the skins of wild animals', painted their faces in black and red and variously wore their hair long, cut short, or even sometimes suffered to hang from only one side when they shaved half their heads. The Récollet priest Sagard-Théodat describes the Hurons as 'tall, well-proportioned, with fine features, healthy and of a cheerful disposition'. Huron women always wore a short skirt which covered their thighs but not their knees; their bare breasts were nearly hidden under numerous necklaces.

While the country was pleasant and the population was welcoming, Huron society continued to surprise Champlain, although he did

The journey of Joliet and Marquette along the Mississippi and Illinois.

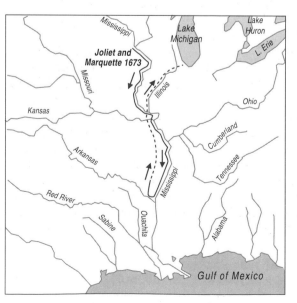

become familiar with most of its outward aspects. As a seventeenth-century Frenchman used to a tight patriarchal family structure and the iron rule of the Catholic moral code, he was totally bewildered by what looked like Huron social incoherence, with its sexual permissiveness for girls and premarital trial periods: 'As for their laws I have not perceived them to have any, given that among them there is no punishment, chastisement or reproval of ill-doers.... Furthermore they recognize no divine being.'

In fact, Huron society was rigidly ruled and structured. Children inherited in the matrilineal line, that is not from their father but from their maternal uncle. The extended maternal family, comprising several nuclear families (father, mother, offspring), formed the economic unit. Residence was matrilocal: a son-in-law lived with the family of his bride. Villages, whether palisaded or not, could include as many as two hundred longhouses.

The dimensions of any of these shelters, built of wood covered in sewn bark, varied according to the size of the extended family who occupied them. The largest longhouses were approximately ten metres wide by thirty to forty metres long, and stood roughly six or seven metres high. Inside, they were bisected by a central walkway which was two or three metres wide; on either side of this walkway extended a lengthy living-platform, upon which each nuclear family enjoyed between six and nine metres of sleeping-space. Cooking fires were lit along the central walkway and one hearth was shared by two families. Food and clothing were hung from the rafters, out of reach of the dogs.

Huron livelihood depended on farming and fishing. Maize and fish formed the basis of daily food and little meat was eaten, despite hunts carried out several times a year by the technique of encircling game. Among the Hurons, land belonged to those who farmed it. Women handled most of the farming, but the men took over the work of clearing. The main crop was maize, but squash, tobacco and hemp were also cultivated.

The Hurons called themselves the Wyandot (French translation 'Ouendat'). They were organized into a confederation which, in Champlain's period, grouped four tribes divided into a defined political hierarchy of eight clans each, distributed among different villages. Each section of a clan had two chiefs, one for war and the other for 'civil' affairs. Village matters were looked after by two councils with specific responsibilities but few coercive powers, no more than the chiefs had. Once a year, the confederation gathered in a general council (*Handbook of American Indians*, vol. 15).

The Hurons believed in the existence of spirits, the most important of which was the Sky in so far as this spiritual being controlled the winds, the sea and other natural phenomena. The two spirits ranking immediately after the Sky were Ataensic the Moon and her grandson Iouskea the

Capitaine de La Nation des Illinois, il est armé de sa pipe, et de son dard.

Captain of the Illinois tribe, *with his peace-pipe* (calumet) *and lance. From the* Codex Canadiensis. *Seventeenth century. [Bibliothèque nationale, Paris. Photo © Bibl. nat.-Photeb]*

THE FEAST OF THE DEAD AMONG THE HURONS

The women who are to bear the bones of their family members go fetch them in the cemeteries; if the flesh thereupon is not entirely consumed, they pull it off the bones and cleanse these properly; then they wrap these in new beaver pelts, adorned with beadwork and collars of mother-of-pearl (wampum), which family and friends contribute (…).

They also bear all the pelts, axes, knives, cauldrons and other offerings with a large quantity of victuals to the destined place, where they are put aside and kept separate; the victuals are set on one side, to be partaken of in the feasts; and the bags and furnishings are hung up in the lodges of their hosts, while awaiting the day in which it should all be buried together with the bones.

The pit is dug outside the settlement very wide and deep, capable of holding all the bones as well as all the furnishings and pelts dedicated to the deceased. A platform is raised high on the side, whither all the sacks of bones are borne; then the entire pit, bottom and sides, is lined with new beaver pelts; then a bed is made of axes, then another of cauldrons, of beadwork, of collars and bracelets of mother-of-pearl (wampum), and other things donated by family and friends. When this is done, from the top of the platform the Captains empty all the bundles into the pit amongst the goods, which they then cover with more new pelts and bark; after this they cast earth upon it and thick logs of wood, for fear of animals; then they drive into the earth stakes of wood all around the pit and pull a cover over it all which lasts as long as it may, whereupon they feast and take leave of one another, rejoicing and well pleased that the souls of their deceased family members and friends have enough share of wealth to make themselves rich that day in the other life.

Father Gabriel Sagard-Théodat

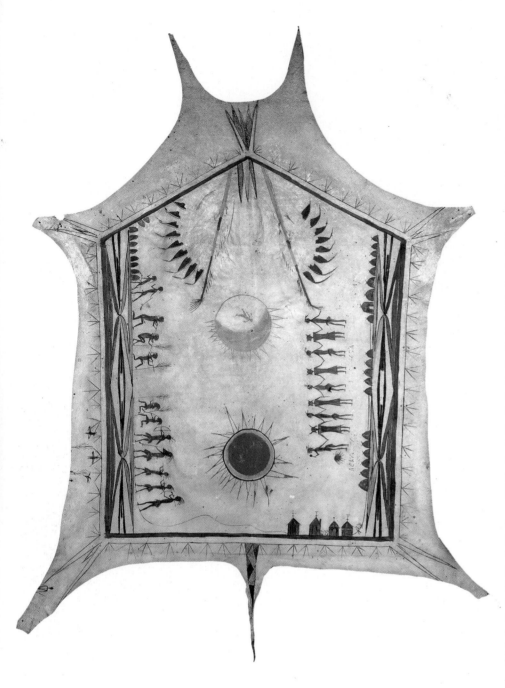

common grave after rejoicings in their honour lasting several days. Each skeleton was carefully cleaned of all the remaining strips of flesh, which were then burnt. Those corpses which still preserved a more or less complete appearance were laid out on litters, while scattered bones were wrapped in beaver pelts. All the dead were then borne into their particular village where a celebration was held in their honour. Then each village carried its dead to the common meeting-ground selected for the Feast.

Here an immense pit was dug. As the funeral processions arrived one after the other, each family bade a final farewell and first cast the bones wrapped in beaver pelts into the pit; upon the pile of these bundles were laid the intact corpses; then, from the platform dominating the pit, further bundles of bones were cast, along with offerings to the dead. Finally, the common grave was covered over with mats, which were woven from bark and then spread with a heap of dirt. This was then reinforced with logs and surrounded by upright stakes. The funeral offerings were shared between the organizer of the ceremony and the participants generally. Some of the offerings cast into the pit were broken beforehand, in order to liberate the souls of the objects, thereby enabling these gifts to accompany the souls of the dead on their long journey (Father Gabriel Sagard-Théodat).

The Hurons believed in the existence of two souls. Until the Feast of the Dead both souls remained close to the body. The first of these souls was freed by the Feast and could be resuscitated through rites connected to the Ceremony of Name-Giving. The second soul, wrapped in its beaver-pelt robe, travelled along the Milky Way to the Village of the Dead, very similar to those of the Living and where existence continued much as it had on earth. Even the souls of dogs proceeded to the same Village of the Dead, although along a different path (Sagard-Théodat p.74).

The Hurons are undoubtedly the best-known and documented North American Indians of the seventeenth century. This is because, from Champlain on, Frenchmen constantly lived among them. The missionaries especially, beginning with Champlain's companion Father Caron, have made a fundamental contribution to our knowledge of Huron culture through their writings. After they were dispersed in 1649, many Hurons found shelter in the village of Lorette, near Quebec, and their descendants still live there.

Cartier had opened up Canada to French penetration through the St Lawrence waterway from the Gaspé peninsula as far as Montreal, but Champlain pushed much farther inland, reaching the Great Lakes and securing solid local allies there for France. The French thus inaugurated the European drive into the American West which culminated in the nineteenth century with the annexation of the last free Indian territories. But the pattern of Western expansion was first set by the seventeenth-century French.

Painted moose skin, Quapaw Indians. Robe made of tanned skin painted with geometrical and realistic designs. Two peace-pipes, the Sun and the Moon occupy the centre of the drawing. On one side, three naked warriors armed with rifles protect a village from the attack of seven enemies, armed with bows and arrows and dressed in loincloths. A painted line runs from these warriors to a group of European-type buildings; two men smoking a pipe are seated between two houses, another armed with an axe is following the line in the direction of three villages, above which nine people are holding hands and following the leader of the line, who is holding a rattle and in front of whom is painted a scalp. [Museé de l'homme, Paris]

Sun. Iouskea the Sun created the lakes and rivers, caused all the animals to emerge from a cave and revealed the secret of fire to mankind. All living creatures came under his care. Ataensic, for her part, presided over death and took charge of souls. These two spirits lived much like human beings, but rejuvenated whenever they grew old. Dreams were of great importance, their interpretation was considered crucial in the life of every individual and played a major spiritual role. Elderly men took responsibility for officiating in religious ceremonies.

One of the most important Huron ceremonies was the Feast of the Dead, and this took place every eight or twelve years. A religious and social ceremony, it symbolized the cohesion of the group. The date of each ceremony was decided by a general council and made known to neighbouring allied peoples. Except for those most recently deceased, the dead on this occasion were exhumed to be permanently reburied in a large

Myths and reality

Even by the second half of the seventeenth century, the idea of discovering a passage by water to China through North America had not quite disappeared. Hopes even lingered that the fabulous realm of El Dorado might be found somewhere in the North American interior. But the main French preoccupation was with navigable waterways. If the right river could be found leading into the West, it might carry explorers straight to the Vermilion Sea, or as far as California, or perhaps even to the magic kingdoms of Quivira and Théguaio, where it was rumoured that gold mines were to be found in abundance. The seventeenth-century French Jesuit missionaries, in their writings to their superiors, often mention reports of the existence of such a river 'wider than a league and more' and so long 'that the savages (...) after many days' navigation never reached its mouth.' (Jesuit *Relations*.)

'How beautiful is the sun, Frenchman, when thou dost come to visit us'

In 1673, Count Frontenac, Governor of Canada, grasped the importance for France to be the first nation to explore such a waterway. He entrusted this dangerous mission to a Canadian-born Frenchman, Louis Joliet, and to the seasoned Jesuit missionary father, Jacques Marquette.

Aware that they were about to head into the unknown with all its attendant dangers, the two men took due precautions. They gathered 'knowledge ... of those savages who had resorted to those parts' and drew up a map according to the indications they received. 'We had them trace the rivers which we should navigate, the names of the peoples and places among whom we should pass, the course of the great river....' (Marquette, *Récit des voyages et découvertes*', Montreal 1974; Jesuit *Relations* vol. II p. 244).

Painted moose skin (*enlarged detail from the illustration on the left-hand page*). *Roman letters identify the first of the three villages as being Akansea, a village inhabited by Quapaw Indians, at which Marquette arrived towards the end of his journey. The houses have a domed roof and each shelters several families. According to Marquette, 'the men went about naked but the women wore poor quality skins'. [Musée de l'Homme, Paris]*

MOOSE
The French word 'orignal'
comes from the Basque 'oreg-
nac', which means a deer. In
the jargon spoken between the
European fishers and the Indians, it referred to the Canadian elk. It was picked up by the
first travellers in the sixteenth
century and now forms part of
the Canadian language.

On 17 May they left the mission of St Ignace, at the entrance to the Lake Des Illinois (Lake Michigan), and paddled across the north of the lake towards the Baie des Puants ('bay of the stinkers', modern Green Bay), on the northernmost shore of which they made their last halt in familiar territory among the Menominee Indians: known to the French as 'the people of the Wild Oats' on account of the enormous quantities of wild rice which grew on their lands, likened by Europeans to wild oats. These Algonquian-speakers farmed maize, squash and beans in little gardens, but mostly depended on harvesting the wild rice and also on hunting and fishing.

The Menominee had been in contact with missionaries for some years. They sought every possible argument to discourage the French from pushing on: the great river, they said, was very dangerous, full of ghastly monsters which devoured men and canoes; a demon was supposed to dwell beneath its waters and his cry could be heard from afar; the peoples who lived along those distant banks 'never forgave strangers who came among them and crushed their heads for no reason'. (Marquette p. 274.) Such an attitude of course recalls that of the people of Stadacona, nearly a century and a half before, attempting to dissuade Cartier from travelling upriver to Hochelaga/Montreal. And again like Cartier, Marquette ignored this sort of pressure.

Marquette's party paddled southwards along the west shore of Green Bay, reached a river mouth, followed the way upstream, portaged around the rapids, and came to the territory of the Mascouten Indians, the so-called 'Nation of Fire'. This was unknown land, beyond the utmost limit ever discovered by the French. Had French missionary influence, however, already indirectly trickled so far? For a cross stood planted in the middle of the village, 'adorned with several white furs, red belts, bows and arrows', which reassured Marquette and convinced him to ask for two guides to continue his journey. Two Miami Indians, allies to the Mascouten, were selected. Marquette describes them as polite, open-minded and sturdy men, excellent warriors and of handsome appearance. These guides took Marquette and Joliet by portage to the banks of the Mescousing (Wisconsin River), which flows into the Mississippi. Marquette and Joliet reached the great river on 17 June.

Just as Cartier before the St Lawrence and Champlain in Huronia, Marquette dwelt on the beauty of the landscape he discovered, the abundance of birdlife and the sleekness of the fish. Further south, along the west bank, they saw some *pisikiou* (bison) for the first time. On 25 June the explorers were deeply stirred to see signs of human life for the first time since leaving the land of the Mascouten: a track leading up from the river into fine prairie country. Boldly, Marquette and Joliet decided to follow this path. After two leagues' walk they saw a village by a stream and two others on the side of a hill: 'We recommended our souls to God and implored his help... then came so close that we could hear the Savages speaking. We thought then that it was time we should discover ourselves, and did so by shouting with all our strength while not proceeding any further. Upon hearing this cry the Savages promptly emerged from their lodges... with no reason to be wary, for we were only two men and had warned them of our coming. They sent four elders to speak to us, of whom two bore finely adorned pipes... decked with various plumage. They walked with measured steps and raised their pipes to the sun as if presenting them to it to smoke thereof.' (Marquette p. 260.) Reassured by this calm and solemn welcome, Marquette spoke first, was answered, found he could follow their Algonquin dialect, and asked who they were: 'They told me they were Illinois, and as a sign of peace they presented me with this pipe to smoke.' (Marquette p. 260.) Once in the village, the visitors were led to a lodge, before which stood a naked man, with hands stretched out towards the sun, who addressed them thus: 'How beautiful is the sun, Frenchman, when thou dost come to visit us; all our village awaits thee, and thou mayest enter in peace in all our lodges.'

The welcome was warm, devoid of fear or hostility. Indeed any surprise or fear were felt by the two Frenchmen even though they had mentally braced themselves to meet new peoples. The Illinois had never seen any French before, but rumour of their existence had reached them and they had most certainly been forewarned of the party's coming by village lookouts. The explorers were invited to pay a call upon the main chief of this nation, who welcomed them standing naked before his lodge, between two elders also entirely unclad. The chief held his pipe turned towards the sun, then proffered it to the newcomers. In his answering speech, Marquette offered alliance with France and asked information concerning those peoples among whom they should expect to pass on their way to the sea. To show he accepted the French alliance, the chief gave to Marquette and Joliet a little slave boy to attend them, and also a pipe whose symbolic importance was immediately realized by the experienced Jesuit missionary. But the chief shied from volunteering any information on the waterway to be followed and attempted to induce the two Frenchmen to stay with him.

These Illinois, of whom Marquette instantly became fond, were to remain staunch allies of the French. In 1673, the Illinois lived along the Mississippi in what is now the state of Missouri. Although Algonquian-speakers and hence culturally akin to the other Algonquin peoples of the Midwest, they also shared many social traits with the Sioux family farther west. They seemed to have been organized into a confederation of five tribes, members of which lived in large villages at some distance from each other. The settlement which Marquette and Joliet had just visited belonged to the Peoria tribe. Livelihood was, again,

THE DISCOVERY OF THE BISON

Bison hunt in winter with snowshoes. *Painting on canvas by George Catlin. [Musée de l'Homme, Paris]*

Having descended unto the latitude of 41 degrees 28 minutes, following the same direction, we found that turkey-cocks had replaced other game, and that the place of other animals had been taken by the pisikiou, *or wild cattle.*

We call them wild cattle because they are markedly similar to our domestic animals; they are no greater in length, but more than one half again as thick and corpulent; our people killed one, and three men had great difficulty in budging it. Their head is very thick, their forehead flat and a foot and half wide between the horns. These horns in every way resemble those of our cattle, but are black and much longer. They have a great hanging dewlap and a rather high hump on their backs. Their whole head, neck and part of their shoulders are covered with a thick mane, like that of a horse. This mane is tousled and a foot long, rendering them hideous and falling over their eyes, preventing them from seeing before them. The rest of the body is covered by a thick curly fleece, somewhat like that of our sheep, but much tougher and thicker. They shed it in the spring, and the skin then becomes as soft as velvet. This is when the Savages make use of it to work into fine robes, which they paint in varied colours. The flesh and fat of the pisikiou *are excellent, and make a choice dish at feasts.*

Moreover, they are most vicious, and there is no year in which they do not kill a Savage. When attacked, they attempt to take a man in their horns, lifting him into the air and then throwing him to the ground. They trample him with their feet and kill him. If one fires at them from afar with a rifle or a bow, one must drop to the ground as soon as the shot has been fired and hide in the grass.

Father Jacques Marquette

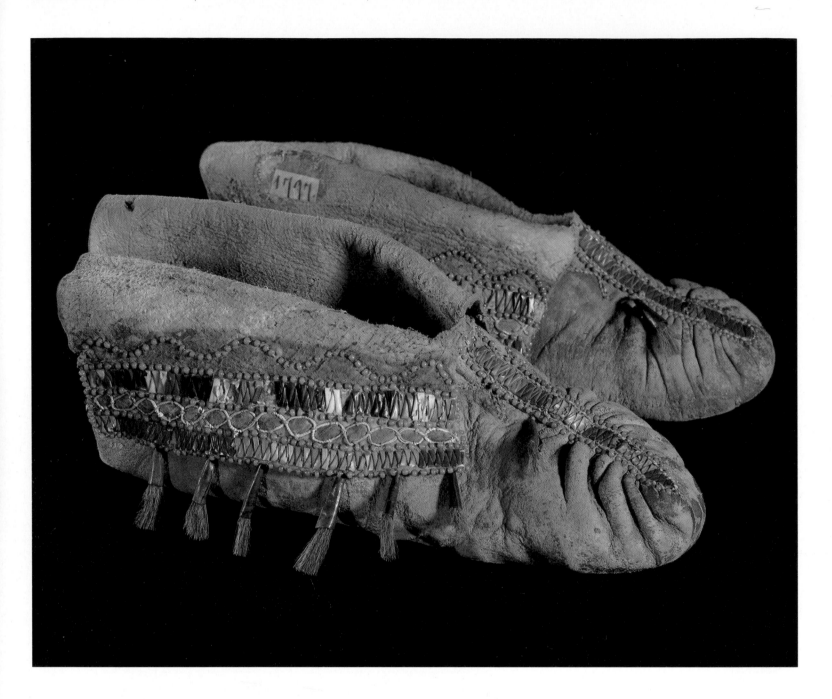

Small pouches, *Huron and Iroquois. At the end of the eighteenth century, the fashion for elaborate tattoos, which all the Indians in the forest regions wore on their body, had disappeared, no doubt due to the fact that individuals wore more clothing. But it seems that many of the symbolic designs used in the tattoos were to be found on certain pouches which, worn next to the body, contained amulets. [Musée de l'Homme, Paris]*

the farming of maize, beans and squash, supplemented by fishing and hunting. Semi-permanent villages along the waterways were set up from March through August. During these months the women sowed and harvested, while the men left long weeks for communal bison hunts. Summer villages were substantial: the Peoria boasted 300 lodges and the Kaskaskia, 351. In September, the summer settlements were abandoned for winter hunting grounds.

Marquette describes the Illinois as bold fighters, handsome, skilled, fearsome to those peoples of the West and South on whom they made war to capture slaves which they then sold to allied tribes. The women, of whom their husbands were 'most jealous', always went very modestly dressed, according to Marquette, although the men 'were not so particular about covering themselves'. Two Illinois cultural traits caught Marquette's attention. While he could not fathom the deep-

lying reason for this, he noted that some males wore female dress from a very young age and kept this all their lives; they never married and their activities were those of women. They went to war but only wielded a club, never a bow and arrows. Likewise, although they participated in the pipe ceremony they did not dance then; but they were members of the tribal councils where nothing could be decided without their advice.

In fact, both among the Illinois and the neighbouring Sioux (so many of whose cultural traits they borrowed), adolescent boys on the threshhold of ritual adulthood were expected to go 'seek a vision' bestowed by the supreme Being, the Master of Life. Upon this vision hinged the social role of the adult-to-be. If the tutelary deity which appeared to the visionary to take him under its protection wore a feminine aspect, then the boy also had to observe a feminine appearance from then on. Nothing proves that such men who

donned the apparel of women were necessarily homosexually inclined. Their social role being out of the ordinary, they were respected, listened to, and many of them also officiated as priests in the pipe ceremony.

Marquette was also struck by the social and ritual importance of the pipe: 'Nothing is more mysterious and worthy among them than the pipe. No more honour is rendered by us to the crowns and sceptres of kings than is rendered by them to the pipe. It seems to be the god of peace and war, the judge of life and death.' (Marquette p. 268.) It was enough to bear such a pipe and show it to pass safely among enemies. The pipe for peace and that for war differed in the colour of the feathers which adorned their shafts: white for peace, red for war. The pipe dance marked important occasions: a declaration of war, sealing a treaty of peace or alliance, honouring a visitor of distinction. In such ceremonies, the red stone bowl of the pipe

Detail of a belt with an arrow motif.
This hand-braided belt reflects traditional Huron and Iroquois techniques. The arrow motif was an integral part of Huron dress. The Hurons settled in N.-D.-de-Lorette, near Quebec at the end of the seventeenth century. [Musée de l'Homme, Paris]

Left-hand page, top
Pair of moccasins, *Huron Indian. Tanned skin decorated with porcupine quills, beads and cones of European metal securing horsehair tufts. The label 1797, visible on one of them, was applied by French Revolutionary authorities then organizing an inventory of property confiscated from French nobles who had fled their country, in order that they could be regrouped, along with treasures from the royal collections, in the new French National collections. [Musée de l'Homme, Paris]*

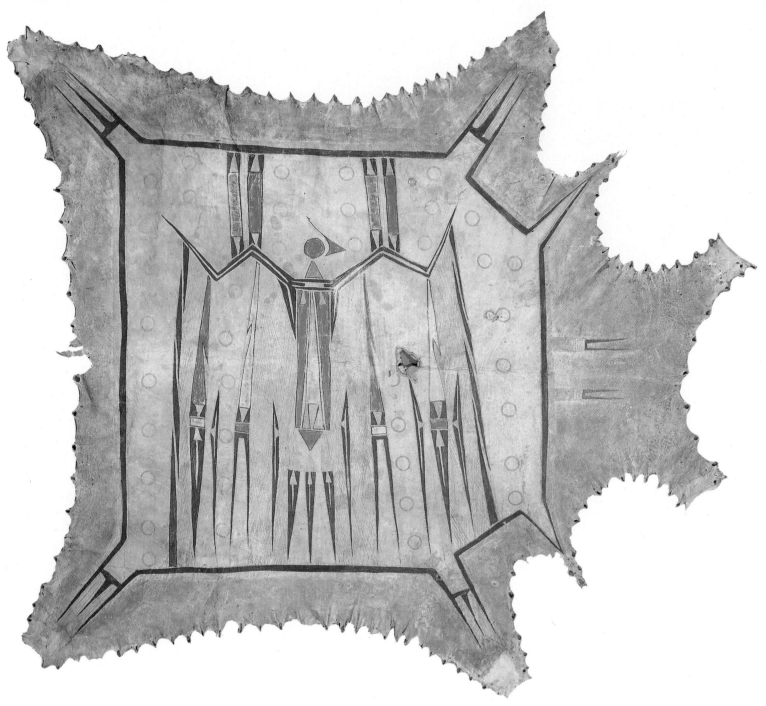

Painted buckskin, *Illinois Indians. This robe represents a stylized Thunder Bird. The ornithological identity of this bird has not been clearly established. According to mythology, thunder and lightning during the redoubtable storms on the plains and in the forests were produced by gigantic birds. The Thunder Birds were greatly feared, and any person struck by lightning who did not succumb might become a great shaman. This painted skin, along with three others, formed part of the collection kept by the King in Paris, in what has now become the Musée d'histoire naturelle. It is possible that it was given to Father Marquette when he was adopted by the Illinois Indians, which would make it the oldest one currently known.* [Musée de l'Homme, Paris]

symbolized the earth, a hearth for the tobacco whose smoke rose to the sky as a link between mankind and the supreme Being. The pipe was one of the most sacred objects in North American Indian cultures, and even served the purpose of a passport for envoys and travellers.

Joliet and Marquette insisted on pursuing their descent of the Mississippi. Reluctantly, the Illinois accepted their departure and presented them with a pipe with which to open their way among all the nations whom they were to meet. The two Frenchmen embarked once more. Soon the climate turned much warmer, mosquitoes harassed the men and the peoples encountered along the banks seemed almost hostile. Still the French party paddled stubbornly on. The landscape changed, prairie gave way to thick forest cover and at length the two Frenchmen distinguished a village among the trees. This time the attitude was one of open hostility. Men armed with bows and

clubs and protected by shields occupied the banks and slid canoes into the river to cut the French party's way both upstream and down. A frightened Marquette waved his pipe as a token of peace until an elder finally saw the object, threw down his bow and arrows, calmed the warriors, and resorted to sign-language, since he did not understand the Algonquin words which Marquette spoke to him. The French were offered food and lodging for the night and they were made to understand that they would find the answer to all their questions the following day, in the village of a neighbouring people called the Akansea.

The travellers spent a somewhat worried night among these people: the Michimeagas were members of the Illinois confederation but sought no alliance with Europeans and were opposed to allowing any of them to penetrate their homeland. On the next day, Marquette and Joliet followed the Mississippi down to the village of the Akansea,

Engraved shell pendant. *Mississippi tradition (700-1600). From the eighth century to the seventeenth century, there existed in the valleys of the Mississippi and Ohio a complex society, associated with which were specific iconographic elements: the cross, eyes, trophy heads, mythical beings and so on, all apparently linked to a religious ritual known as 'the cult of the south'. [Musée de l'Homme, Paris]*

Acadian man. *Engraving from* The Encyclopedia of the Voyages, *by J. Grasset-de-Saint-Sauveur, 1796. [Bibliothèque nationale, Paris. Photo © Bibl.nat.-Photeb]*

Preceding page
Mandan warrior known as 'Old Bear', *oil on canvas by George Catlin: 'He is shown here in the costume of a sorcerer or doctor, his mystery pipe in his hand, and foxtails attached to his heels.' [Musée de l'Homme, Paris]*

where men in two canoes met them with a pipe to smoke and some food, then guided them to their settlement where the people stood assembled. Here, thanks to an interpreter who spoke the Illinois dialect of Algonquin, the two Frenchmen learned that they were only about ten days' distance from the sea. But the Akansea could tell them little of the peoples who dwelt farther south: the Akansea themselves were blockaded in that direction by hostile tribes who barred their own way to the sea and prevented them from making contact with the Europeans (Spaniards) on the coast. Moreover these enemy peoples were warlike, owned guns, and 'continually raided along the river,' which convinced the Frenchmen that it would indeed be too dangerous to proceed: in the light of the kind of reception they had just seen from the Michimeagas, Marquette and Joliet agreed that it was better to turn back north.

Marquette and Joliet realized from the direction of the flow that the Mississippi's outlet could only be the Gulf of Mexico and not, as they had hoped, in the area of California. If they pursued their exploration to the river mouth, they risked being killed either by the Spanish or by the Spaniards' Indian allies, hence all news of their discoveries would be lost. On 17 July 1673, therefore, they left the Akansea to travel back to Peoria. Paddling the Mississippi upstream is hard work, but fortunately the Illinois were able to show them, upriver from the site of the future St Louis, 'another stream which much shortened the way and took us with little hardship to the Lake of Illinois.' (Marquette p. 288.) This river is still called the Illinois.

Better known under the name of Quapaws, the Akansea people spoke a language of the Sioux family. They were descendants of the so-called Mound-Builders, the culture which dominated the lower Mississippi valley between the eighth and the end of the sixteenth centuries and which the Spanish expedition of Hernando de Soto certainly saw in 1541-1542: the chronicler Garcilaso de la Vega speaks of the superb fortified villages to be

encountered in this region. In 1673, Marquette mentions no such fortified villages, but does note the Akansea's nagging fear of their enemies, which 'made them miserable as to their sustenance' because they dared not emerge from their immediate homeland to hunt bison. Fortunately the warm climate allowed them to stave off hunger with three maize crops a year. Marquette describes how they cooked in well-made clay pots and used fired-clay utensils for many other purposes. But their appearance was primitive, 'the men go naked... and the women are dressed in wretched skins... and possess no rare thing with which to adorn themselves.' (Marquette p. 286.) What Marquette saw here were the fallen heirs of a great civilization, mere survivors of the terrible European epidemics which the Spaniards had left in their wake. Marquette's Quapaws had already abandoned whole stretches of their territory and many of their villages. Cut off from access to the sea by the Spanish along the coast of the Gulf of Mexico, harassed from the east by peoples allied to the French or English, the Quapaws by the end of the seventeenth century were a nation racked by war and disease, already doomed by the very fact of the European presence on their continent. The disintegration of their society under such pressures at the close of the seventeenth century clearly foreshadowed the rapidly approaching fate of nearly all the North American peoples.

The exploits of Joliet and Marquette made a tremendous impact on thinking in French Canada. But the French authorities in Quebec were not immediately prepared to take advantage of their explorations, for they had first to fend off attacks by the Iroquois allied to the English on the eastern sea-board, who were trying to disrupt and seize France's monopoly of the North American fur-trade. Only after a decade of intermittent Anglo-French colonial warfare in the north-east did René Robert Cavelier de La Salle secure permission to navigate the Mississippi to its mouth in April 1682 and take possession of the delta region on behalf of King Louis XIV of France whose name he bestowed upon the new land: Louisiana.

By annexing the lands watered by the Mississippi to those of the St Lawrence, France's riverborne North American domain had indeed turned into 'an empire on the scale of a continent.' (Ph. Jacquin.) But the dawning eighteenth century would bring to the Indians of these vast lands the shock which the colonial French described as the *Grand dérangement*, 'the Great Disturbance'. Buffeted between the different imperial European nations struggling for control of North-eastern America, overwhelmed by the steady advance of colonists moving west, and finally dislodged from their own homelands, the Indian nations would be snuffed out. Less than two centuries after Marquette's journey, no more than a handful of Indians survived across the territory of what had once been the empire of New France, lingering ghosts of the first people to inhabit America.

AMERICAN CURIOSITIES

ANNE VITART

Preceding page
Barbarian festival. *Engraving from Grands voyages, by Théodore de Bry. [Service historique de la Marine, Paris. Photo © Lauros-Giraudon]*

Below left
A wooden club. *This Tupinamba club is very probably the one brought back by Thévet and donated by him to the cabinet de curiosités of the King. It therefore belongs to Quoniambec who, according to Thévet, 'is supposed to have eaten thousands of his enemies as well as a goodly number of Portuguese....' [Musée de l'Homme, Paris]*

Below right
The execution of an enemy. *Engraving from Grands voyages, by Théodore de Bry. [Service historique de la Marine, Paris. Photo © Lauros-Giraudon]*

'Our world has just found another one,' wrote France's greatest Renaissance thinker, Montaigne (1533–1592), and this new world was a surprise, set in the middle of the ocean, blocking the way west to the spice islands and China, and inhabited by peoples hitherto unknown to European cosmography: a new world whose very existence disquieted and fascinated both by its wealth and by its many aspects so difficult to understand.

America had to be explained because it had not been expected, hence its existence had to be proved, and this could only be done empirically. To a Europe which had just, quite suddenly, become the 'Old' World, it was therefore necessary to bring evidence: 'New' World plants never heard of before but nonetheless very real, animals, and most especially, human beings and the things they wrought. Christopher Columbus himself brought back to Spain, from his first voyage, tobacco leaves and an ear of maize, artefacts and the men who made them.

From then on, sixteenth-century crossings of the Atlantic Ocean increased, mainly towards Brazil, in search of precious woods. There the traders and corsairs met peoples 'naked, ferocious and cannibal', as the German Hans Staden wrote of his stay as a captive for several years, around 1550, among the Tupinambas (*Nus; Féroces et Anthropophages*, p.17 n.).

The French friar André Thévet, cosmographer to Kings Francis I and Henry II, travelled among these same Tupinambas and brought back as a sample of their remote land a robe of feathers, in which, he said, they paraded their prisoners before killing them: 'They are very beautiful to see both from afar and from up close. On my return from my first voyage I gave one to the late Lord Bertrandy... who, since it was a rare thing, presented it to King Henry II....' In addition, Thévet brought back a wooden club used by these people to smash the heads of those prisoners who were to be eaten: 'Their swords are thick, massive and very heavy. I have still in my present house the sword of Quoniambec, capable of stunning an ox.' (*Histoire d'André Thévet Angoumoisin*, unpublished manuscript, Bibliothèque Nationale, Paris.)

This Quoniambec to whom Thévet refers was a powerful mid-sixteenth-century Tupinamba chief allied to the French. Thévet spent some time with him and witnessed the ritual killing of a prisoner, felled by a powerful blow with this club 'upon the topknot of his head, a smiting so well assured that it cast him down, followed by redoubled blows that clean smashed his head.' (Thévet *op.cit.*)

Such objects, which officially proved the existence of the 'New World', were normally presented to the French Kings, as Thévet reports, and began to accumulate in their various royal residences alongside precious manuscripts from the Levant, jewels and implements from India, ostrich eggs, stuffed crocodiles and lizards, medicinal plants, precious rocks, and medallions from every country in the known world.

Thévet was indeed the first curator, as it were, charged by King Francis I with keeping and displaying this motley collection in a specific place. But just as such objects entered the first *cabinets de curiosités*, or 'curio rooms', the first 'Americans' themselves touched French soil. On 1 October

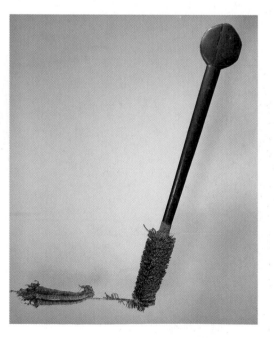

The dance of the Brazilians at the Saint Ouen bridge *in Rouen in 1551. Anonymous. [Bibliothèque municipale, Rouen. Photo © G. Dagli Orti]*

1550, Henry II and his Queen, Catherine de' Medici, were received at the port of Rouen by 'three hundred men naked, sunburnt and bristle-haired', authentic Indians newly brought from Brazil, among whom mingled sailors, themselves 'attired and equipped in the manner of the savages of America'. On a meadow by the banks of the Seine, trees were planted in serried rows, their trunks freshly painted and their branches hung with fruit 'of diverse hues and kinds imitating the natural', among which flew and chirped parrots and other multi-coloured birds. In the middle of this stage-set, men busied about and enacted scenes of savage life: hunting, fishing, dancing, transporting wood, and the like. This idyllic scene was suddenly interrupted by the attack of a group of hostile Indians, and the ensuing hand-to-hand combat was further dramatized with some huts set on fire.

Beneath surface appearances, the purpose of this performance was political and designed to convince Henry II to establish a permanent colony in South America in order to encourage the trade in 'brazilwood', for which Rouen was a major port. In itself, however, this Brazilian masque was to inaugurate in France a long period of curiosity in American peoples, indeed set a fashion.

On 12 April 1613, fashionable Paris rushed to see an important event: Monsieur de Rasilly had returned from Brazil with six Tupinamba Indians 'and several rare things from the land of Brazil'. In the church where the *Te Deum* was sung, such was the press of princesses, court ladies and gentlemen to see the Tupinambas 'dressed in their habit and plumage according to their fashion, each holding in their hands their *maracas* (dancing rattles)', that the Indians had to be taken to the convent of the Capuchin monks, and guarded by armed soldiers.

These six men who had aroused such a fever of curiosity were ambassadors, chosen by their people to render homage to King Louis XIII on behalf of their nation. The then twelve-year-old King welcomed them to his chamber in the company of the Regent, Queen Mother Marie de' Medici. The Indians offered alliance, which the King accepted, and the date of 17 July was reserved for the christening of the envoys. Unfortunately, within days, three of them sickened and died, felled by European germs. They were christened all the same *in extremis*, and period engravings by Duviert depict them under their double names, both Christian and Indian, but always dressed in their own 'savage' attire: François Carypyra for example, armed with bow and club, clad only in a breechclout of feathers, with his body almost entirely covered in geometric tattoos. According to the missionary, Capuchin Father Claude d'Abbeville (*Histoire des missions des pères capucins en l'isle de Maragnan*), this Carypyra had been an illustrious war chief, victorious in twenty-four battles, and his tattoos were no mere complicated adornment, but a reminder of his glory, as if it were a manuscript written 'not on paper, nor on brass, nor on the bark of trees, but on his own flesh'.

The three other Tupinambas to be christened fortunately survived the onslaught of European microbes unscathed and were duly baptized on 17 July in the church of Capuchins, decorated for the occasion with rich silk hangings worked in gold and silver, while the altar was 'covered with gold and riches: and all was silk carpeting on the steps and surrounding flagstones'. The Bishop of Paris officiated in the presence of the King, the Queen Mother and the whole court. Two Capuchin fathers accompanied each of the three Tupinambas.

The Duke of Guise, dressed as an American King. *Engraving by François Chauveau from* Courses de testes et de bagues faites par le Roy... en l'année 1662, *by Charles Perrault, 1670. [Bibliothèque nationale, Paris. Photo © Bibl. nat.-Photeb]*

François Carypyra and Louis Marie, *two of the six Tupinambas brought to France by Monsieur de Razilly. Anonymous engravings from* Histoire de la Mission des Pères Capucins en l'isle de Maragnan..., *by Claude d'Abbeville, 1614. François Carypyra was a famous war chief, as his tattoos show. [Bibliothèque nationale, Paris. Photo © Bibl. nat.-Photeb]*

The young King stood as a godfather, so all three were christened with the name Louis, and with a second name to identify them: Itapoucou became Louis-Marie; Ouaroya, Louis-Henri; and Iapouia, Louis de Saint-Jehan. The same engraver shows them dressed in the long white robes of catechumens, holding a lily in their right hand and the cavalier-style hat then coming into fashion in their left; nothing any longer remains of their previous identity; even their original names have now disappeared; the savage has entered into the orderly classification of the Old World: he has become a 'good' Indian.

We know very little about what happened to these men after this very Parisian affair. Only the contemporary court poet Malherbe, in his correspondence from Paris with the provincial magistrate Peiresc in Carpentras, makes several references to their marriages to French girls. In a letter dated 23 June (three weeks before the christening ceremony) he writes: 'There are wives already made for them. I believe that they are only waiting for the christening before holding the weddings and sealing the alliance between France and the island of Maragnan.' In another letter, dated 29 June, he adds: 'The Capuchins, to show all courtesy to these poor people, have resolved to persuade some devout girls to wed them, I believe they have already started to....' While Malherbe

seems to betray some reservations concerning this ploy of marrying off the strangers to French girls, he was as taken as everyone else at court with the typical dance of the Tupinambas, then all the rage, and did not hesitate to send his friend Peiresc a copy of the music of a *sarabande* inspired by these exotic tunes: 'I am sending Marc-Antoine a *sarabande* which Gauthier has composed from the dance of the Tupinambas; when he has learnt it he will give you the pleasure of it: it is held to be one of the most excellent pieces that one may hear.'

This fashion for the '*sarabande*' represented the first true artistic flowering in France of a taste for things American which had by now existed among curious Europeans – and indeed fascinated them – for more than 150 years. But the 'American' craze in France reached its pitch in the second half of the seventeenth century, under Louis XIV. Not that this monarch was particularly interested in France's empire in America as such: by the end of his long reign, the Sun King had successively lost Acadia, Hudson Bay and Newfoundland to the English by the Peace of Utrecht in 1713. But, while real-life Indians gradually disappeared from France's political scene, an allegorical vision of America began increasingly to leave its mark on the art of the age, in its architectural ornament, in its interior decoration, in the masques which enlivened the festivities celebrating the birth of the Dauphin, or in Rameau's operas: as if, it has been said, this American allegorical image was powerfully fraught with the symbolism of 'a (pre-revolutionary) ideology as yet not even aware of its own subconscious existence'. In the same period, in a *cabinet de curiosités* built in the King's gardens, were collected 'all things rare in nature' and especially 'the habits, weapons and tools of the newly discovered peoples' brought back by French travellers on royal commission since the days of Francis I; these included a Tupinamba war-hammer and the Tupinamba head-shattering mace taken by Thévet, as well as several pairs of moccasins, bags and belts found by Cartier in New France: 'The rafters were hung with all sorts of weapons, attires and apparels of savages...as well as four large aprons or cloaks of skin painted after the fashion of the Illinois', a plain reference to the painted buffalo robes given to the Jesuit Jacques Marquette by the Illinois and tangible proof of French penetration of the Mississippi valley.

Towards the middle of the eighteenth century, however, under the influence of the naturalist Buffon, the peoples of the New World and their artefacts began losing their character of mere 'curiosities' and started to be classified as objects of science. The *cabinets de curiosités* gradually changed into *cabinets d'histoire naturelle* – natural history rooms.

In 1783, the Marquis de Sérent, tutor to the children of the Comte d'Artois, younger brother to King Louis XVI, decided to open a room of natural history in which to house objects of all sorts, but especially artefacts of people from far-off and little-known lands. He addressed himself to a former royal commissioner to France's American colonies, Monsieur de Fayolle, who had gathered an important collection from his various journeys. Fayolle complied and sold his collection, which was moved to the Marquis de Sérent's town house, and included shells, minerals, insects, stuffed rare animals, petrified woods, but also 'the complete dress of a savage of Canada' reconstituted on a painter's dummy as an evocation of the world of the American Indian. On the eve of the age of the French Revolution, Indians had certainly stopped being perceived as awesome ambassadors from exotic nations for quite some time, nor were they regarded any more as mere 'curiosities'; however, they had yet to be intellectually integrated into a comprehensible social order, hence their status in late-eighteenth-century French eyes was coldly placed more in the order of 'nature', along the lines of fossils and other elements of natural history.

Ways of thought were evolving quickly and the War of Independence, of which La Fayette had made himself a champion in France, further transformed European perceptions of the New World. 'America' was no longer seen as a land of Indians, but as the country of the colonists who had occupied its soil for two hundred years. 'America' had become White, and the Native

SAUVAGES AMENEZ EN FRANCE POUR ESTRE INSTRUITS DANS LA RELIGION CATHOLIQUE, QUI FURENT BAPTISEZ A PARIS EN L'EGLISE DE S. PAUL LE XVII JUILLET 1613.

Americans faded away before the glare of this new state whose very building-up required the seizure of their territories and 'the spatial, political and cultural banishment of the Indian peoples' (J. Rostovski and N. Delanoë, *Les Indiens dans l'histoire américaine*, Paris 1991).

But, on 21 April 1845, it seemed as though history were suddenly reversed: King Louis-Philippe welcomed to the Tuileries Palace a delegation of twelve Iowa Indians (including their own interpreter) accompanied by the American painter George Catlin, who had spent ten years in the Great Plains recording the traits and habits of the native peoples, and had dedicated his life-work not only to creating a museum to the American Indians but also to perpetuating their memory and legend; indeed he had brought with him to Paris an 'Indian Gallery' of his paintings. Just as had happened with the Brazilian Tupinambas in the early seventeenth

Brazilians brought to France to be baptized. *Engraving by Joachim Duviert, seventeenth century. These people came from the region of São Luís de Maranhão, on the northern coast of Brazil, where François de Razilly and Daniel de La Ravardière founded a colony in 1612 [Bibliothèque nationale, Paris. Photo © Bibl. nat.-Photeb]*

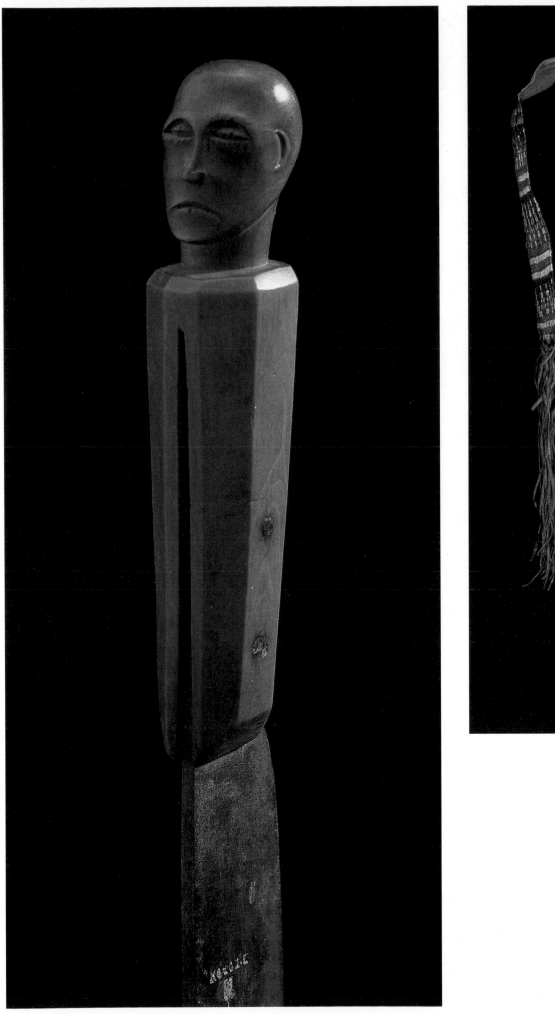

A knife with a carved wooden handle. *The sheath is made from skin decorated with porcupine quills. From the forest regions in the East. This is a particularly accomplished example of the art of wood carving among the Hurons and Iroquois. This knife was part of the clothing of the 'Canadian savage' in the Hôtel de Sérent. Like the small vermillion pouch, it hung from the belt of the model. [Musée de l'Homme, Paris]*

Left-hand page
Feather head-dress, Mundurucus Indians. *In the middle of the nineteenth century, the Mundurucus Indians were still wearing head-dresses similar to those of the Tupinambas of Razilly. [Musée de l'Homme, Paris]*

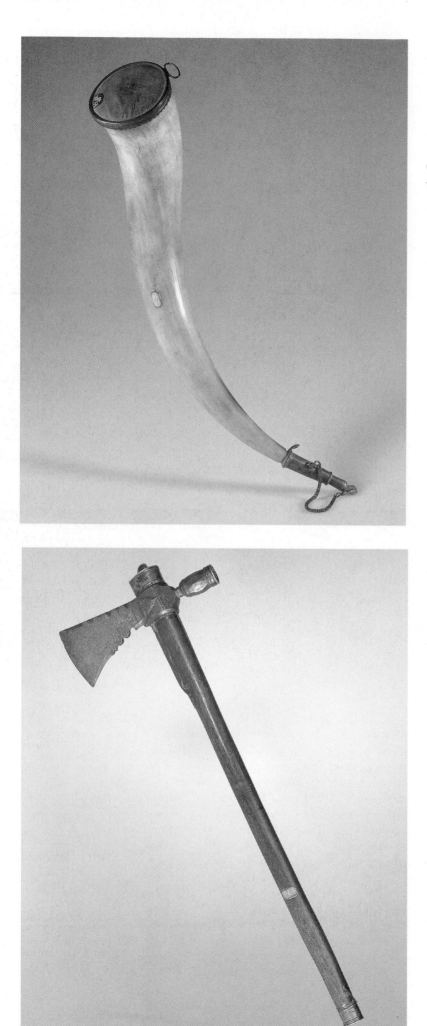

Above, left
A powder horn from the forest regions in the East. *The use of powder horns was introduced by the Europeans. This one was in the Hôtel de Sérent. [Musée de l'Homme, Paris]*

Above, right
A sketch of the model in the Hôtel de Sérent. *Line drawing from* Versailles illustrée, *1897-1898.* [Bibliothèque de Versailles]

century, the arrival of the Iowas caused a Parisian sensation. The famous woman novelist George Sand wrote a long article: 'Relation d'un voyage chez les sauvages de Paris' published in *Le Diable* in 1846. The poet Baudelaire also referred to them and the painter Delacroix drew pictures. An American Indian fashion stirred back to life, fed not only by Catlin's paintings but also by Chateaubriand's and James Fenimore Cooper's novels. King Louis-Philippe and his Queen were thrilled by these men 'wearing their magnificent costumes of buffalo robes embroidered with porcupine quills and fringed with scalps taken from their enemies'. (Catlin, *Catalogue* to the 'Indian Gallery'.) After presentations and a lengthy talk, the King gave a gold medallion to each chief and a silver one to each warrior. By way of thanks, the war chief, Walking Rain, in the middle of his harangue, offered the King a splendid pipe whose stem, nearly a metre long, was decorated with

porcupine quills. The Indians were led to the ballroom, where they performed the Eagle Dance and the War Dance, in the course of which one warrior, Little Wolf, moved towards the spectators and 'after several violent cries by which he told how he had killed and scalped an enemy of the tribe of the Pawnees, placed his tomahawk between the hands of the King, saying: "Since I have come to this country, I have become convinced that peace is better than war; I bury this tomahawk between your hands...I shall fight no more...." ' (Catlin, *op.cit.*)

These Iowa Indians, come to France with Catlin, had just escaped from the 'natural' order in which the eighteenth century had confined and classified them. Their decades-long struggle against the United States government to preserve their lands had virtually forced Europeans, willy-nilly, to recognize them as participants in a social order. At least for the duration of their embassy to the King

of France, they were not only 'curiosities' but again the envoys and representatives of the American Indian peoples. But the Lakota (Sioux) Indians who came to France only thirty years later with Buffalo Bill, for the Paris Universal Exhibition of 1878, had relapsed into the status of 'curiosities', to be exhibited from one place to another.

So what now remains of this European curiosity, which may have peaked or waned but has remained with us for the last five hundred years? The artefacts preserved in the *cabinets* were catalogued and classified during the French Revolution and have survived various historical upheavals. They are to be found in French museums as motionless witnesses to a bygone age. Yet on occasion we bring them to life and allow them to tell their story. Thus Paris' Musée de l'Homme, heir to the royal *cabinets*, preserves to this day the mantle of feathers and the war-mace of Quoniambec, brought back by the monk Thévet, as

Indians in Europe, *brought across with Buffalo Bill's circus during the* Exposition Universelle *of 1889. [Photo from the Roland Bonaparte collection, Musée de l'Homme, Paris]*

Left hand page, below
A tomahawk-pipe, Canada. *This was a combination of the peace pipe and the famous war axe, entirely European in creation and manufacture. These tomahawk-pipes quickly became valued trading objects for almost all the Indian tribes in North America. The one shown here was held by the Sérent model. On a flat surface below the bowl can be read the date, 1763, and the interlaced initials RL. The blade of the axe is decorated on one side with an engraved, shining sun and on the other with a quarter moon and a fleur de lys. [Musée de l'Homme, Paris]*

King Louis-Philippe watching the dance of the Iowa Indians. *Oil on canvas by Girardet. In the picture can be seen the Indian child portrayed by Catlin (right-hand page).* [Château de Versailles. Photo © RMN]

Right-hand page
Portrait of an Iowan child. *Painting by George Catlin.* [Musée de l'Homme]

well as Brazilian feather head-dresses and the Illinois buffalo robes which once hung from the rafters of King Louis XIV's rooms. The museum, which also inherited the *cabinet* of the Marquis de Sérent, proved that it was possible to recreate its original aspect, restoring new life to artefacts, arranged so as to represent the eighteenth-century European way of looking at them.

Men taken to France, and who lived and sometimes died there while others returned home, have also left traces of their passage among us. The images of the Tupinamba Indians depicted as 'savages' and then as royal godsons remain with us; Catlin left with King Louis-Philippe his portraits 'of these brave people whose proud and free character and noble expression he has superbly rendered....' (Baudelaire, comments on the *Salon* or painting exhibition of 1846); even the haughty, determined features of one of the Sioux who came with Buffalo Bill's circus to Paris in 1878 were immortalized in marble by a sculptor of the time.

The rage for things American is with us still, but it has been diversified because we are now confronted with so many different Americas. One of them, White America, remains potent in our imaginations as a model we envy and reproduce. Although it was born as a mere colony, La Fayette contributed a lot to forge its image – which became a symbol – of a land of liberty. But Indian America returns to haunt us. After three centuries of resistance, Indian voices, which we had thought forever stilled, are being raised again loudly and clearly. These peoples who have fascinated us for five hundred years are returning with pride to the world stage. Once again, our Old World finds itself under a charm. As we see American Indians defend their rights by dealing skilfully with the highest US and international courts and making themselves so eloquently heard, many of us still tend to look upon them again as 'Noble Savages': that is, people who lived in harmony with nature and are re-emerging as champions for the safeguarding of our world.

THE COEXISTENCE

THE CONVERSION OF THE INDIANS, from Santo Domingo to Mexico

CHRISTIAN DUVERGER

MERIDIAN LINE
This limit was moved to 370 leagues beyond the Cape Verde islands by the Hispano-Portuguese agreement of Tordesillas, signed in June 1494. This new dividing line, further to the west, permitted the Portuguese to settle in Brazil.

However strange it may seem today, the christianization of the American Indians was originally a judicial requirement. To understand the context of the discovery of America at the end of the fifteenth century we must go back to the time of Pope Innocent III (1198–1216). He imposed on the sovereigns of Christian Europe the idea of a *potestas*, a spiritual 'power' superior to the temporal power of princes. According to this doctrine, the Pope could dispose of the lands of 'pagans, idolators and infidels' in order to grant them to a Christian prince whose responsibility it would then be to ensure the evangelization of the newly subjugated peoples.

These dispositions, which were originally devised to stimulate the spirit of the crusade, were still in force in the fifteenth century, and the Portuguese were not slow to have all their African discoveries systematically confirmed by papal bulls. In a strong position because of their advance

beyond the Gulf of Guinea, they obtained from Sixtus IV, for example, the bull *Aeterna Regis* (1481), through which Portugal was granted all the territories south of the Canaries. It is therefore scarcely surprising that the status of the new lands discovered by Christopher Columbus in 1492 had been subjected to scrutiny by papal authority.

But in 1492, a Spaniard, Rodrigo Borja (italianized to Borgia), had just been elected Pope under the name of Alexander VI. And this Pope, born in Játiva, intended to give America to Spain. Through the famous bull *Inter caetera* of 1493 he decided to concede to the Catholic Sovereigns, Isabella and Ferdinand, all the lands situated to the west of a meridian line passing one hundred leagues to the west of the Azores. But the judicial requirement applying to the attribution of territories by the Pope remained: the Spanish monarchy had to commit itself to evangelizing the new lands and to sending 'men of good morals,

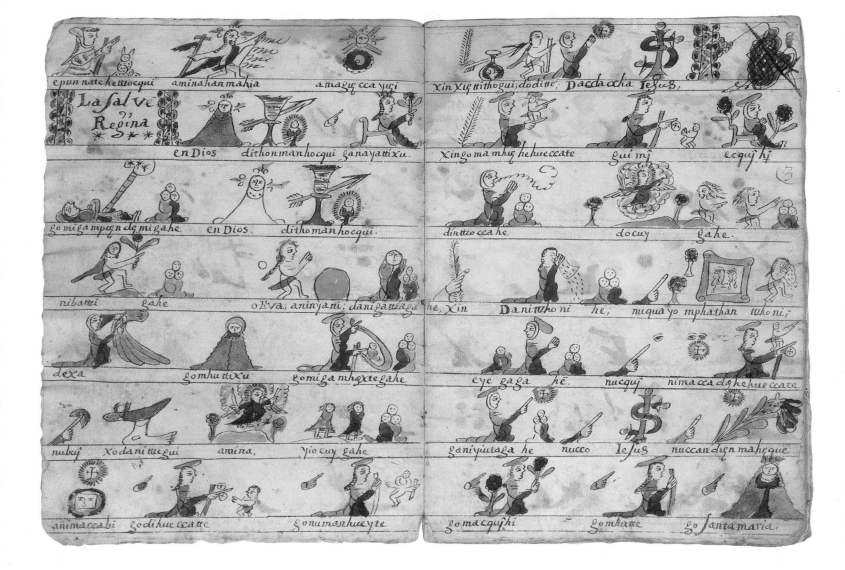

honest and God-fearing, learned, wise and experienced, in order to instruct the inhabitants in the Catholic faith'. This requirement was hardly likely to displease Ferdinand and Isabella, who had just distinguished themselves in the defence of Christianity by obtaining the surrender of Granada, the last Moorish kingdom in the Iberian peninsula, and so completing the *reconquista*.

So everything was done to ensure that, starting with Columbus' second voyage, the work of evangelization could begin in America. In accordance with the powers which the *patronato* had conferred on him, King Ferdinand designated one of his intimates, Brother Bernardo Boyl, as vicar apostolic to the Indies. He had this choice ratified on 25 June 1493 by the bull *Pius fidelium* of Pope Alexander VI, which conferred on this priest full powers in terms of administration of the Church and evangelization of the Indians. Then a dozen priests were designated to accompany

Columbus' expedition to Hispaniola. On 25 September 1493, at Cadiz, as part of a large flotilla, this first mission took to sea in order to try to convert the Indians.

The scenario in the Antilles: the failure of the conversion and the extermination of the Indians

It is now known that the missionary work in the Antilles during the years of discovery was a total failure. The monks showed themselves completely incapable of protecting and converting the inhabitants of the islands.

The figures are overwhelming. The general estimate is that, in 1521, when Cortés became master of Mexico, 80 per cent of the indigenous population of the island of Hispaniola had been killed. The chronicler Gerónimo de Mendieta

A pictographic catechism. *Mexican manuscript. About 1540, the Franciscans in Mexico had the idea of composing catechisms and collections of prayers by using a system of pictographs, inspired by pre-Columbian tradition. The aim was not only to make the learning of Christian doctrine easier for the Indians, but also to capture the sacredness attached to the language of the ancient glyphs. The two pages shown here transcribe the Salve Regina in Otomi language (Central Mexico). [Bibliothèque nationale, Paris. Photo © Bibl. nat.- Arch. Photeb]*

MISSIONARIES
It seems that no churchmen accompanied Columbus on his first voyage.

The House of the Rope, Santo Domingo. *This house, which dates from 1503, is said to be the first European stone house erected in the New World. It was built by Francisco Garay, a member of Columbus' first expedition and the future Governor of Jamaica. The rope of the Franciscans, which decorates the façade, shows the influence of this order on the islands from the beginning of the sixteenth century. [Photo J. Duverger]*

indicates an even higher figure. In 1516, according to him, 90 per cent of the inhabitants of the island were already dead. (*História ecclesiástica indiana*, bk. 1, ch. 17.) In the space of thirty years almost a million and a half men perished, exterminated not just by force of arms, poor treatment, slavery and diseases from Europe, but also by sheer demoralization linked to the loss of their land and culture. By the mid-sixteenth century the native population of the Greater Antilles had almost completely disappeared.

Columbus and his master plan are certainly in the forefront of those responsible. No matter that the Admiral of the Ocean Sea was granted the honour of canonization proceedings with a view to making him a saint, nor that secular hagiography praised his Christian faith and the depth of his religious convictions, nor even that he ostentatiously wore the cowl of a Franciscan monk. Despite all this, the avowed aim of his expeditions was glory, wealth and power. As for the ambition of most of his companions, it was limited, pure and simple, to getting rich. Even though Columbus demonstrated his respect for the formalities and took possession of the new lands in the name of God and the King, in practical terms his concern for evangelization was less than convincing.

On the other hand, he excelled at converting the fruits of discovery into personal gain for himself and his family. He needed no persuasion to accede to the greed of his expeditionary corps, granting the Spaniards *repartimientos* of Indians who were promptly transformed into slaves to extract the gold from Cibao.

Neither Columbus, nor his brother Bartolomeo, who was second in command in Santo Domingo while he explored Cuba, was ever seen to intervene to check the Spanish demands on the natives. Moreover, Columbus was openly pro-slavery. In 1494, for example, he sent five hundred Taíno slaves as a present to his partners. The President of the Council of the Indies accepted the gift; but the Archbishop of Seville immediately sent the twenty Indians intended for him back to their island, accompanied by two Franciscans to ensure their 'return to freedom'. It is not beyond the bounds of possibility that Columbus' pro-slavery leanings actually hindered the project of evangelizing the Indians.

In Castile, custom permitted non-Christian prisoners of war to be made slaves. In Columbus' view, therefore, it was acceptable to maintain the pagan status of the Indians so that he could retain the possibility of legally making them slaves.

The first Vicar Apostolic

It is easy to see that relations between Columbus and the monks might have been rather strained. This conflict of authority had in fact started at the outset of preparations for the second voyage. Columbus wanted to give the religious supervision of his expedition to Father Marchena, who had done a lot of work towards the finalization of his projects while he was superior of the Franciscan convent of La Rábida.

The King decided otherwise, and designated Brother Bernardo Boyl. What a strange person this well-read firebrand was! He came from a powerful Catalan family. As a Benedictine monk, he had made his vows at the monastery of Montserrat. But he was like a hermit at court, living in the orbit of King Ferdinand. He successfully carried out special missions: he quelled a rebellion in Sardinia, and was sent as personal ambassador of the King to Charles VIII of France to negotiate the restoration of Cerdaña and Roussillon to Spain. In 1492, while he was staying in France, he decided to change orders and joined the Franciscans: he took the cowl of the Minims of St Francis of Paola. When Ferdinand chose him to accompany Columbus to the Indies, it was obviously with the aim of keeping a close watch on the Admiral. Columbus, who was well aware of this, did everything he could to discourage him. He opposed the idea that the Vicar Apostolic should travel with him in the flagship, and relegated him to one of the sixteen accompanying ships. While he could not stop him officiating at the first mass celebrated in America, on the day of Epiphany in 1494 at La Isabela, he cast him aside from the presidency of the *junta de gobierno*. Instead, he entrusted the task to his son Diego, who could speak only a little Castilian. The Admiral systematically opposed Boyl's decisions, claimed absolute control and, to put an end to disputes about his authority, ordered the monk's supplies to be cut off.

The ecclesiastical group was too disparate to constitute an effective counter to the imposing administrative and military power of Columbus and his twelve hundred men when they disembarked at La Isabela to colonize the island of Hispaniola. As if to conceal this inglorious episode, history does not record the names of these first twelve missionaries. There were supposed to be six Franciscans, two Mercedarians, a Hieronymite, and three others whose identity scholars still dispute.

Of these pioneers, only three stand out. The two Frenchmen among them, lay brothers of the Minorite order, were called Jean Tisin (or Cousin) and Jean le Rouquin (Juan de La Duela, called El Bermejo, 'the red-headed one'). Both were natives of Picardy, which belonged at the time to the duchy of Burgundy, and they were the spearheads of the Franciscan mission which was officially founded in Santo Domingo in 1500. The third was a Catalan, Ramón Pané, another lay brother who belonged to the Hieronymites and who is America's first anthropologist.

But at La Isabela in 1494 these monks lived as recluses while the Spaniards were launching numerous violent actions in their quest for Cibao. Boyl and his acolytes – with the notorious exception of Ramón Pané – decided to return to Spain to denounce Columbus' actions. In September 1494 they requisitioned one of the ships which had just brought to La Isabela Bartolomeo Columbus, whose brother the Admiral, hastened to nominate him *adelantado*. Did this action by Boyl constitute capitulation or a strategic withdrawal? In any case the departure of the Vicar Apostolic – who certainly lacked determination – removed the top men from the nascent American Church. It would be 1511 before three sees were created: Santo Domingo, Concepción de la Vega and Puerto Rico. But the first Bishop of Santo Domingo, the Franciscan García de Padilla, died in Spain before occupying his see; and his successor, an Italian secular priest, was scarcely of the calibre required by the situation. As for Boyl, his disappointment was eased by his nomination as Abbot of Saint Michel de Cuxa in Roussillon. Against that, the impetuous Genoese was confirmed in his office as Governor of the Indies, his brother Bartolomeo as *adelantado*; in addition, his son Diego arrived in Santo Domingo in 1508 with the title of viceroy! Obviously protection of the Indians was not yet the order of the day.

Of course, destruction of the indigenous population was not part of the plans of the Spanish Crown which continued, all through the sixteenth century, to proclaim the principle of the freedom of the Indians and the obligation to pay them for their work, and reiterated over and over again the prohibition of slavery and serfdom. But in the field, first of all in the Islands, then in Mexico and Peru, these principles were blithely held up to ridicule by the *encomenderos*. As a consequence, from the outset, the mendicant orders who were to operate in America associated their work of evangelization with safeguarding and protecting the Indians.

On the island of Hispaniola, the situation was hopeless. However, the monks did not give up. As soon as he arrived, Ramón Pané began to learn the native languages (Taíno and Macorix) in order to be able to preach in the vernacular and to

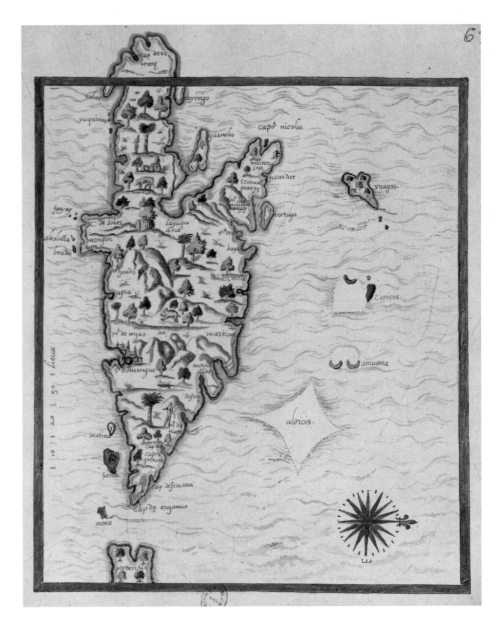

The ruins of the Franciscan monastery of La Vega, *Cibao, Dominican Republic. Founded in 1502 by the Minor Brothers at the same time as the monastery of Santo Domingo, this monastery was situated in the richest and most populous zone of the island of Hispaniola. Unfortunately, the extermination of the Indians quickly rendered the Franciscan mission obsolete. [Photo © G. Dagli Orti]*

understand the myths and local beliefs. With his *Relación acerca de las antigüedades de los índios*, he started the ethnological research which would be systematically carried out by the monks. He was able to arrange the first christening in the history of the American Church, that of the Indian Juan Mateo of Macorix Province on 21 September 1496.

In 1502 the Franciscans had already established two monasteries, Santo Domingo and La Vega: they applied themselves to educating young people there, notably the sons of the *caciques*. In 1505 the Seraphic order had about twenty-five monks on the island; they founded the Province of the Western Indies, which denoted their intention to have a permanent mission there. The Dominicans arrived at Santo Domingo in 1510, with Pedro de Córdoba at their head. From the following year, the missionaries distinguished themselves through the steps they took in support of the Indians – already in the process of extermination – and Antonio de Montesinos was to pronounce in front of Diego Columbus and the *encomenderos* his famous sermon on the fourth Sunday in Advent, 21 December 1511 – 'I am the voice crying in the wilderness...' – in which he denounced the behaviour of the Spaniards. It was in 1514 that Bartolomé de Las Casas was 'converted'. He had participated in the Indian wars launched by the governor, Ovando, and had lived the life of a greedy colonist, exploiting the Cibao gold and then an *encomienda* in Cuba. He joined the Dominicans and, in order to expiate his sins as a colonist, ceaselessly denounced the exploitation of the Indians.

Nevertheless, the actions of the religious orders were to be ineffective in the Greater West Indies for two reasons. Firstly, they came too late: throughout the first ten years, the collision of civilizations had already happened and the cultural catastrophe was complete. The Indians were already in the process of being exterminated and their traditional societies totally destabilized when Governor Nicolás de Ovando, who completed the barbarous process of destruction, arrived in Santo Domingo in 1502. As a consequence of all this, the local population completely rejected conversion to Christianity because it was associated with the religion of the despised conquerors. How could a message of love and peace be preached when the Christians already present in the islands were providing examples of the worst forms of cruelty and outright greed?

The only logical choice for the indigenous population was refusal. They could copy the *cacique* Enriquillo, who, having been brought up in the Christian faith by the Franciscans of Santo Domingo, eventually revolted in 1519 and led a guerrilla war in the Sierra de Pedernales which lasted for fourteen years.

The Mexican scenario: from the eradication of idolatry to respect for the Indian way of life

In 1506, when Columbus died in Valladolid in Spain, Hernán Cortés had already been two years in Santo Domingo. He lived in a house which was superb yet austere, at the junction of the first two roads built in the New World, a few hundred yards from the residence of Governor Ovando. Invested with rather vague administrative responsibilities, he nevertheless knew everything that was happening in the little capital of the West Indies. He followed, without direct involvement, the progress of the wars of pacification on the island and observed as a privileged witness the premature downfall of the system instigated by the Spaniards.

When Diego Columbus took up his post as viceroy, his thoughts turned to Cuba, which was under his jurisdiction and was still an unexplored territory. In 1511, Diego Velásquez conquered the island in a bloody replica of the Haitian scenario. Cortés, who this time was a member of the expedition, received a *repartimiento* of slaves and a land concession and was chosen as secretary to Velásquez, who was appointed Governor of Cuba. For eight years, as a planter and a civil servant, Cortés lived at the heart of the colonial system. He watched a repetition of the failure in Santo Domingo: the Indian people who refused to surrender were decimated within a few years. When Cortés took command of the Mexican expedition he had learned some lessons from the West Indian disaster. He knew his conquest would endure only if it did not turn into a war of extermination of the Indians. In order to make his project succeed, the *conquistador* had a key idea: miscegenation.

After stopping off on the Caribbean coast of Yucatán and the island of Cozumel, Cortés entered the Gulf of Mexico. However, when he wanted to disembark, he was forced to do battle with the Mayans of Tabasco. After a brief engagement in which the heavily armoured horses of the Spaniards

Left-hand page
A painting made from feathers, *representing St Luke. In 1529 the Franciscan Pedro de Gante created a school in Mexico for young people specializing in the plastic arts. Religious themes were treated in the spirit and technique of pre-Hispanic art, as shown in this work which continues the Aztec tradition of featherwork into the sixteenth century. [Musée de l'Homme, Paris]*

133

Codex Fejevary Mayer. Pre-Columbian manuscript from Central Mexico, on deer skin which has been stuccoed and painted. Here the nine 'lords of the night' are represented; they govern the ritual calendar of 260 days, whose signs are organized according to the four directions of the universe. [Liverpool Museum. Photo © The Board of Trustees of the National Museums and Galleries on Merseyside]

carried the day, the Mayans made an alliance with Cortés. The two sides exchanged gifts. Among those offered by the Mayans were twenty women, including the famous Malinche (Malintzin), a princess of Nahuatl descent who was to become, a few months later, the *conquistador's* companion and his personal interpreter. Without hesitating, Cortés accepted the women. He had them baptized forthwith and gave them to his lieutenants, as official concubines. All the way to Mexico, the local chiefs acted in the same way: they offered women to Cortés. It is known, for example, that the sovereigns of Tlaxcala gave three hundred. Each time the scenario was the same: after a perfunctory baptism the chief of the expedition handed the women over as companions to his men.

This was a most opportune coincidence between an ancient pre-Hispanic tradition and one of the most secret plans of Cortés, who dreamed of the union of the two races. The conqueror himself

showed an example by living first with Malinche and then with one of the daughters of the Aztec emperor Moctezuma, whilst at the same time forbidding his legitimate Spanish wife, Catalina Juárez, to come and join him in Mexico. She defied the order and was 'mysteriously' strangled in her bed, three months after arriving.

In his desire for the mingling of the two races, Cortés was logical to the very end. Even after they had been conquered, former dignitaries were not excluded from affairs. In Coyoacan, where the new master of Mexico had installed his court, the former *tlatoques* were entertained daily at his table; they kept their titles and privileges. Cortés tried at all costs to rely on the native élite, because he had no desire to create a second Spain in Mexico at the expense of the Indians. Rather, he wanted to encourage the emergence of a New World where the best of the two cultures could unite, through the merging of a Castile, stripped of its medieval

backwardness and an Aztec world freed from its idolatry. Was this a pipe dream?

For their part the mendicant orders, who had been given very broad authority from Rome to set up a new American Church, had also learned lessons from the Caribbean failure. Even if the term 'millennarianism' often applied to the ideology of the Franciscans in the New World is arguable, it has to be admitted that at the heart of the order there existed an idealized vision of the mission which opened up to the monks with the discovery of the West Indies. The project of the Minor Brothers, who had broken free from the moral corruption rife in the Old World, was to use the Indian as an example of the New Man. Since he was free of all European contamination, the Kingdom of God on earth could be embodied in him. But in order to create this Church which would ultimately conform to the evangelical ideal, they had to be able to count on *living* Indians. All

the skills of the Franciscans of Mexico would therefore be deployed to convert local people while keeping them Indian. It was this apparent paradox which determined the missionary strategies and the apostolic techniques employed in Mexico and then South America throughout the sixteenth century.

Recourse to indigenous languages

In 1519 the revolt of Enriquillo, *cacique* of San Juan de la Maguana on the island of Hispaniola, forced the Franciscans into a profound examination of their conscience. The predominant idea at the time the missions were set up in Santo Domingo was that conversion came through education. So the first Franciscans were to be seen teaching the sons of the indigenous nobility to read and write – but in Castilian! The anti-Spanish reaction of the persecuted Indians made them rapidly reject both

The Franciscan Monastery of Cuernavaca, *Mexico. Constructed between 1533 and 1538, the church of the former monastery of Quauhnahuac is used as a cathedral today. It is a beautiful example of Renaissance architecture. [Photo © Fiore-Explorer]*

example, how were they to transcribe with the letters of the Latin alphabet the glottal occlusive and the eight vowels of Otomi, or the aspirated consonants of Tarasco? How were they to put on paper the tonal languages of the Oaxaca, where differences in intonation corresponded to differences in meaning? Nevertheless, the evangelizers of Mexico took up the challenge.

Having resolved the problem of alphabetical transcription, they started to write dictionaries and grammars to help new arrivals to learn. They also wrote a large number of religious works: catechisms (*doctrinas*), anthologies of sermons, confession manuals, translations of the Epistles and the Gospels, psalms and prayers, lives of the saints, and so on. These writings date, for the most part, from the years 1540–1550. They circulated among monasteries not just in manuscript form but also as printed books, for in 1537 the Franciscans had had a printing press brought from Seville to enable the publication of works for use in the apostolate. It is significant that the first book printed on the American continent was edited by a Franciscan in an Amerindian language. It was a catechism in Nahuatl, the anonymous *Breve y más compendiosa doctrina cristiana en lengua méxicana y castellana*, published in Mexico in 1539. Of the first hundred books printed in Mexico, two-thirds are works by Franciscan, Dominican and Augustinian monks designed to support the apostolate in the indigenous language. Renouncing the Castilianization of the Indians in Mexico was clearly not an idle threat !

The ethnographic view

It would be pointless to try to conceal that between 1524 and 1529 Mexico had been the scene of a brutal 'idol hunt'. This was an era when the pioneers of evangelization, who were still few in number, carried out a spectacular destruction of the temples, shattered the statues of Aztec gods and ostentatiously burned their images. They wanted to make it quite clear that the Christian God must replace the indigenous polytheism and not be lumped in with the innumerable cohort of Mexican gods. But this ostentatious policy of idol destruction might very easily have been transformed into a counter-productive persecution. Once the incompatibility of the religion of one God with the indigenous polytheism had been well established, the monks interested themselves more freely in the beliefs of the population and thus became archivists of the very paganism whose destruction was supposed to be their mission.

Among the Franciscan ethnologists made famous by their chronicles, three names stand out: Andrés de Olmos, who put together his *Tratado de las antigüedades méxicanas* between 1533 and 1539 in the large urban concentrations of central Mexico; Motolinia, who undertook his research between 1536 and 1541 in the region of Tlaxcala;

the Christian religion and the Spanish language. Accordingly, from the very start, the evangelizers of Mexico wanted to dissociate themselves from the Spaniards, and that included their language.

When the famous mission of twelve Franciscan 'apostles' arrived in Mexico in June 1521, they were careful to present themselves to the civil and religious Aztec chiefs as papal envoys (see '*Les Colloques des Douze*' in Christian Duverger's '*La Conversion des Indiens de la Nouvelle-Espagne*', Paris, 1987, pp. 71-111). As men of God, they were the representatives of a spiritual power situated above temporal power.

As for education, it would for choice be given either in Latin or in the vernacular. This was not a neutral decision. Teaching the Indians Latin would give them access not only to the language of the Church but also to the scholarly and scientific language of the age. It was therefore assumed that the Indians were capable of knowledge – a humanist concept which contrasted strongly with the prejudices of the day. As much as fifty years after the discovery of America, certain people still refused to admit that the Indians could have souls! In addition, the act of preaching in local languages, not only created a link between the preacher and his audience but also attributed a cultural value to the vernacular. It constituted, in fact, statutory recognition of the values of the Indian world. Abandoning Castilian Spanish as the medium of conversion to Christianity marked a decisive turning point: it opened indigenous Mexico to the word of God, and unmistakably installed the monks in the camp of the Indians.

Once the principle of using indigenous languages was accepted, they had to be spoken fluently. When one thinks about it, the linguistic enterprise into which the monks launched themselves was extraordinarily complex.

The first obstacle was the ethnic diversity of Mexico. Certainly there was a dominant language, Nahuatl, and it was spoken throughout the territory previously controlled by the Aztecs. But it would have been detrimental and sometimes ineffective to have systematically used the language of the former masters of Mexico. So, respecting both ethnic diversity and avoiding taking the side of the strongest group, the monks spoke to almost all the peoples of Mexico in their own language, involving some twenty dialects. In so doing, the monks found themselves face to face with forms of language totally unknown in the Old World. For

and finally Bernardino de Sahagún, who from 1546, the date on which he became a teacher at the college of Tlatelolco, until his death in 1590 continued to collect and order the material of his *História general de las cosas de Nueva España*.

In this vast encyclopedia of the Aztec world, Sahagún brought together information concerning the religion and its rituals, the calendar, omens, rhetoric, moral philosophy, astronomy and traditional medicine. The life of the priests, the nobles and the merchants is described along with the vices and the virtues of the people. He includes observations on funeral customs, education systems and the proverbs in use in pre-Columbian times. And he draws up genealogical lists as well as giving an overview of how Mexico was actually populated. Accompanying it is a full description of the natural history and an account of the Spanish conquest up to the fall of Mexico City. This is a work of great documentary value, collected from the mouths of local informants who were competent and reliable. In its definitive version, expertly handwritten and illustrated between 1576 and 1580, Sahagún's work includes 1223 folios and 1842 illustrations in the form of vignettes inserted into the text. It is bilingual, in Nahuatl and Spanish.

In spite of its serious nature and the outstanding quality, the *História general* was never printed. The reason is that throughout the sixteenth century there existed in Spain a strong current of opposition to the publication of works related to the 'idolatry' of the Amerindian nations. The interest of the mendicant orders in the indigenous cultures appeared paradoxical, and indeed suspect, to certain zealots of a Catholicism still haunted by the prospect of heresy or schism. This preoccupation of the missionaries with the local religions becomes much easier to understand in the Mexican context.

The monks put the pragmatic aspects of their initiative first and foremost. In the same way as a doctor should get to know his patient's illness in order to treat it, the priest should get to know the foundations of ancient idolatry in order to destroy it. But behind this 'official' argument a more ambitious and more complex plan emerges. The basic desire of the evangelizers was to understand every detail of the thought processes and psychology of the population, because they wished to adapt the Christian message to local idiosyncrasies. They were trying to initiate a policy of capturing what was sacred to the local people, in the knowledge that Catholicism could be imposed only by being grafted on to the religious feeling predating the arrival of the Spaniards. So the Franciscans built their monastery on the site of former pagan temples or pressed into service as fonts the *quauhxicalli* which had previously been used to receive the heart and blood of sacrificial victims. They reactivated the tradition of codices by inventing pictographic catechisms; they produced evangelizing plays which included some elements from the former pagan ceremonies.

Most often, the Christian devotions were a substitute pure and simple for pre-Hispanic cults: the Virgin of Guadalupe, so dear to Cortés, replaced Tonantzin, 'our venerated mother'; at Chalma, a miraculous Christ took the place of Oztoteotl, who reigned in the depths of a sacred grotto. At Chiauhtempa, a monastery dedicated to St Anne, the mother of the Virgin Mary, tapped the faith of the former worshippers of the goddess Toci, 'our ancestor'. If the Indians might have danced in honour of their gods, they would now dance in the church squares singing Bible verses translated into Nahuatl, Mixtec or Matlatzinca. All this was because the monks had taken up the challenge of inserting Christian practices into the ongoing tradition of pre-Hispanic cultures.

The anthropological approach of the Franciscans corresponded to a more political vision of their mission. Not only did the Minor Brothers consider it important to respect the foundations of the indigenous society in their daily activities – at least when these were compatible with Christian dogma – but they also strove to improve the status of the history and cultural tradition of the inhabitants of Mexico. By transcribing, for example, the corpus of myths, beliefs and other historical genealogies into Latin script, the monks were trying to give the indigenous population the attributes of civilization, acknowledging and emphasizing the existence of a body of knowledge, of wisdom, of virtue, of a sense of the divine, all associated with a respectable antiquity. In this idealization of the 'noble savage' – a cannibal perhaps, but a cultivated one; a reasonable man but led astray by the devil – we find both the justification of the mission of the evangelizers, who by the revelation of the true God could free the souls of the natives from the influence of the devil,

Square of the Three Cultures, Mexico. *In this symbolic square are united the remains of the pre-Hispanic ceremonial centre of Tlatelolco, the church of the Franciscan convent of Santiago, founded in about 1530 but rebuilt in 1690, and modern blocks of flats. The ones shown here were destroyed by the earthquake of 1985. [Photo G. Dagli Orti © Arch. Photeb]*

CHRISTIAN CONSTRAINTS
The church's rejection of polygamy, traditional among the nobles, was both a source of friction and a factor in destabilizing the indigenous society.

The Ozama Fortress, 1504, Santo
Domingo. The entrance to the arsenal.
This facade is typical of the austere
architectural style of the beginning of the
sixteenth century, medieval in inspiration.
[Photo J. Duverger]

and a more or less explicit condemnation of the
Spanish colonizers, who, faced with the Indians
and their thousand-year-old culture, found
themselves devoid of legitimate reasons for their
territorial occupation. Throughout the whole
period of the glory of the mendicant orders, up to
1572, this bias in favour of the Indians was
nourished both by great suspicion of the
encomenderos and by a genuine fascination for these
sweet and intelligent Indians who recited the Pater
Noster with such conviction in Nahuatl.

From the Middle Ages to the Renaissance

In contrast with the disastrous results of the
conversion of the Antilles, the evangelization of
Mexico was a success. Missionary groups and
monastic settlements grew steadily: the
Franciscans, who were first to arrive, founded 20
convents by 1531. In 1559, according to
investigations by Mendieta, the Minor Brothers
had 80 houses and 380 monks, while the
Dominicans and the Augustinians each had 40
monasteries and respectively 210 and 212 monks.
In 1596, the Franciscans had a network of 200
monasteries run by about a thousand monks, the
Dominicans 90 and the Augustinians 76. Given
the number of candidates for conversion, the
Franciscans organized mass baptisms. By 1531, after
seven years of activity in Mexico, they had
baptized about a million people. In the year 1536,
Motolinia estimates they had reached the order of
'four million souls'. Two years later, the chronicler
produced the figure of six million Indians baptized,
or a third of the population of central Mexico!
Thus conversion to Christianity had become an
incontestable reality twenty years after the arrival
of the Spaniards. The contrast with Hispaniola is
striking: there the bishopric of La Vega had had to
be withdrawn because there was no congregation.

The success of the Mexican evangelizers was
due to two factors. Having learned the lessons of
the Haitian episode, they were able to take the side
of the Indians without being afraid to stand up
against the colonizers' greed. It was probably
because the Indians considered the monks their
defenders that so many wanted to place themselves
under their protection and seek baptism.

The personality of the actors in this drama is
critical. Quite independently of their intrinsic

qualities, the Franciscans who devoted themselves
to the Indians loved Mexico and its inhabitants,
and entered into a relationship of profound
complicity and mutual understanding. For all those
monks who made their mark on the history of New
Spain, Mexico was neither a fleeting adventure nor
a stepping stone in some kind of honorary career.
All of them made it their adopted country, their
true homeland. Two examples illustrate this: Pedro
de Gante, who arrived in 1523, and Bernardino de
Sahagún, who arrived in 1528, died at the age of
ninety-two without ever returning to Europe.

Over and above this, it is clear that the
'Indianization' of the Catholic religion greatly
helped the phenomenon of mass conversion.
Respect for certain pre-Hispanic traditions,
superimposing Christian and pagan cults and the
adaptation of certain Catholic rites created a
syncretic religion, sufficiently Christian for it not
to bring down the wrath of Rome and sufficiently
Indian not to turn away the indigenous masses.

In the end, time did its work. Twenty-nine
years passed from the discovery of the West Indian
Islands to the fall of Mexico. In one generation, the
Old World passed from the Middle Ages into the
Renaissance. It is unjust to accuse Columbus of
being a man of his time, but everything about him
was medieval: his concept of power in terms of
fiefdom, his concept of the Other as a non-being,
his concept of the future just in terms of prophecy.
It is also unjust to accuse Ovando of being a man of
his time; but everything about him was equally
medieval. Look at the town he built on the bank of
the Río Ozama. Go through the old streets of Santo
Domingo and observe the massive and austere
architecture; nothing but fortresses, loopholes,
thick walls and smooth facades. In Mexico, the
post-Cortés architecture is already inspired by the
Renaissance, vibrating with grace and subtlety
through the elegance of its embellishments, the
balance of its proportions and the originality of its
inventiveness. In the interval, the wind of history
had blown. But it was America herself which
inspired this great intake of air and swept in
modernism from the Old World. It was this
encounter with otherness, this inevitable rendering
of the European cultural models as purely relative,
this enlargement of the intellectual realm which
stirred the minds and spurred the imagination of
thinkers. The evangelizers of Mexico, forty years
after the first crossing, were wholly men of the
Renaissance, men of the New World.

INDIAN
NORTH AMERICA,
in the turmoil
of colonization

PHILIPPE JACQUIN

'There is not a single savage who does not think himself infinitely happier and stronger than the French.'

On 22 July 1701 the colonists in Montreal witnessed an awe-inspiring spectacle. Two hundred canoes approached the modest little town; almost eight hundred Indians landed on the Ile St Laurent, marching past the spectators in an incredible variety of costumes and hairstyles, and talking in unknown languages. One of the most noteworthy delegations was led by Chief Kondiaronk, nicknamed 'The Rat' by the French, at the head of his Huron braves. The colonists had already seen Ottawas, Ojibwas, Nipissings and Miamis; but here were also the Crees from the tundra, the Sauks and the Fox from Lake Superior, the Potawatomis and the Illinois from the upper Mississippi and even the Sioux from the western marches.

The day before, the public had felt a thrill of apprehension with the arrival of a hundred Iroquois. Since the landing of Samuel de Champlain in 1608 hostilities between the Iroquois and the French had hardly ceased. But now, at the very start of the eighteenth century, with this Great Peace of Montreal, the latent insecurity of the colony was about to end for the first time. A century after the settlement of the French in Quebec, the diplomatic conference in Montreal offered another opportunity: it brought together the thirty Indian nations who were allies of France in order to put together a map of the expanding New France. This was an unprecedented expansion in North American colonization, to such an extent that the English had begun talking of the 'French empire'. Cavalier de La Salle had already opened up the Mississippi, while Louisiana, founded in 1699, had brought to fruition the efforts of the colonial explorers and administrators with little help from a mother country which was more eager for European glory than American laurels. There was, however, no word for 'empire' in any Indian language – and in any case, just how real was this empire in the eyes of the Indian nations who constituted it yet in no way considered themselves subject to it?

Throughout America these 'people from afar', these Europeans, inspired curiosity, anxiety and sometimes fear. The Indians could not imagine the presence of a land across the ocean, in much the same way as the Europeans had not imagined America. Being excellent sailors, the Indians of the north-eastern coast took to sea in their canoes and did not hesitate to approach these 'strange floating islands' on which men in coloured clothes gestured to them and gave them things they had never seen before. The Micmacs were sure that on board was their hero, White Man-Rabbit, who had gone to the east. Other tribes who located the kingdom of the dead on some vague marine horizon wondered if their ancestors had returned. Contacts with the fishermen of Newfoundland and fur trappers at the start of the seventeenth century quickly dispelled any ambiguity, but the Indians were deeply impressed by the many new objects that came into their possession, from metal to glass beads, and were disconcerted by the 'silent invasion' of epidemics which decimated the coastal populations and quickly moved along the commercial routes.

Contrary to a widespread concept, the French did not discover people 'of biblical times'. The

'savages' – this name was used throughout the colonial period – were not 'without faith or law'; even less were they Jews who had escaped from the Promised Land. The French, who observed them with all the prejudices inherited from the Middle Ages and a superiority derived from Christianity and current scientific knowledge, suddenly realized they were dependent upon them. From the beginning of the seventeenth century, several elements combined to compel the conquerors to modify their policy, as Champlain quickly realized.

The flow of French emigration to North America was only a thin trickle, which had almost dried up by the time Louisiana was reached. In New France, barely ten thousand French came to settle on the banks of the St Lawrence. Although numbers are uncertain, some Indian tribes were of considerable size: there were at least twenty thousand Hurons and thirty thousand Iroquois, many of them warriors. The French penetration started from the St Lawrence axis, pivoting round the Great Lakes and, to the south, the Mississippi. In a climate and landscape which could often be harsh, voyages and explorations required knowledge which only the Indians possessed. The 'conquest of the West' could only be achieved by establishing friendly relations and commercial links. British superiority in trading and population finally led the French to seek an Indian alliance. The 'French empire' in reality was a huge network of inter-tribal links in which the French immersed themselves, by means of a policy of offering gifts and imposing outright commercial pressure.

In 1608 Samuel de Champlain, colonizer and fur trader, received authority from the Montagnais, Algonquins from Labrador, to establish a trading post in the Strait of Quebec. The French could venture westwards on condition that they did not trade, for the intermediary tribes wanted to preserve the favourable trading position acquired before the Europeans arrived. There were two separate crossflows of commerce in the Great Lake and St Lawrence basin. With the good weather, bands of hunter-gatherers such as the Ojibwas, Crees, Nipissings and Montagnais brought furs, unrefined copper, antlers, dried fruit, moose skins and fish to the southern farmers of the basin: the Hurons, Iroquois and the neutral Eries. They were offered in return maize, squashes, tobacco, filleted fish, squirrel skins and seashell beads bartered with the Susquehannocks on the coast.

The Winnebagos came from the west with bison skins and pipestone (catlinite). The Algonquins of the lower St Lawrence, and in particular the Hurons settled near Georgian Bay, held exceptional positions as middlemen because the lakes and the river were the only means of rapid communication between the two main economic zones. All these commercial relations favoured political links and, consequently, military alliances. So the Montagnais, assisted by the Algonquins, ejected the Iroquois from the St Lawrence valley in the course of the sixteenth century and joined the Hurons in their struggle against the Iroquoian league, whose Five Nations (Mohawk, Onondaga, Oneida, Seneca and

THE SILENT INVASION

Isolated from the rest of the world, America suffered none of the pandemics which had spread terror across Europe for centuries. With their lack of immunity the Indians fell victim to smallpox, influenza, head colds and the 'many fevers' that were brought by the sixteenth-century explorers and fishermen of Newfoundland. The viruses spread along the commercial routes and penetrated the heart of the continent well ahead of the Europeans. The Hurons, for example, suffered attacks of smallpox and dysentery (1634), of influenza (1636) and then of smallpox again (1639). The missionaries estimated that the population fell by a third.

In the following year, 1610, Champlain renewed his military exploits. Along with Hurons and Algonquins, he attacked a Mohawk fort on the River Richelieu. Here again, victory was complete; the defeat brought the Iroquois closer to the Dutch and reinforced the links between the French and their Indian allies. In accordance with Indian tradition, the alliance was substantiated by an exchange of warriors. The Huron Savignon followed Champlain; Iroquet, the Algonquin chief, took the young Etienne Brûlé. The French youth spent the winter with the Hurons, shared the hospitality of Iroquet, and learned the Algonquin and Huron languages. He then became the first *coureur de bois* (traveller) and interpreter in New France. By familiarizing themselves with the Indian languages and customs, these *coureurs de bois* would play a major role in the fur trade. Throughout the time of the French presence, fur was a kind of 'brown gold'. Beaver skins were obtained cheaply by the French and sold throughout Europe, where they were used to make hats – beaver fur was much appreciated for its waterproofness and insulating qualities. As the main export of the colony – wood never rivalled fur – the beaver brought in considerable revenue for the colonists. However, trade required close collaboration with the Indians.

Indian forest encampment. *Engraving by W H Bartlett. Nineteenth century.* *[Photo © L. de Selva-Tapabor]*

Cayuga) remained ensconced in their fortified villages on the southern shore of Lake Ontario. As part of this logical diplomacy the Algonquins and the Hurons, allied to the French, surprised two hundred Mohawks: the arquebuses 'did wondrous well', bullets pierced the wooden breastplates, and some fifty Mohawks including two important chiefs were killed. Champlain had reinforced his alliance with the Hurons but the French had also made inveterate enemies: the Iroquoian league. The latter turned towards the 'men of cloth', the Dutch, who had begun to settle on the Hudson. The Iroquoians promised to supply them with furs in return for arquebuses. These arms and the determination of the Iroquoians would eventually ensure supremacy to the enemies of the French.

Brown gold: the fur trade

Because of the demand, the Indians of the north-east coast, who had been exchanging furs with European fishermen for a century, were obliged to increase their purchases from the interior. This was possible by virtue of the enormous value of iron, glass beads and other objects gleaned here and there in maritime trade. However, the Indians who tried to find out what value the French attached to these goods, succeeded in changing the unfavourable rate of exchange established when contact was first made. On the internal market, even in the seventeenth century, the Montagnais bartered ten skins for an axe, which they had obtained for two.

The settlement of the French on the St Lawrence, the presence of a trading post in

---

THE OTTAWAN COURTING CEREMONY

Right-hand page
An Iroquois mask, made from maize leaves *sewn together, the braided fibre assuming the shape of a face. The members of the Husk Face Society in the seventeenth century incarnated the spirits of agriculture by wearing these masks at the great annual ceremony of the Fête de l'Hiver, in February. [Musée de l'Homme, Paris]*

'Business takes Diéreville, a trader, to Canada, where he learns about the native Indian customs. The missionaries showed rather less tolerance with what they regarded as immoral behaviour among the Indians, namely their attitude to sexual relations among young people. Normally, love is a duty which is fulfilled first, but a man's passion, here as it is there, is not always satisfied with the same person. And there are means of acquiring another: you must avail yourself of a box of matches and, in the evening, go to the huts where you know the young girls to be. Once inside, you should strike several matches, which become a torch of love. Wave the flame in front of the eyes of the most pleasing young girl and, if by some common stroke of luck, one of them should blow it out while in your hands, it is a sign of good fortune and you may be assured that your desires will be fulfilled. And if you spend the night in that hut, your loving will not be disturbed.'

Sieur Diéreville, Relation du voyage du Port Royal de l'Acadie à la Nouvelle-France, *Amsterdam 1708, p.201.*

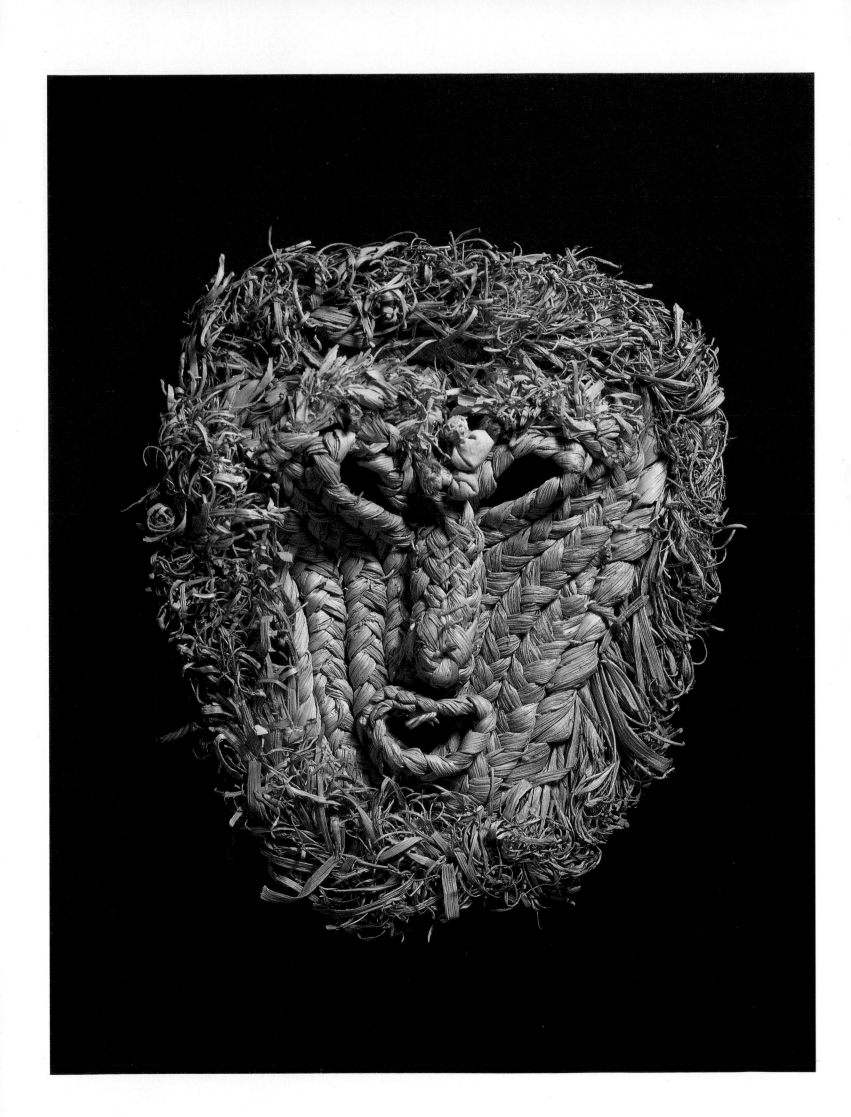

Montreal since 1642, and the establishment of posts around the Great Lakes during the eighteenth century upset the existing trade structures. Even more so than the French merchants, the fur traders ventured into the hinterland and made contact with the bands of hunters on the Laurentian shield. Because of the enormous distances involved, the main threat for the French in the 1670s was the establishment of English posts along the coast of the Hudson Bay: the English, supplied by ships, could offer merchandise more cheaply to the Crees and Chipewyans of the tundra.

In the carrying out of the fur trade the Indians were initially able to impose their commercial conventions on the French. Exchanges of gifts, military alliances and even marriage settlements were accepted by the newcomers. The *coureurs de bois* shared the daily life of the Indians, and, in spite of the damage being wrought by the Jesuits, helped to keep the Indians in the Great

Lake basin in the French camp. But even though it was easier for the French to adapt to the Indian way of life than vice versa, the development of the fur trade transformed attitudes in the course of the century. The intrusion of market forces destroyed the main element in social relationships: sharing. A chief or even a simple brave did not accumulate exotic products, but shared them in the form of presents. Generosity was a source of power and influence in the Indian community, and the main motive for trade was more the acquisition of prestige than personal enrichment.

In addition to tempting the Hurons and Algonquins with unknown objects which created new needs, the French imprisoned them with even more alien products, such as alcohol and credit. The simple fact was that, as soon as the French traders gave credit to the trapper, they dragged him into a closed circuit of dependency which made him ignore his obligations to his own community in order to dedicate himself to 'producing' more fur; this led to over-hunting, which deprived him of the meat and skins necessary for his own economy. He was then forced to appeal to the trader in order to obtain, at considerable cost, food and clothes. Even in the agricultural communities of the Hurons, trade led to overworking. The women had to increase the amount of arable land in order to obtain better yields of maize, an essential product if they were to obtain more skins from the bands of hunters. So not only did the system cause fierce competition between individuals, but it also led to the supply of game drying up and thus forced the Indians into inter-tribal conflicts.

In the seventeenth century the 'fur wars' were to plunge New France into bloody conflict. The Iroquois never gave up their attempts to disperse the Hurons, whose commercial position as intermediaries and allies of the French harmed Iroquois interests. In 1640–50 the Huron confederation was broken, for the French did not want to arm their allies – only those Hurons who had converted to Catholicism received firearms – for fear of the rifles being turned against them.

The disappearance of Huronia placed the young colony in a very delicate position. The Iroquois could cut the fur route, and the disappearance of the intermediary role of the Hurons had forced the French to reorganize their trading connections. Faced with Iroquoian supremacy, the Indians of the Great Lakes nonetheless chose the camp of the 'men of iron', the French. They had the top position in trade because they had the European outlet for fur. However, they lacked the means for their expansionist policy. The two thousand colonists huddled together on the St Lawrence in 1660 occupied only a thin strip of land; the Iroquoian harassment was paralysing their economic life, and so the colony risked asphyxiation.

In 1663 New France became a royal province. Louis XIV's chief minister, Colbert, wanted to develop immigration and, to attain his profiteering objectives, he considered that the new province should furnish the metropolis with the raw materials essential to the military ambitions of the young king. While Colbert's policy thus tripled the population of New France, the Governor, Frontenac, launched campaigns against the Iroquois. The arrival in 1665 of twelve hundred men of the Carignan-Salières regiment worried the Iroquoian league. During the summer of 1666 there was a campaign of outright extermination, with crops being burned and Mohawk villages destroyed. The eighteen years of peace that followed enabled the French to launch their conquest of the West.

Exploratory expeditions multiplied, benefiting from the trade profits, and according to the Governor, 'the explorers are looking not for the Western sea (the passage to China) but for beaver.' After the success of Cavalier de La Salle, groups of coureurs de bois ventured west of the Great Lakes. In 1688 Jacques de Noyon forged links with the

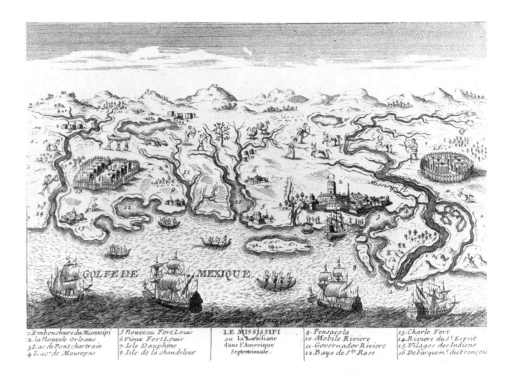

Assiniboians near Rainy Lake, on the threshold of the huge Canadian prairie. The coureurs de bois crossed Lake Superior in their canoes equipped with sails and, by means of portages where there were no navigable waterways, reached Lake of the Woods and Lake Winnipeg at the start of the eighteenth century. Pierre Gaultier de La Vérendrye and his sons then attempted, with a handful of coureurs de bois, to encircle the English posts on Hudson Bay. The plan was to establish forts (in reality 'mean cabins') where they would stock munitions and alcohol, with a view to stopping the Crees and Assiniboians on their way to the bay. The French installed themselves on the rivers Assiniboine and Saskatchewan, thus controlling the river basin near Lakes Manitoba and Winnipeg.

The La Vérendrye offspring distinguished themselves in the West. Pierre, the oldest, sailed down the Missouri in 1738 where he encountered the Mandans, the Hidatsas and the Arikaras – to the annoyance of the Assiniboians, who feared the French would sell rifles to their traditional enemies. Here again the French were being trapped in a net of politico-economic rivalries, to which should be added the contraband trade of the coureurs de bois. Guns, alcohol and beads were forwarded via the Illinois to the Missouri, the 'land of the Sioux'. South of the Great Lakes, on the frontier of New France and the young state of Louisiana, coureurs de bois pursued their own political ends. Some set up with tribes to the west of the Mississippi.

Smuggling and disputes cost the life of Pierre La Vérendrye, his brother Jean-Baptiste and twenty coureurs de bois, massacred on an island in the upper Mississippi by the Sioux in July 1736. Other coureurs de bois were killed by the Fox Indians. Using other Indians as agents, the French tried for years to wipe out this tribe which lived on the edge of Lake Superior.

Mississippi or Louisiana in northern America. This map, probably engraved by Bonnart in the 1730s, since it shows New Orleans, offers some interesting information on the Indians and local fauna. Two large fortified villages with long houses seem to indicate the territorial limits of the province. The Indians are hunting bison, alligators and turkeys. The Indian canoes are approaching the ships, but there is no hostility apparent in this map, in which the villages with their churches resemble those back in France. [Bibliothèque nationale, Paris. Photo Jeanbor © Arch. Photeb]

ADOPTION
The young French trapper, Pierre Radisson, was captured by the Mohawks (Iroquois) in 1652, then adopted by a widow. 'She coated me in grease, combed my hair, removed the paint which the warriors had smeared on my face, brought me toasted Indian corn (maize), a blue blanket, gaiters, moccasins and material to make a pair of breeches. She examined the clothes to see if there were any fleas; if she found any, she crushed them between her teeth as though they were a delicacy. I slept beside her son, the man who had captured me. I did everything in order to accustom myself to the Mohawks.' [Voyages of Peter Esprit Radisson, Being an Account of His Travels and Experience Among the North American Indians From 1652 to 1684. Edited by Gideon Schull, Boston 1885, pp.38 and 39.]

Otter skin made into a bag, *decorated with brass plates and used by a shaman when officiating at healing rituals. It was probably a bag containing migis, the sacred shells revealed to the Ojibwas, symbolizing the path of truth. In the ritual of the* midewiwin, *the migis symbolically kill the novice who wishes to enter this society of healers at the moment when the officiant presents him with the body of the otter. Brutal subjugation, epidemics and inter-tribal conflicts led the Crees and Ojibwas to create this secret society with its therapeutic purpose, the* midewiwin, *in the seventeenth century. [Musée de l'Homme, Paris]*

Another son of Pierre La Vérendrye, Le Chevalier, decided to launch an expedition to the west, across the plains. Between April 1742 and July 1743 he travelled across the region west of the Missouri, guided by Indians, perhaps even meeting the Big Horns in present-day Wyoming. The spirit of independence and the fighting qualities of the semi-nomadic tribes that he met made him very cautious. At the end of all this, he concluded that the commercial potential of these immense treeless spaces was very limited. The West would have to wait another century before the tumult of colonization descended upon it.

In the valley of the Mississippi French colonization was marking time; only lower Louisiana experienced some slight development from 1735 onwards with the cultivation of indigo, tobacco, rice and cotton. This young colony, too, suffered from a lack of investment on the part of metropolitan France, as well as a low rate of immigration into a region where the climate and 'fevers' decimated the population. Under the Regency, while Louis XV was still a minor, the schemes of the Scottish financier Law, who acquired a trade monopoly in Louisiana in 1717, inspired a brief interest in the 'land of the Sioux'. Colonists settled in and around New Orleans, some even daring to create plantations along the banks of the river. A servile labour force worked in these plantations: just as in Canada, there was a policy of 'volunteers' – poor devils shipped to the Americas who, even Frontenac admitted, 'were treated like slaves'. The colonized zone extended as far as the country of the Natchez and the Red and Arkansas rivers. It comprised tiny groups of settlers made up of disbanded soldiers, three hundred German colonists recruited for John Law's trade concession, Swiss attracted by promises of making their fortune, and adventurers living with their Indian concubines. During the reign of Louis XV there was a policy of deporting to Louisiana whores, vagabonds and beggars, undesirable sons and nephews, and deserters. The colonists lived to the rhythm of the ships from the Antilles and France, and undertook a little trade with nearby Mexico.

Just like New France, Louisiana was almost swamped by the immensity of the continent in which it was located. The main artery of the Mississippi nourished trade with the Illinois, and along its banks could be found communities of mixed Franco-Indian blood as well as one or two forts around which a few farmers were settled. To the west of the Mississippi, 'the father of rivers', spread an ocean of grass in which a handful of *coureurs de bois* operated. The Missouri was the most widely used route, with the French living side by side with Mandans and Sioux, the latter having just emigrated south from the Great Lakes to settle in the upper Missouri.

Further south were the Cheyennes, Osages and Pawnees – tribes to which the Comanches sold horses. These animals, having returned to the wild since the arrival of the Spanish in the south-west, were captured by the Apaches and the Caddos and had become part of the trade of the Great Plains which ensured their distribution northwards during the eighteenth century. The horse changed the way of life of the hunter-gatherer societies of the plains. Hunting bison on foot or with traps was abandoned in favour of the use of horses. Mobility and prestige combined to make the horse the 'sacred dog', as it was called in their language by

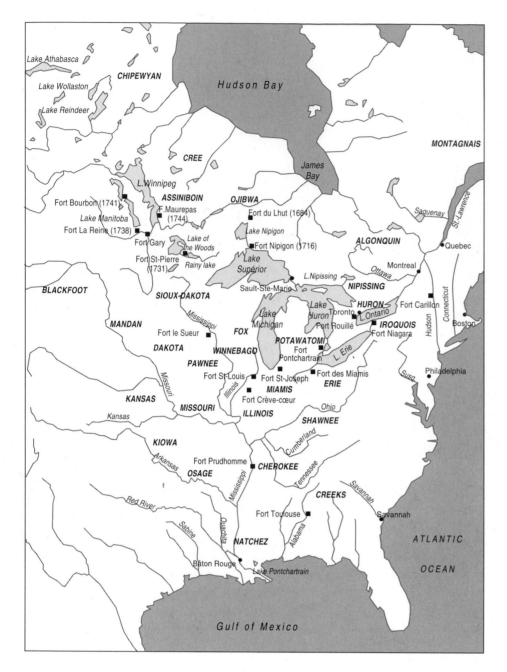

The Indian tribes in the east of North America.

The majority of the names given to the Indian tribes were based on their first contacts with the Europeans. When the French met the Dakotas in the west, they called them the Nadowessioux, 'poisonous serpent', a phrase used by the Ojibwas, who were at war with them. Dakota means 'the seven councils' and Ojibwas means 'make folds', the Algonquin name for moccasins. As for the Montagnais, the Algonquins of Labrador, the French gave them this name because they came from the nearby 'mountains' of the St Lawrence.

the Sioux who used it to replace their unruly dogs in pulling their *travois*. Along the Arkansas and Red rivers, the French were in contact with the Wichitas and the confederation of twenty-five Caddo tribes, one of which – the Tesas – gave Texas its name.

Beyond the Mississippi, Louisiana in those days extended as far as the Rocky Mountains and stopped at the Spanish possessions in Mexico. The French did not pay much attention to this immense western region where little-known tribes lived as nomads. Their sole concern was their disputes with the Indians in lower Louisiana, particularly the confederation of Creeks, Taensas and Natchez. Natchez society operated like a theocracy. The prince – the Great Sun – was surrounded by nobles, the 'honourable ones', and held to be the reincarnation of the supreme star. He was deeply respected by the Puants, 'the stinkers', which is what the French christened the general populace.

The construction of Fort Rosalie near the village of La Pomme, the brutality of some colonists towards the 'honourable ones', but above all the pretensions of the fort commander, Captain Etcheparre, and his scorn for Great Sun, led to a general rebellion by the Natchez. On 28 November 1729 the 237 French soldiers in the fort were massacred. The colony was taken completely by surprise, and the population fled to the capital.

Repression was merciless. A military expedition burned the Natchez villages, killed the braves, and took the women and children to be sold as slaves to the Antilles. The families of the survivors who took refuge among the Chickasaws were pursued and punished to the very end of the French occupation. It was not by accident that the Natchez took up with this tribe, whose determination in opposing the French was well known to them.

During the establishment of the colony in 1699–1700, Le Moyne d'Iberville and his brother Bienville had met the Choctaws: they needed the support of a powerful tribe and the Choctaws, at war with their neighbours the Chickasaws, sought aid from the French. This began half a century of mutual hostility, broken every so often by military expeditions trying to get the better of the Chickasaws who, naturally, equipped themselves with arms from the English in Carolina, smuggled through the Tennessee valley.

In 1736 the French were saved from catastrophe by the Choctaws of Chief Red Shoe. The campaign of 1739 failed because of bad weather combined with personal rivalries between officers, some of whom were incompetent. In the American colonies, the high-ranking administrators and officers who had come to seek fame and fortune were constantly denigrating one another, with accusations of misappropriation and of contraband – that was when they were not fighting duels over matters of precedence!

For Louisiana, the threat lay to the east. Its frontiers stopped at the Appalachians, whose valleys were frequented by English traders. The Creek confederation, which included the Cherokees, Chickasaws, Choctaws and Creeks, inhabited the Appalachian range itself. It observed a certain degree of neutrality with regard to the Europeans, limiting itself to intervention during the revolt of the Natchez and not taking at all seriously the Choctaw alliance with the French. In order to avoid invasion of its territory the Creek confederation agreed to trade with the English in Carolina and Georgia, but it refused to allow them to build schools and missions.

The French colony was still a matter of great concern to the confederation, which would support the English during the Seven Years War of 1756–63. Because of their trade relations and political traditions, the Indians found themselves involved in every conflict between the French and British forces. Some tribes preferred to move west; others hoped that the war would save their own

A calumet. *'Smoking is praying', said the Indians. The name 'calumet' is derived from the French word* chalumeau. *The bowl of this pipe is made of catlinite, a soft stone from a quarry in Minnesota, bearing the name of the artist George Catlin (the first man to have it analysed). [Musée de l'Homme, Paris]*

independence, or ruin their traditional enemies. The French retained the support of the tribes of the Great Lakes, while the English counted on the Iroquois and on the Creek confederation.

With the Treaty of Utrecht in 1713, France had already ceded to England Acadia and Newfoundland, and recognized its rights over an immense territory near Hudson Bay. The Treaty of Paris in 1763, at the end of the Seven Years War, put an end to the French presence in North America. Western Louisiana returned to Spain, whilst the eastern half and New France became part of Britain's Thirteen Colonies. In the same year a Delaware shaman known as the 'Prophet', preached rejection of white culture and a return to the traditions and unity of the Indians. The Ottawa chief Pontiac united the Shawnees, the Chippewas, the Potawatomis and the relics of the tribes scattered around the south of the Great Lakes. Some French even joined the cause.

In May 1763 the Indians besieged Detroit and the British garrisons were massacred in the Ohio valley. But the following year, weary of war, the Indians gave up the struggle. A smallpox epidemic, probably spread by blankets offered to the Delawares, decimated the combatants. Pontiac surrendered and the French fled westwards. It was not by chance that the revolt had been sparked off by a 'holy man', because at a very early stage the shamans, whom the French considered to be 'sorcerers', had appealed for defiance from their brothers and respect for traditions.

Few Frenchmen aroused such passion and became the focus for so much hatred as the missionaries. They were quick to arrive, following behind the first colonists. In 1615, four Franciscan Récollets arrived at the request of Champlain and, in 1629, two Jesuits settled in Acadia. However, Cardinal Richelieu, who was France's principal statesman at this time, wanted to hand the region

over to the Capuchins. The Jesuits returned in force to Quebec in 1632 and, over the next century, some thirty of them divided up responsibility for this 'mission' country which is the size of a continent.

Missionaries and Sorcerers

Rivalries between religious orders existed in the colonies. The Seminary of Foreign Missions wished to have a monopoly of the apostolate of the 'savages of the Mississippi'. When Louisiana was founded, the seminary contested the presence of the Jesuits among the Illinois. The conflict was renewed in 1720 when John Law appealed to the Carmelites to come and evangelize Louisiana.

The majority of these missionaries, particularly the Jesuits, were 'veritable soldiers of the faith': they were ready to undertake any sacrifice, with martyrdom the ultimate reward. The Jesuits acquired a special status, since they tried to adapt to the Indian way of life, learning the languages and converting the natives in a reasonably flexible manner. They have left us their *Relations*, letters written to encourage donations from metropolitan France. These represent an incomparable source of ethnographic information; most of the writers spent years in the Indian communities, naively setting down on paper the reactions of the Indians to these 'Black Robes'.

For a long time the Indians simply could not work out the precise role of these unarmed bachelors, who were so interested in their beliefs and their traditions. However, they did quickly realize the fundamental difference between their own religion and Christianity. They noted that the

A scalping scene on a powder horn. *An incision in the scalp, a sharp tug, and the warrior tore away the trophy from the corpse of his adversary, and at the same time acquired the strength and courage of his enemy. This American ritual is very old, as is proved by skeletons discovered in archaeological excavations in pre-Columbian sites. [Musée de l'Homme, Paris]*

An Iroquois who has killed two enemies. *This somewhat imaginative drawing, taken from the Codex Canadiensis, shows an Iroquois warrior with a bow in his hand, covered with tattoos and with scalps blowing in the wind. The Iroquois is like 'a demon from Hell': little flames radiate from his legs, and a strange hairstyle crowns his face of an avenging angel. [Bibliothèque nationale, Paris. Photo Jeanbor © Arch. Photeb]*

Beaver hunting. *An engraving by J. L'Hernault. Nineteenth century. [Photo © Kharbine-Tapabor]*

Transgression of a taboo or forgetting a ritual could chase away the game, cause a drought or create an illness. Among the Hurons there were three main causes of illness: natural agents, unassuaged desires and sorcery. An illness which was natural in origin could be quickly cured by dieting or sweating or infusions. But if none of these remedies was successful, this meant the illness was the result of sorcery or the patient's soul was suffering from some unfulfilled desire. In delicate cases, the family would appeal to a specialist, the shaman. He identified the nature of the desire or removed the source of the spell – dog's teeth, bones, feathers – which a sorcerer had planted in the body. For the Hurons, envy was the source of all witchcraft, hence the importance of sharing gifts with one's neighbours. The shamans were also able to talk to the spirits and the souls of the dead.

For many Indians the missionaries seemed to be some kind of shaman. So, when epidemics broke out and traditional remedies proved to be ineffective, the Indians turned to the missionaries. Why were they able to resist these 'mysterious ailments' so well? And if the French insisted that the Indians welcome these men, was it not for some sinister purpose? While smallpox epidemics decimated tribes the Jesuits baptized the dead and continued to invoke a terrible after-life instead of praying for the cure of the patient. They also tried to discredit the cures of the shamans, 'these charlatans who create a great obstacle to the conversion of the savages'.

The shamans, meanwhile, with their power under threat, and worried about the inefficacy of

French had an exclusive and unbending dogma, while they, as Indians, could integrate personal spiritual experience into the ritual of the tribe. The Indians were familiar with the religions of the communities with which they traded, but never tried to make them change. As animists, they invested nature with forces and spirits, life being the process of reconciling oneself with these spirits and fending off the more evil of them. Since man was part of nature, in the same way as animals and plants, the hunter had a social relationship with his prey; similarly there were feasts and sacrifices in order to help plants germinate and to make it rain.

MARRIAGE AMONG THE NATCHEZ PEOPLE IN THE VALLEY OF THE MISSISSIPPI

'When a young man thinks to get married, he must present himself to the father of the young woman or, if he be lacking, to the eldest brother: they agree a price, which is settled in furs or other goods of value. Although a woman may have led a life of dissolution, this in no way impedes their choice, for they do believe that she will change her ways when she is married. Moreover, they worry not from which family she comes, caring only that she pleases them. As regards the parents of the woman, their sole concern is to know whether he that seeks her is a skilled hunter, a noble warrior or a good ploughman. Such qualities diminish the price which might then be asked of them for the marriage.

'When the two parties are in accord, the husband-to-be sets off on a hunt with his companions: and when he has acquired, be it game or fish, sufficient to regale the two families contracting the marriage, they foregather at the habitation of the parents of the woman; they serve principally the newly-espoused, who share each dish. When the meal is over, the man offers a pipe to the parents of his wife and then his own parents, after which all the guests retire. The newly-wed couple stay together until the next morning, whereupon the husband takes his wife to his father-in-law, and he stays there until the family has constructed for him a separate cabin. Whilst this is being built, he spends the entire day hunting, in order that he can provide sustenance to those working on the building.

'The laws allow the Natchez people to have as many wives as they wish: however, the lower members of the clan normally have but one or two. The chiefs have more, they having the privilege of their fields being tilled by those beneath them at no cost to them, so that the number of their wives is no burden to them.

'The marriage of these chiefs proceeds with less ceremony: they merely send for the father of the woman that they wish to marry and tell him that they are taking her to put among their wives. Thus the marriage is made; however, they do not fail to offer a gift to the father and mother. Even though they may have several wives, they keep but one or two in their cabins: the rest remain with their parents, where they go to see them when it pleases them.'

Jesuit Relations, *volume 68, pp.140 - 142*

their therapy and magic, analysed the situation. They accused the missionaries of spreading death by offering the sick 'the snow of the French' (sugar), 'signs which speak' (writing), and embroidered surplices – but above all pictures. The Indians invested symbols with a life of their own, and the Jesuit image of hell was all the more terrifying for them since, for the Hurons in particular, the 'village of the spirits' was like life here on earth.

The ravages of the epidemics did not persuade the Indians to convert. Instead, ritualism spread, which is a testimony to the dynamism and robustness of the Indian beliefs. In spite of the fear and distrust which the missionaries inspired, the Algonquins and Hurons did not dare to murder them, for the Indians depended on the French for trade. This dependence was also evident among the Iroquois when, after the destruction of Huronia, the Jesuits opened a mission in 1654 among the

Onondagas. By accepting the Black Robes, the Iroquois were attempting to set up commercial links with the French. At the same time, many Iroquois thought that the Jesuits were favourable to their cause, although they were often taken hostage in the event of disputes. There were also captive Huron Catholics among the Iroquois, who encouraged their masters to welcome the priests.

The proselytizing of the missionaries was made particularly delicate because of the Indian tradition. Father Le Jeune spent the winter of 1633–4 with Montagnais families and followed them on their nomadic treks. During the winter, the Algonquin hunter-gatherers dispersed over an enormous area between the northern and sub-Arctic forests, in order to track the caribou of the far north, as well as beavers, bears, lynxes and porcupines. During this period life was very harsh and the families were constantly threatened with famine. When the weather was good the families

War jacket *from South Dakota. In the plains, the jacket, made from wapiti or buckskin, was worn by men. It was often decorated with strips of porcupine quills. The quills were dyed in a concoction of natural dyestuffs, in this case a yellow obtained from the wild sunflower. Then the quills were flattened with a bone mallet; the embroidery consisted of winding them around a thread sewn into the skin. The Sun, the central motif, frequently appeared in plains decor, for it was an object of veneration. [Musée de l'Homme, Paris]*

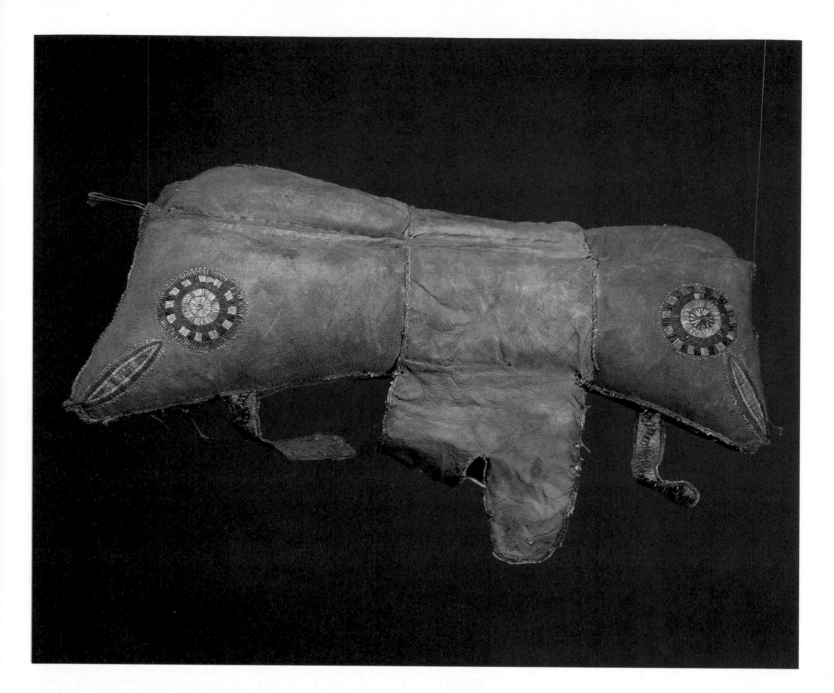

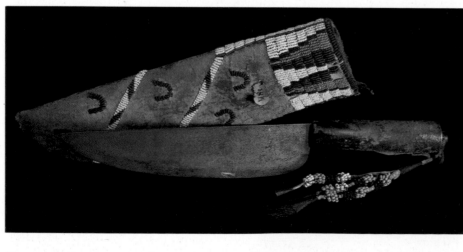

Top
Dakotan saddle (Sioux). *A model inspired by the small Spanish saddles of the sixteenth century, which were copied by the Comanches. It is stuffed with horsehair and decorated with solar designs made from porcupine quills. [Musée de l'Homme, Paris]*

Above
A 'trader's' knife. *From the seventeenth century, this knife circulated in the fur trade. It was used for hunting and fighting, and women wore it at their side. The tracery of beads is the mark of the owner. [Musée de l'Homme, Paris]*

would group into bands to fish or to hunt seals, with the women picking fruit. Le Jeune realized that this nomadic way of life made evangelization very difficult, and he wanted to establish bands of Indians near forts, although he never achieved his aim. In 1634 Father Brébeuf arrived among the Hurons. As a settled tribe the Hurons offered easier access to the Jesuits. The mission of Sainte-Marie-aux-Hurons, inaugurated in 1639, comprised several stone buildings, including a chapel, workshops and forge. It was transformed into a fortified camp during the Iroquois campaign. Some fields, cows and chickens enabled the missionaries to break free from a diet of *sagamité*, the maize gruel of the Hurons. In the middle of Huron territory, this mission was a symbol of French might.

Father Lalemant sent missionaries out to the Huron villages every day. The Jesuits tried to convert influential married men, and particularly older men whose opinions were respected; in 1646

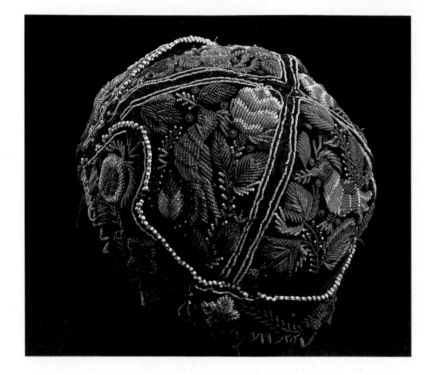

Huron bonnet, *decorated with multi-coloured birds and flowers. From the seventeenth century, Europeans imported beads made from Venetian glass, which they bartered for furs, and the Indians were enchanted by their iridescent colours, as well as by those of the European clothes. Mother-of-pearl and porcupine quills, which entered into the geometrical or symbolic compositions decorating the Indian head-dresses and costumes, were replaced by glass. The bonnet is inspired in shape by that of European women's in the eighteenth century. [Musée de l'Homme, Paris]*

Preceding page
Cockscomb head-dress, *a male fashion very popular in the Great Plains. To a wide strip of skin were fixed porcupine quills or badger hairs, among which also appeared one or more eagle feathers. The wearing of this head-dress was restricted to special ceremonies and other important occasions. Apart from their aesthetic aspects, the feathers had a very specific meaning since they indicate the brave acts undertaken by the wearer in war or in hunting. [Musée de l'Homme, Paris]*

about 560 Hurons seem to have been converted. However, contrary to the hopes of the missionaries, the converts had to give up any public function they had and, as a result, they cut themselves off from their community. Huron society was thus torn apart by segregation, which weakened its capacity to respond to the Iroquois invasion. On 16 March 1649 the Iroquois seized Brébeuf and Lalemant, who were accused of sorcery and tortured to death. Sainte-Marie-aux-Hurons resisted attack, but panic spread through the other Huron villages whose inhabitants took refuge with their Indian allies.

Among the Iroquois the Jesuits met with some success after the peace of 1667. Some Mohawks hoped to escape the war by placing themselves under Jesuit protection; others preferred to trade with the French or fled the alcoholism that ravaged their villages. Today, Catholic Hurons live in the village of Lorette and Catholic Mohawks in suburban Montreal.

'The savages are not as savage as people think they are in France and I can say in all truth that the spirit of several is in no way inferior to ours.' The *Relations* of the Jesuits are scattered with such observations, and those contributed, at the start of the eighteenth century, to the birth of the idea of the 'noble savage'. It was assisted by the

publication in 1703 of the *Supplement to the voyages of the Baron de La Hontan in which are found curious dialogues between the author and a savage of good sense who has travelled*. The Huron Adario, 'a Machiavelli born in the forests', in Raynal's phrase, spoke with La Hontan about the collision of cultures in America. He took the role of accuser and judge, condemning the conquest, while idealizing the savage. La Hontan admitted – and Jean-Jacques Rousseau, with whom the concept of the noble savage is most closely associated, would not have denied it: 'Solitary life attracts me and the manners of the savages are entirely to my taste.' The myth of the noble savage, which from the eighteenth century nourished the fantasies and hopes of the West – the 'nostalgia for the neolithic', as Claude Lévi-Strauss has put it – has its roots in French America.

The cultural conscience of the Indians

Our perception of the history of the French in America has been modified because of the research of ethno-historians. Far from being passive agents, the Indians always tried to derive some advantage from the invaders. They negotiated alliances in order to exploit their own strategic and commercial interests. They constantly tried to understand these strange men from a far-off world they simply could not imagine, but whose behaviour showed they had no reason to envy them.

Although impressed by technology, the Indians were nonetheless well aware of the value of their own culture, for as one chief remarked to a French missionary: 'I ask thee to believe that, miserable as we might seem in thy eyes, we yet esteem ourselves much more happy than thee, insomuch as we are very contented with the little we have, and I think again that you are much mistaken if thou dost try to persuade us that thy country is better than ours. For if France is a little paradise on earth, why then dost thou think to leave it, why abandon wives and children, relations and friends, and hazard thyself at whatsoever season it may be to the storms and winds of the sea to come to a foreign and heathen land which you esteem the poorest and most miserable in the world.... Know then, my friend, once for all, for I must open my heart to thee, that there is not a single savage who does not think himself infinitely happier and stronger than the French.'

COLONIAL AMERICA:
a land of synthesis

GEORGES BAUDOT

The spirit of synthesis has never engendered so many combinations and fusions of different cultural elements, as during Europe's encounter with the Americas. The expression 'meeting of two worlds' has never more truly realized its full symbolic import than during the events which, at the end of the fifteenth century, plunged a surprised America into the history of the planet – at that time being led at a brisk pace by a Europe which was sometimes just as bewildered. In the sixteenth century, cultural interchange would overtake the tragedy represented by brutal confrontation with the political and religious desire for slavery which marked the Iberian enterprise.

The unknown lands of America had been the theatre of a fabulous human development between the time when Siberian hunters first migrated across the Bering Straits in the Pleistocene age (forty thousand years BC) and the classical splendour of Tikal, Copán and Palenque in the sixth and eighth centuries AD, or even the post-classical urban marvel of Mexico-Tenochtitlán at the very moment of the encounter. Unfortunately, at this early stage, the Amerindian world seemed to matter very little in the eyes of the European when faced with the Other. Otherness in this case seemed to be irreconcilable with continuity, and a desire to surprise and destroy was stronger among the new arrivals than a willingness to understand. The Other from across the sea was himself, of course, at the peak of a human cultural flowering of enormous potential. Behind the Spanish *conquistadores* and evangelizers lay the legacy of almost ten thousand years of growth, dating from the first ear of wheat grown on the banks of the Euphrates and the first villages of Palestine. Above all, the Iberian world could take pride in some five thousand years of urban civilization and of intellectual and literary influence. It was the heir of Sumeria, of Egypt, of the Greeks and the Romans. Down the centuries it had also been transfused, to its undoubted benefit, with subtle Chinese, Arab and Hindu contributions which had enriched the message it had to bear.

Not that any comparison of the cultures should be considered as disastrously unbalanced. The quality and elegance of Mayan astronomy, the brilliance of Inca or Aztec architecture, the depth of Nahuatl philosophy, as well as the beauty of the verse of Nezahualcoyotl, are as much part of humanity's common legacy as Pythagoras' geometry and Virgil's poetry.

In spite of this, the confrontation in the late fifteenth and early sixteenth centuries expressed itself in a brutal clash of armed force so unequal that the weight of military technology prevailed over any other consideration. The triumphal language of António de Nebrija and the Christian faith of the Catholic Sovereigns, shaped by more than a thousand years of the Church (before the storms of the Reformation and the counter-attack of the Council of Trent), were bound to be overwhelming and unyielding. From this moment, enlightened Amerindian cosmology, which represented a major insight into the world based on subtle languages with incomparable expressive capacity, would start a long decline which led its dead gods into oblivion or museums, to re-emerge only as latter-day peasant witchcraft.

In these circumstances, synthesis was the sign of a new universe forged from the ruins – initially underground, then as inescapable as it was obvious. And the symbols could be viewed on equal terms: the bloody liturgy of the pre-Columbian sacrifices found its response in the sinister glow of the stakes of the Spanish Inquisition, for man is always immolated in the name of something trans-cendental. But the two worlds, which clashed so harshly across a land which produced colonial society, where the conqueror seemed to have excluded the conquered, intermingled with such intimacy that they gave birth to a new way of speaking, understanding, producing and living. They started a new page of human history; and today more than 400 million Latin-Americans have to find themselves and their identity.

The men and women

Iberian-American colonial society inaugurated the spirit of synthesis by mingling its human foundations – that is to say, the men and women who inhabited its territories. Prodigious inter-breeding between races presided over the birth of a new society. A new kind of human being seemed to emerge from the clash of the two worlds; the Mexican philosopher José Vasconcelos has written that America became the homeland of a new race '...rich in all the potentialities of the races which came before, the final race, the cosmic race...'.

The human reality of this land of synthesis had three foundations. First were the Amerindians, who arrived in the continent almost forty thousand

15. De Yndio, y Meſtiza nace Coyote.

A 'coyote' *was the nickname given by the Spanish to a child, born of an Indian father and a half-caste mother, who would have been placed quite low in the racial hierarchy, according to the classification used by Gilberto Fereyre. Table of cross-breeding. [Musée de l'Homme, Paris]*

years ago. At the time of the encounter with the Europeans they were one of the most important population groups on the planet, numbering seventy or eighty million. But the consequences of this encounter were disastrous, and the first century of their integration ended in a demographic catastrophe without precedent, which would decisively change the terms and conditions by which colonial society was created. At the end of the 1980s, demographic historians at the University of Berkeley in California were able to put forward some impressive figures for Mexico and the Caribbean. In Mexico, the Amerindians numbered just over twenty-five million at the time of the *conquistadores'* arrival, yet only about two and a half million remained in 1568, some forty-seven years after the conquest. By 1605 the population was even lower, at about one million. In the Antilles, the destruction of the original population was even more brutal. On the accession of Philip II of Spain in 1566, not one of the four or five million natives who encountered Christopher Columbus in 1492 – or their descendants – remained. Even if the figures for South America are less well known, the demographic cataclysm still attained terrible proportions.

Ascribing the responsibility for these deaths is not easy. Major roles were certainly played by the military events of the conquest, bad treatment, and the brutality of a systematic exploitation of the Amerindian workforce distributed to the *encomiendas, repartimientos, obrajes* and other drudgery, like the sinister mining *mita* of Potosí. But the principal cause of death seems to have been the murderous shock of Old World diseases brought over by the Europeans, notably smallpox, influenza, typhus, typhoid and mumps. These European illnesses were responsible for practically seventy-five per cent of the disaster which annihilated the Amerindians. The Indians, isolated

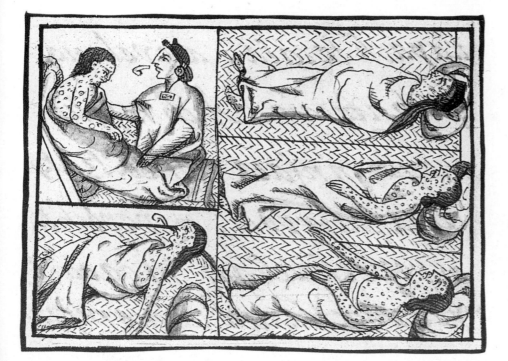

Mexican Amerindians suffering from smallpox *at the time of the conquest. História de las cosas de Nueva España, by Fray Bernadino de Sahagún, Florentine Codex, sixteenth century. The first smallpox epidemic, introduced by a black slave from Panfilo de Narvaez's army, at the time of the conquest of Mexico, decimated the Aztecs and crippled their resistance against the invaders. The last Aztec emperor but one, Cuitlahuac, himself succumbed to the disease in November 1520. The epidemic would spread so quickly that it had reached the Inca empire of Peru before the arrival of the conquistador Pizarro. [Biblioteca Medicea Laurenziana, Florence. Photo Donato Pineider, © Photeb]*

since the Upper Paleolithic age by the two largest oceans on the planet, were not able to develop immunity against the germs of the Old World. So the encounter with the men from Europe culminated in almost forty million dead Amerindians in the course of the sixteenth century. It is easy to understand that the human landscape of America was completely changed as a result.

In fact, this depopulation greatly reduced the workforce available and the productive potential of the continent. The conquering Europeans very quickly attempted to compensate by importing a huge workforce of black slaves from Africa, which were to become the second element in the melting-pot. The first black men had arrived in America in the baggage of the *conquistadores* as servants or auxiliaries, and their qualities of endurance and courage had made them highly appreciated workers. The need to import more was very quickly realized. In 1518, Charles V granted to his friend Laurent de Gorrevod a licence for four thousand. In the reign of his son, Philip II, the import of black African slaves was organized by handing out individual promises to pay which were worth, in 1578, some thirty ducats a man. At the end of the sixteenth century, a convention of public law, the *asiento de negros*, regulated the conditions of the slave trade. The first of these *asientos* granted by Philip II was for thirty-two thousand black slaves to be furnished over a period of nine years to the port of Cartagena, New Grenada, with the sum of nine hundred thousand ducats payable to the Crown of Spain. The sale price of slaves was left to the good judgement of the beneficiary of the *asiento*.

At the end of the first century of colonial rule the black population of the Americas must have reached seventy five thousand, the great majority originating from the Gulf of Guinea or Senegambia. Slaves were especially necessary for the plantations in the low tropical lands of the

Caribbean basin, as well as in the Antilles and on the coasts of present-day Colombia, from Santa Marta to Cartagena, from present-day Venezuela towards Cumana, and on the Pacific coast at Guayaquil in Ecuador. But their presence was equally important in towns, where they formed the bulk of domestic servants and in certain trades. At the beginning of the seventeenth century Mexico possessed twenty thousand black slaves.

Finally there was the White population, dominated by the conquerors and the European colonists. We are reasonably sure of their numbers and composition during the sixteenth century. In 1574 the chronicle of Juan López de Velasco, the famous *Universal Geography and Description of the Indies*, mentions some 225 villages or towns peopled by Spaniards, comprising approximately twenty-three thousand households of five, six or seven people. These figures, corrected by modern historical demography, give us a total of almost two hundred and twenty thousand Spaniards in America at that time.

About fifty years later, this figure had more than doubled. If we are to believe the *Summary and Description of the West Indies* of Fray Antonio Vázquez de Espinosa which appeared in 1628, there were 77,600 Spanish households; this gives a total of 465,000–540,000 Spaniards established in the Americas only one century after the conquest of Mexico. These figures are confirmed in part by the number of departures registered in Seville during the embarkation of the galleons for 'a career in the Indies', which contemporary historical analysis puts at a quarter of a million passengers for the sixteenth century alone. A fact to note is that Spanish women made up 5.6 per cent of the passengers for the period 1493–1519 and reached 16.4 per cent for the period 1540–1559, with 54 per cent of them unmarried.

In fact, the most striking aspect of colonial synthesis is the widespread inter-breeding which eventually became the most significant trait of the American population in a colonial society organized by race and skin colour. Today the term 'pigmentocracy' is used to define its social hierarchies. Sexual miscegenation started very early, from the time of Columbus' attack on Guanahani and during the exploration and then the conquest of the continent. The beauty of the Amerindian women had won over most of the rough conquerors who went to battle in the densely populated high plateaux of Mexico and Peru. The

Als die Fundgruben keine Außbeut mehr geben wolten/werden die Nigritten zum Zucker sieden angehalten. II

chronicler Cieza de León wrote of the north Andean women that they were 'beautiful, more than voluptuous and very much in love with the Spaniards'; while the German mercenary foot-soldier, Ulrich Schmidel, who participated actively in the discovery of the Río de la Plata and who confessed his admiration for the Jaray women said: 'In my opinion, very beautiful, and marvellous lovers, affectionate and physically ardent.' The result was a sort of general concubinage, a *barraganía*, with the Spaniard sometimes living in the middle of real harems. The Church, of course, tried to oppose this, but without much success. Eventually it tolerated these sexual relations on condition that they were only established after the baptism of the Amerindian belle. A decree issued in Cartagena in 1538 stipulated that, '...no soldier was to sleep with an Indian woman who is not baptised....' If one adds to that the fact that interbreeding between European masters and black

slaves was also widespread, one can understand that racial complexity would become one of the essential characteristics of American society. In a society which, in about 1570, was made up of 96 per cent Amerindians, 3 per cent blacks and half-breeds, and about 1 per cent Europeans, the number of half-castes and *mulattos* progressively increased to the point at which, in 1650, they alone represented more than 3 per cent of the American population. By the eighteenth century there was an impressive racial kaleidoscope in which colour prejudice had invented a range of up to sixteen socio-ethnic differentiations, each one of which had its own name.

Obviously, such intimate and complex mixtures have created quite an original human landscape, in both town and countryside. Dress and diet in particular show remarkable living examples of racial and cultural synthesis. At the end of the sixteenth century peasant dress still remained

Sugar production, circa 1540. *America pars quinta,* engraving by *Theodore de Bry, 1595. [Bibliothèque nationale, Paris. Photo © Bibl. nat.-Photeb]*

lo. De Chino, ê Yndia, nace Cambujo.

A 'cambujo' (reddish donkey). This was the epithet given by the Spanish to a child born of an Indian mother and a chino father. From a series of colonial paintings illustrating, with quaint terminology, the wide variety of human types produced by inter-racial breeding in Spanish-America. The Europeans tried to impose a hierarchical order of classification on these various ethnic strains. [Musée de l'Homme, Paris]

largely pre-Columbian. In Central Mexico, for example, where the loincloth (*maxtlatl*) and coat (*tilmatli*) had been partly retained, or Peru, where in the district of Huamanca in 1586 'the clothes and dress worn now, were worn in the Inca era, a wool shirt down to the knees and a blanket which serves as a cape.' (*Relaciones geográficas de Perú.*) In the towns breeches became more and more common until they became predominant in the seventeenth century – largely under pressure from the Church, which was obsessed with modesty as far as dress was concerned.

Food evolved in a similar fashion. The peasant diet remained almost the same as in pre-Columbian times, with staples of maize, beans and peppers in Mexico, or the potato and *quinua* (mountain rice) in Peru. But in the towns pre-Hispanic dishes, as consumed, in times gone by, by the Amerindian nobles, had undergone Spanish 'improvements', which sometimes turned them into

pure works of art. Take pre-Columbian *molli* in Mexico – which was a sort of turkey stew with cocoa and tomatoes. Revised and improved by the nuns of the convent of Santa Clara in Puebla for their bishop's table, it became the incomparable *mole poblano* of smart colonial society and is still enjoyed today. So syncretism was present in all domains in the new America inaugurated by the European invasion.

Tools and products; rural and mining landscapes

In the countryside, perhaps more than anywhere else, we can measure the degree of synthesis which comprised so many elements from each of the two worlds. Mines or towns were places which bore the full imprint of the Europeans; metal-bearing mines were in practice an almost uniquely European

8. De Yndio, y Negra. nace Lobo.

A 'wolf' (lobo) *was the nickname given to a child born of a black mother and an Indian father. Another picture from the same series. [Musée de l'Homme, Paris]*

enterprise. It was not that the Amerindians did not know of them in pre-Columbian times. But on the scale that collection and extraction of gold and especially silver was organized during the colonial age – in Mexico at Zacatecas, Taxco and Pachuca, and in the vice-kingdom of Lima at the famous *Cerro rico* of Potosí – the business was to remain strictly an invention of the Europeans, even if the workforce was massively Amerindian or sometimes black, as in Buritica in Colombia.

As for the towns of colonial America, they also rapidly became European interpretations of the way that space should be occupied. The brilliant and successful pre-Columbian cities, like Mexico-Tenochtitlán, Texcoco, Tlaxcala, Iztapalapan, Cuzco, Quito, Vilcashuaman and Chanchan, were either razed by the conqueror or gradually and insidiously relegated to such minor roles that they gave up and regressed, invaded by silence. The towns where synthesis operated were imported from Europe. Sometimes they followed designs which owed much to the inspiration of the utopian urbanists and architects of the Italian Renaissance; but more often they accorded to the plans and arrangements prescribed by the Council of the Indies, which aimed above all to make urban organization the symbol of European domination. These towns were in the first instance, for reasons of safety and control, the place of residence for the Europeans. But they were also the base unit of colonial society, the centre *par excellence* of decision-making in the exercise of political, religious and economic power. The Amerindian, black, half-caste or mulatto population of the towns was represented in the main by slaves, servants, small tradesmen and the drop-outs who swarmed the streets.

However, the countryside remained essentially Amerindian, sometimes even pre-Columbian, even though major upheavals had

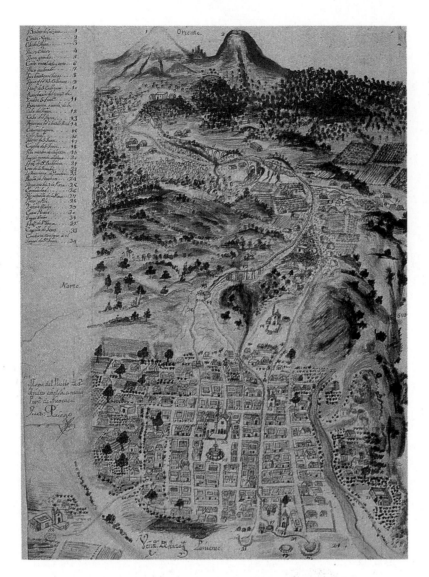

The village of San Andres Chalchicomula (Puebla). *Anonymous engraving, 1764, illustration to La Formación de la hacienda en la época colonial, by Gisela von Wobeser. This is a unique pictorial record of a colonial country landscape in the eighteenth century. [Photo © F. Delebeque]*

occurred as a result of crops, tools and domestic animals imported from Europe. In the high plateaux the tools, crops, habitat and peasants remained Amerindian. They continued to cultivate, using the traditional digging stick, beans, peppers, plants of the gourd family, agave and, of course, maize, the miracle cereal of the neolithic Americans. In the fertile soil of the tropical lowlands, the sweet potato, manioc and cocoa tree also bore witness to the significant influence of Amerindian cultivators. However, wheat, imported from Spain after some unfruitful trials in the Antilles, appeared on the continent during the first third of the sixteenth century. It did quite well in a few areas such as around Lima, the valley of Atlixco in central Mexico and the valley of Santiago in Chile. Wheat completely transformed the rural landscape.

The valley of Atlixco in the Puebla region, which at the end of the sixteenth century, had a population of several hundred specialist Spanish farmers, produced almost 55,000 hectolitres of wheat while the neighbouring valley of San Pablo, with about sixty Spanish farmers, provided 40,000 hectolitres. The central valleys of Chile even managed to export wheat to Peru, which needed

extra supplies to feed the large workforce in the silver mines.

Sugar cane offers another striking example. The plant was first imported by Columbus from the Canaries in 1493, and cane-growing spread considerably between 1520 and 1580. The countryside of Cuba, Jamaica and Puerto Rico was transformed by it; then the canefields, the *canaverales*, invaded the east of Mexico at Jalapa as far as the warm western region at Michoacan. Little by little the crop reached the south, the valleys of the Pacific coast of Peru, then Arequipa and Ayacucho. From this success undoubtedly arose the immoderate taste for sweet foods, which characterized the cuisine of colonial America and which still survives in Mexico and the Andean countries.

The cultivation of indigo also developed remarkably. It began to be exploited near Cuernavaca in Mexico in about 1570, and from 1576 it was to prosper so well in Yucatán and Guatemala that production reached some 10,000 *arrobes* (120–150 tonnes) at the end of the century. But these examples of crops imported from the Old World should not make us forget that they coexisted with authentically American ones, even if European intervention had modified the way they were grown and the yields achieved. Cochineal and cocoa are prime examples.

Cocoa, which had been 'domesticated' in neolithic times by the peasants of Central America, was already an important product pre-Columbus, since the cocoa beans served as money and indeed continued to play this role until the seventeenth century. Cocoa's development during the colonial age arose mainly from the fact that chocolate quickly became a fashionable drink in both colonial and European society. In spite of the financial stake which they represented, the plantations remained, oddly enough, under Amerindian control for the most part. Their output allowed the native communities to pay their tribute in 'contributions' of cocoa, each of about 24,000 kernels. To give an idea of the amounts involved, the regions of Soconusco, and that of Los Izalcos in Guatemala and El Salvador, respectively collected almost 55,000 contributions.

In Mexico the cochineal insect, from which a valuable carmine dye is obtained, was bred on a cactus called the *nopal* by the Amerindian peasants, who harvested the product every three months and sold it on under Spanish control through 'cochineal officers'. For both these two American products, even though production remained in the hands of the Amerindian peasant the management of the other phases of the trade, before and after, was Spanish. This was a clever form of synthesis in the economic area.

New crops like wheat, sugar cane and indigo, and the ancient Amerindian crops which were being developed in an infinitely more productive way to meet a demand outstripping that of pre-Columbian times, necessitated a complete and profound change in agricultural techniques and

therefore in the tools used. The Amerindian peasant might keep his digging stick and hoe for use on his own fields of beans and maize; but on the colonial properties, where he owed days of drudgery under the terms of the 'allocation' contract, he had to learn to use tools from Europe, in particular the plough. It appears that he learned without any great conviction, if we are to believe the correspondence between the *encomenderos* and the viceregal administration. The plough required a pair of oxen to pull it, which represented considerable expenditure on the part of the peasant if he was ever to consider using one on his own. Nevertheless, in the seventeenth and eighteenth centuries there were many Amerindian peasants who were wealthy enough to have one at their disposal. So the presence of this tool from elsewhere became more and more extensive and significant. In one single year, 1597, Spanish galleons off-loaded more than 12,000 ploughshares in Mexico; and this equipment slowly but surely changed the landscapes.

However, these transformations of the countryside were unimportant when compared with the deep trauma caused by the appearance of European cattle. This was the most spectacular innovation to arise from the meeting of the two worlds. In fact, a certain rural landscape which seems today to symbolize America – vast expanses of pasture land, where horsemen, *gauchos*, cowboys, *llaneros*, *vaqueiros* and *jaguncos* live in complete freedom in the midst of immense herds roaming endless plains – was born in this founding sixteenth century. After Columbus' second voyage, horses and pigs appeared in the Antilles, then sheep and cattle quickly afterwards. The breathtaking rate at which they multiplied on the rich virgin grazing lands of America was like an unexpected tidal wave spreading over the pre-Columbian landscape. It reached the stage that a herd of cattle left to its own devices reverted to the wild state, making up the *ganado cimarrón* which was considered

communal property for use by any man as he wished. Thus in 1574, in Santo Domingo alone, 400,000 cattle were officially owned, plus perhaps a million animals which had reverted to the wild. In central Mexico, at Toluca, in twenty years the herds of cattle amounted to more than 150,000 head, and around Oaxaca the breeding *estancias* even had to be closed down in three valleys.

This extreme abundance also applied to horses and sheep. Near Querétaro, in central Mexico, more than 10,000 mares were counted in 1543. The increase in sheep saw the creation of the Mesta, the association of breeders on the Castilian model, in 1537 in Mexico. This was followed in 1543 by the Mesta of Oaxaca, and one in Michoacan in 1563.

Obviously these changes not only transformed the American landscape but disrupted the lives of the Amerindian peasants, who watched powerlessly as the sheep, horses and cattle proliferated and chased them from their maize fields and villages. For the most part left unsupervised, the herds devoured the holdings, completely occupying all the agricultural land and so destroying the Amerindians' food crops. In 1551, the Franciscan monk Francisco de Guzmán was alarmed to see that the indigenous farmers were no

Labourers in the colonial age. *Drawing from* La Formación de la hacienda en la época colonial, *by Gisela von Wobeser.*

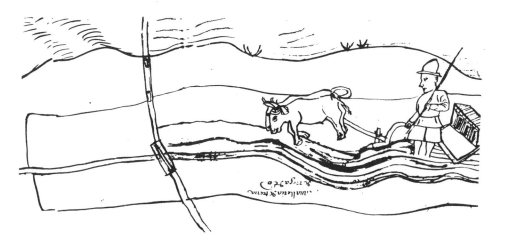

La Plaza Mayor, Mexico City.
Painting by Cristobel Villapando, 1695. In the seventeenth century, Mexico once again became the largest city of the Americas. On the site of the old sacred enclosure of pre-Columbian times the great central square (today known as the Zócalo) was laid out with the viceroy's palace, the Cathedral and the town hall. Private patrician residences, palaces and churches, often of sumptuous design, reflected the splendour of the capital city, whose glory shone throughout what had once been pre-hispanic Mesoamerica, now transformed by European colonialism. [Corsham Court, Wiltshire. Photo © Bridgeman-Artephot]

than eighty. In the 'imperial town' of Potosí, in High Peru, there were a massive 800 drinking places, although admittedly this was an exceptional mining town of 120,000 souls. To some this problem concerned the conquest of hearts and minds, and its failure was obvious. It was a question of a new society, and new discourses, in which the humble Amerindian could hardly participate in the light of the conditions which had been imposed upon him.

Altarpiece from the Chapel of St Xavier, *the Jesuit convent, Tepotzotlán, Mexico, 1762. [Photo © Ch. Lénars – Explorer]*

longer sowing seeds but were fleeing to the mountains before these invasions of cattle. The viceroy of Mexico, Antonio de Mendoza, even went so far as to warn his successor in 1550: 'Your Lordship should know that if you authorize cattle, you will destroy the Indians ....' So cattle ended up as a plague of the Amerindian peasants on a scale comparable to that of the European diseases against which they had no immunity. It should also be noted that they were not even able to take advantage of the cattle to improve their diet. In fact, on the pretext of holding down rising prices, the *audiencia*, or High Court of Mexico, in 1556–64, and then the viceroy Martín Enríquez in 1574, forbade the Amerindian peasants to eat meat. In 1586 a very serious commission of theologians gravely deliberated the appropriateness of the use of meat among the indigenous population, and the Franciscan, Geronimo de Mendieta, actually stated that meat intake might be the cause of their sneezing: 'Even now babies at the breast sneeze, and they receive this from their parents, because they eat meat...with which they exude superfluous fatty secretions like us and so they sneeze as we sneeze....'

As regards the consumption of new products, it was in the area of alcoholic drinks that the synthesis of colonization and its associated judicial and social changes had tragic consequences. Following the Spanish conquest alcohol, whose use in the pre-Columbian age had been very strictly controlled and was reserved especially for liturgical ceremonies and ritual celebrations, became freely available to the Amerindian peasants. They very quickly succumbed to the attractions of inebriation, which offered a means of escape from a reality which was full of despair. The problem became sufficiently serious for the viceroys, courts and monks to try desperately to combat this frenzy, in which they also perceived some vague resurgence of the pre-Columbian ceremonies which they had abolished. But the frequency of the schedules and decrees forbidding drunkenness demonstrated their very ineffectiveness, in spite of the harsh punishments which they contained – such as the provisions of 1539 which stipulated one hundred lashes in public for the first time any Amerindian was arrested while drunk. None of this did any good and in 1587 the viceroy of Mexico stated in a letter to King Philip II that at Cholula, where there were scarcely one hundred Spaniards, there were sixty taverns, while in Tlaxcala there were more

Evangelization and agriculturation. The discourse of domination

The reality is perhaps that the 'spiritual conquest' of America, founded on the transfer of religious beliefs, of ideological models, of ethnic and even aesthetic norms – all these foreign cultural discourses and structures brought from across the seas – clashed with the colonizing imperative and its apparatus. In theory the European presence in America – Spanish and Portuguese – had only one aim and justification: the evangelization of the Amerindian nations. After Columbus' first journey, in May 1493, the pontifical bulls *Inter Caetera* of Pope Alexander VI Borgia had ceded immense territories to the two crowns of the Iberian peninsula, purely as a means of guaranteeing the evangelization which was considered to be a bounden duty. Therefore, in principle, the main enterprise was the mission. This gave the presence of the Spanish and Portuguese a dimension which was out of the ordinary and defined their approach within spiritual perspectives, eschatological even, conceived on a scale relating to the future of the human race.

Almost the whole of the colonial period was informed by a crucial religious fact which affected everything in a spiritual manner: proper sharing of the Christian message. Culture, artistic or literary creation, speaking in public, education and communication, historical or philosophical discourse, publication and diffusion: everything was conceived and carried out in the shadow of the Church. Sculpture, painting and music, when they expressed major artistic ambitions, were prescribed as part of the process of installing the Church. Even the interest in the pre-Columbian past of the Amerindian novices and the very timid discovery of the plurality of cultures was the work of monks, almost always Franciscans, who only undertook this research within the framework of a project of a utopian society with eschatological aims.

The first great writers of mixed blood, such as Alvarado Tezozomoc, Alva Ixtlilxóchitl and Chimalpahim in Mexico, and Garcilaso de la Vega el Inca and Guamán Poma de Ayala in Peru asserted the importance of the history of the pre-Columbian world, and their vernacular languages (Nahuatl and Quechua) and original cultural identity. But they only conceived it and wished for it within the framework of Christian renewal.

So the installation of the Church and the conquest of souls had exposed the missionaries to the great temptations of synthesis. It is certainly in the domains of the mind, of beliefs and discourses that synthesis makes itself felt with the greatest force. When we consider that the effective preaching of the Christian message involved learning indigenous languages, the perspective offered by America in this area might seem to lead to despair. There were more than 150 families or possible linguistic groupings which brought together between 400 and 2,000 different languages, according to modern classification systems! Fortunately, in the areas occupied by the colonial enterprise there were a few languages used for general communication – such as Nahuatl or the Maya family in Mexico, and Quechua or Aymara in the viceroyalty of Lima – which made the task less discouraging. But they still had to be transcribed into the characters of the Roman alphabet and formed into grammars and dictionaries in order to ensure appropriate communication.

In this area the work of the evangelizers, especially the Franciscans, was extraordinary. In Mexico alone, 109 works of this kind were produced by the end of the sixteenth century, of which 80 are attributable to the Franciscans. Nahuatl or Quechua, transcribed into the Roman alphabet, squeezed into the straitjacket of European signs, defined and fixed in grammatical categories stemming from the works of António de Nebrija – who produced the first grammar in 1492 – were they not hybrid languages, vehicles for the colonial cause? In addition, a royal decree of 1550 formally ordered the viceroys to teach the language of the conqueror to the conquered: 'You should try by all possible means to teach these Indians our Castilian language.' Even if, in the course of the century, this instruction was applied to a greater or lesser degree, Hispanization was considered a necessity which it was hoped would, in the fullness of time, finally be accomplished. In the delicate domain of the notions and theological lexicons of preaching, synthesis sometimes imbued the forms of the impossible semantic task or the confused aspects of the conceptual framework which must have astounded more than one Amerindian novice. One thinks also of the treatise on Spanish witchcraft and spells which a Franciscan, Father Andrés de Olmos, translated into Nahuatl in 1553 for the edification of his flock, thus complicating even further the picture of the dying pre-Columbian beliefs, still only partly understood, by adding to it the mysteries of European demonology.

Despite all the restrictions of the Council of Trent of 1545–63, which defined Catholic doctrine and discipline, America witnessed the emergence of a religion reinterpreted by the indigenous population, especially people of the land. Even the Inquisition did not really prevent the establishment of synthesis, although the tribunal of the Holy Office was officially established in Mexico

Cathedral, Mexico City, *façade of the Sagrario. [Photo © Oronoz-Artephot]*

in 1571. In fact it had already been exercising its virulent power through the activity of the monks, who were charged with watching over the orthodoxy of the newly baptised, or with burning and persecuting those Amerindians who secretly adhered to their former religious practices. The Amerindians, in any case, might have felt themselves excluded from the Church, since they were not admitted to the Catholic priesthood or to religious orders. The imperial college of Santiago de Tlaltelolco, on the outskirts of colonial Mexico, which in the minds of the Franciscans was to be the first seminary for the people of the New World, disintegrated in the last quarter of the sixteenth century. It marked the death of a certain type of conversion to Christianity in America.

However, the Church and thus Christian values were indelibly inscribed on all aspects of colonial America from the sixteenth to the eighteenth centuries. But this was done by following the fashions of Europe and in particular those of Spain, which exported several artistic and architectural styles such as Gothic, Mudéjar, Plateresque and Baroque. The first cathedral of the New World, Santo Domingo, was constructed in late Gothic style, and the making of tiles in the Mudéjar fashion was even practised in Mexico by a Franciscan specialist, Andrés de San Miguel, who wrote a treatise about it. From the second half of the sixteenth century to the first third of the seventeenth the Plateresque style dominated, especially in Mexico; and the monasteries of Acolman, Huexotizinco and Calpan, for example, conveyed some memories of Mudéjar as well.

Everywhere, however, the influence of America made itself insidiously felt. Firstly, of course, that was because the workman, or the craftsman and very often also the artist, was Amerindian. The monks never ceased to praise their knowledge and their skill in adopting and also

adapting the European techniques and forms. This did not, however, happen without some designs of pre-Hispanic inspiration intruding which, here and there, gave pause for thought. But where the Amerindian imagination burst through most obviously was during the blossoming of the Baroque, which was to provide America with one of the most beautiful and most spectacular illustrations of a style which was already sumptuous in Europe. The façade of the Jesuit convent of Tepotzotlán in central Mexico, and even more strikingly the gorgeous retables of its chapels, especially those of St Francis Xavier, are among the marvels of colonial America. Here the masterly influence of the Andalusian Lorenzo Rodríguez, creator of the splendid Churrigueresque façade of the Sagrário in the cathedral of Mexico, blends with the abundant but controlled imagination of the artists or craftsmen of Amerindian or mixed parentage who projected their fantasies on to it. The same applies to Santo Domingo of Oaxaca, St Francis of Quito and many others.

Perhaps here more than anywhere else, in the mysterious and liberated domain of artistic imagination, were played out the dramas of that quintessential synthesis which breathed life into colonial America and foreshadowed its future.

Church of St Francis, Quito. *Quito's entire historic centre has been placed on UNESCO's World Cultural Heritage list.* [Photo © J.-P. Courau – Explorer]

AMERICA: CONTINENT OF MISCEGENATION

RICARDO AVILA PALAFOX

When they think of America, Europeans often have two stereotypes in mind. On the one hand, they associate it with the United States, with its population of European origin, its immense open spaces, its powerful economy and its questionable foreign policy. On the other hand, they think that the rest of the continent – Latin America and the islands of the Caribbean – is populated by exotic native people, living in extreme poverty in the middle of a tropical paradise. These clichés obviously do not match the reality, but they do illustrate some of the reality which a contemporary European may appreciate, or indeed transcend, if he has an open mind, in order to discover great cultural riches. These riches derive, in part, from miscegenation, a phenomenon which is difficult to grasp but which is a key element in the understanding of America.

Miscegenation

Miscegenation goes back to the dawn of time. From an anthropological point of view it owes its origin to a very ancient practice, the abduction of women, which is very common in so-called 'primitive' societies. At the end of the twentieth century this custom still exists in certain places, although it adopts more sophisticated guises. For example, in various parts of Mexico it is common for the men not to ask for the hand of their wife-to-be but to 'steal' her – that is, they persuade her, willingly or unwillingly, to leave her family home for several days, without the permission of her parents. When she returns, her parents have no choice but to formalize the illicit union.

Miscegenation results from the mixing – biological and cultural – of individuals belonging to different ethnic groups, thus creating new societies of a hybrid nature based on elements borrowed from one or other of the original cultures. The result is the creation of new 'cultural products': new customs, new social institutions, new technologies, new artistic expression and even new systems of thought. It might be suggested that miscegenation is a crossroads where paths cross and lead to the discovery of new and different places. Miscegenation is a meeting: it enables races to infiltrate and enrich one another.

To consider the evolution of societies to their present stage of development without taking miscegenation into account is impossible.

Although certain 'philosophies' and racial prejudices have tried to make us believe that the noblest cultural expressions stemmed from a pure ethnic background, we now know for certain that this is an illusion, and that ethnic and cultural purity simply do not exist.

Miscegenation in America is the product of a long and inextricable history which stretches back, at the very least, to the time when Europeans and Americans met each other in the alleged 'New World', five centuries ago. But it is difficult to create a picture of five centuries of ethnic and cultural cross-fertilization in America, for the cultures which came into contact in 1492 were not themselves 'pure' cultures, but rather two great syntheses of several cultures, which gave birth to yet another culture, rich and complex, multi-faceted, and itself different from its predecessors: the hybrid American culture.

The context: a particular view of the universe

Before 1492 the nations living on the 'old side' of the planet had a limited idea and knowledge of the globe which gave rise to extremely confused cosmologies that attempted to explain the world and the universe. As a result of astronomical and mathematical calculations, scholars had discovered and demonstrated that the world was round. But no one imagined that, on the other side of the great ocean to the west there existed a gigantic continent, like 'another world' yet totally different from all the worlds so far explored.

At the end of the fifteenth century, Europe was gradually emerging from the medieval era. There was great excitement in the air, and with it a new wave of expansion of a Latinate culture which was already a thousand years old and rich, itself the fusion of existing cultures from Africa, Asia and Europe. It is in this context that we must relocate the implantation of a transatlantic Latin culture by the nations of western Europe.

In its expansion westwards, the Latin culture did not stop on the American continent. It crossed the Pacific Ocean and reached the coasts of Asia, known in Europe through the travels of Marco Polo and the trans-continental route taken by the caravans of the silk trade. So the spirit of the Renaissance ratified the fact that the planet was round; for the first time the earth was a whole and single world. For Europeans at least the discovery of America marked the advent of a 'modern' world.

The immensity of the New World

The geographical diversity of the new continent, its enormous landmass (more than sixty-six times larger than present-day France), the varying forms of social organization of the American peoples and the very nature of European immigration all determined the degree and complexity of the ethnic and cultural miscegenation, which started at the beginning of the sixteenth century in America.

The exploration, conquest and colonization of the islands in the Caribbean Sea, the Antilles, did not arouse much enthusiasm among the Europeans: they found none of the riches there that would satisfy their spirit of plunder. Accounts of the years immediately following the discovery of America show that the Antilles were the scene of a brutal conquest and of colonization which eliminated the limited 'manpower' resource of the native peoples.

So Europeans very quickly found themselves short of workers to undertake heavy labour, which was a serious handicap in exploiting the recently conquered territories or pushing forward exploration in order to conquer new territories on the huge continent nearby, with its rich promise of plunder. Adept businessmen that they were, the Europeans quickly found a solution to the problem: the slave trade between Africa and America. This traffic would be an important phase in the miscegenation of America. The trade in black slaves mainly concerned the Antilles and the coastal areas of the Caribbean, as well as the Brazilian Atlantic coast which was owned by the Portuguese. In due course the traffic extended to Florida, Louisiana and the south-east of the present United States, but only a few groups were settled on the Pacific coastline of South America.

Moving from the Antilles to the mainland the Europeans discovered, to their great surprise, a great range of people with complex social structures. What they saw with their own eyes far surpassed anything that they might have imagined: for example, the city of Mexico-Tenochtitlán, the capital of the Aztec empire, built in the middle of a huge lake. Even larger than most of the major cities in Europe, Mexico-Tenochtitlán provided evidence of almost perfect urbanism and social organization. It was, along with Cuzco – the Inca capital in Peru – one of the greatest cities in the New World. Together, Mexico-Tenochtitlán and Cuzco presented very elaborate models of society resulting from a long evolutionary process which had benefited from a synthesis of several ethnic and cultural 'crossroads' which the communities had encountered on the American continent in the course of their ancestral migration.

The native peoples whom the Europeans met had not all followed the same path as the Aztecs

and Incas, who had organized themselves into great theocratic and military states. However, contemporary archaeological and ethnological research proves that all the nations living in the huge territories of America, North and South, formed societies which were undoubtedly very complex, evolved and organized.

A typical encounter: Cortés and Moctezuma

Before the arrival of Columbus on the new continent, the American peoples had their own concept of the world and the organization of the universe, and they were astonished to meet Europeans who came from the eastern limits of their territories, for only the gods had the right to do so. At the very beginning, the Indians were extremely cautious. In the reports of the voyages of

The concheros danced in time to the sound of the viol, a European stringed instrument copied by the Indians and made from the shell of the armadillo. The dancing took place at the shrine of Our Lord of Mercy. Milpa Alta, Mexico City, May 1985. [Photo Rubén Paez Kano]

Before beginning the dance of the chocolateros, *the Indians awaited their final instructions* (chcootl: *an acidic, yellow-coloured fruit*). *Milpa Alta, Mexico, May 1985. [Photo Rubén Paez Kano]*

Columbus it appears that he was welcomed in a peaceful and cordial manner, and even received gifts from the natives. The same happened with Jacques Cartier when he met the indigenous people of what was to become New France. And when Hernán Cortés arrived on the Mexican coast, he was welcomed with rich gifts. Subsequently most indigenous Americans reacted in an aggressive manner to the European penetration of the continent.

These communities were inevitably doomed to defeat on the field of battle, in spite of their numerical superiority, because the military technology of the Europeans quickly carried the day. However, this was not the main reason for bringing about the subjugation of the Amerindians. In the case of Mexico, for example, the prime cause was the exceptionally fatalistic concept of destiny among the Aztecs. In this connection it is interesting to recall the interpretation which they ascribed, the emperor Moctezuma in particular, to the arrival of the Spaniards, which appeared to confirm the legend of Quetzalcoatl. This explains the fatalism with which Moctezuma accepted his capture and domination.

When Cortés arrived in Mexico-Tenochtitlán and met Moctezuma, he was fully aware that he was facing a man who was similar to him yet also very different, and he also knew that he could dominate him. Moctezuma, for his part – and in spite of his doubts – had realized that Cortés was a man, not a god. The meeting of the Aztec emperor and the Spanish *conquistador* was the culmination of the meeting of the two worlds, a moment symbolizing the fusion of two cultures which gave birth to the modern world of America.

Hernán Cortés was a clever man and he knew how to exploit situations as they arose. Because of his military skills, but above all because of his undoubted charisma and political astuteness, it took him only two years to overcome one of the two great empires of the New World. The same happened with the Inca empire: in a few years its immense power was reduced to nothing by the skill and audacity of an adventurer, Francisco Pizarro.

After the fall of the American capitals, Tenochtitlán and Cuzco, the process of conquest and colonization of the vast territories of Mexico and Peru was only a question of time. The small states adjacent to the large ones and other native communities – many of them tributaries to the great empires – could not or would not resist the pressure of the *conquistadores* and fatalistically accepted the domination of their new masters. And yet not all these societies survived: some disappeared completely, leaving nothing but a few remains and references to their existence in the chronicles of the time.

The war of conquest and colonization effectively lasted until the end of the nineteenth century in North America, when the last Indian nations were finally defeated. In the interim, many indigenous communities had succumbed: their social organization had been torn apart and they were confined within reservations, allowed only limited contact with the European colonists.

In South America, settled on the coasts and the high plains of the hinterland where the climate was favourable, the Europeans did not venture far into the interior of the continent unless there was a possibility of economic advantage. In the case of Peru, for example, where there was a dense population in the colonized regions, ethnic miscegenation was under way from the beginning of the sixteenth century, although many of the native community had left the coast and emigrated to inhospitable regions which the Europeans did not invade.

But in the wide plains of Argentina and Chile, where the population was scattered and mobile, the Indians avoided contact with the Europeans until they were forced to engage in a war of resistance which they could not win and finally, at the end of the nineteenth century, had to assimilate or disappear. This explains in part the relative lack of miscegenation in the most southerly part of South America, although the Jesuits, for example, tried to encourage it in their missions to upper Paraguay. In the nineteenth century the increase in population and new waves of immigration from Europe, together with technical and economic advances, made possible the complete subjugation of these territories, and miscegenation grew. In the same way the impenetrable tropical forest of Amazonia remained outside the sphere of conquest and colonization, leaving the indigenous populations free of miscegenation until the mid-nineteenth century. During the second half of that century, colonization and exploitation of these lands began, but miscegenation between Indians and colonists scarcely existed. The Indians retreated into the most remote regions while the colonists launched into exploitation of the forest's riches, in particular rubber and precious woods. Among the indigenous population these new conditions caused poverty, alcoholism and finally degradation, as is still the situation today.

The Europeans in America

A critical element in miscegenation derives from the diversity of the Europeans who landed in America and the cultural tradition to which they were the heirs. The Spaniards quickly interbred with the Amerindians of Mexico and Peru, thus initiating the great mixing of blood, unlike in other parts of the continent. In North America, for instance, the French were more interested in trading with the indigenous population than in mixing with them, although they did not avoid doing so. The northern Europeans, however, and in particular the English, completely avoided any kind of inter-ethnic relationship with the Indians, preferring instead to colonize the land destructively.

The dance of the concheros. 'Here is our god,' the Indians cried as the dance of the concheros began, around the standard of the pre-hispanic virgin, Tonantzin. Milpa Alta, Mexico, May 1986. [Photo Rubén Paez Kano]

European immigration to the New World brought with it in the main a Latin culture, but one transmitted by a variety of sources each having their own distinctive traditions. The purest Roman tradition was transmitted by the Spanish and Portuguese and, to a lesser extent, the French. The Anglo-Saxon tradition, however, was strongly imbued, in a quite important manner, by Latin culture, and the English were its main means of transmission. For quite specific historical reasons people of direct Latin origin, in the classical sense, settled south of the Tropic of Cancer, while the Anglo-Saxons established themselves north of this latitude. These two principal waves of immigration, each with its own cultural traditions, determined the two types of ethnic and cultural miscegenation in America once they came into contact with the indigenous populations.

The first Europeans to cross the Atlantic and settle on the new continent were basically adventurers who had no hopes left in Europe. They were men looking for new frontiers, be they geographical, social, political or even spiritual. This was also true of the missionaries belonging to the various mendicant orders who made possible – largely by the utopian aspect in which they cloaked their spiritual initiatives – the conversion to Christianity and through it the conquest of countries like Mexico and Peru.

Although European women did join the colonists quite quickly, the men were for a few years left alone with the women of the indigenous nations. When Hernán Cortés arrived on Mexican soil the local chiefs offered him several young girls whom he shared out with his senior captains, keeping one for himself. By taking as his concubine an indigenous woman (he was already married to a European, living in Cuba) and making her his

Top
Dance of the Tecuanis. *This dance, deeply rooted in prehispanic culture, is performed in the regions of Guerrero and Puebla. [Photo Rubén Paez Kano]*

Above
An attack by the Tecuani, *which would have been repulsed by the mixed-blood men of today. Acatlan, region of Puebla, November 1986. [Photo Rubén Paez Kano]*

interpreter, counsellor and mother of one of his children, Cortés made la Malinche or Doña Marina an example of the miscegenation that would take place in the New World.

When the European women arrived in Mexico the *conquistadores* kept up their intimate relationships with the Amerindian women whilst giving their European partners a place as 'first ladies' in order to uphold their reputation in society. In this way the Spanish institutionalized *amancebamiento* – a society – tolerated unofficial extra-marital relationships with another woman. This practice which attached one or two indigenous women to a Spanish household became so common in colonial Mexico that there was a saying: 'Better a good mistress than a bad marriage.'

The example of multiple concubinage had been introduced into Spain by the polygamous Muslims, who occupied part of the country for eight centuries. This custom has survived among the Mexicans into the twentieth century: having one or more *casas chicas*, or 'second houses' – that is, unofficial liaisons with one or more mistresses, is still common, although no one admits to it publicly. Similarly in Brazil the Europeans had so many black concubines and mulatto offspring that the master-slave relationship of the colonial period collapsed in the nineteenth century, enabling present-day Brazilian society to acknowledge openly its mixed blood.

The Spaniards, like the Portuguese and French, had a long and significant inter-ethnic tradition because many different populations – Iberians, Goths, Visigoths, Basques, Occitans and Moors – had intermingled among them. In contrast, the strong puritanical ideology of the Anglo-Saxon Protestants prevented them from having relationships with members of the native population, although there were doubtless some exceptions to this rule.

That is why, with the discovery of the New World, two great cultural regions were created in accordance with the nature of the European immigration: in the north, Anglo-Saxon – where the socio-cultural exchanges were mainly between the Europeans themselves, with less spectacular results – and, in the south, Latin. In both regions the cultural interaction was intense, bringing about the appearance of a variety of socially rich nations, each having as common denominator a profound ethnic and cultural miscegenation.

Syncretism

Miscegenation was also encouraged by Christianity, which brought the spirit of the Renaissance to the new continent. The discovery of America drew Franciscans, Augustinians, Dominicans, Jesuits and many other orders to the American territories in order to preach the 'true faith'. Mexico is a good example of the importance of the 'spiritual conquest'. As soon as Cortés landed, he realized that his plan for victory could not omit the spiritual dimension. So mass was celebrated as soon as they reached shore and the place was baptized 'Vera Cruz' or the 'True Cross'. He succeeded in persuading the local population to place Christian symbols, especially the cross, on their altars. The Mexican adventure was the inspiration to the European priests to dedicate themselves to evangelization of the Indians, although the latter transposed the teachings of Christianity to their own cultures and vision of the world.

Religious syncretism is one of the most remarkable products of miscegenation in America: it reinterprets and combines elements of cultures which overlap with each other. In Mexico, for example, it is most strikingly exemplified in the Virgin of Guadalupe. Before the Europeans arrived the Aztecs had important places of pilgrimage. One of these was Mount Tepeyac where they worshipped Coatlicue-Tonantzin, the goddess of the earth and by extension mother of everyone and everything that exists on Earth. During the first years of colonization, the Franciscans, spreading the gospel in the country, realized the importance of the Aztec system of beliefs and in particular the indisputable presence of this goddess. They appreciated the significance of this particular place and appropriated it for their own purposes, spreading the story that on Mount Tepeyac had appeared the Virgin of Guadalupe. She was supposed to be mysteriously endowed with indigenous characteristics which were the opposite of those on European virgins – for instance, she had a dark skin and was not European in appearance like all the images of saints brought

Above
Tecuani, the ferocious jaguar, *the central figure in the dance, representing man's dominion over the wild beasts. Acatlan, region of Puebla, November 1986. [Photo Rubén Paez Kano]*

Left
Dance of the Tecuanis. *The pagan men drop to their knees as they enter the Christian cemetery, where they will dance in honour of one of their companions. Acatlan, region of Puebla, November 1986. [Photo Rubén Paez Kano]*

175

from Spain. They built a church in her honour, and thus the goddess-mother of the earth, Coatlicue-Tonantzin, was transformed into Our Lady, the Virgin of Guadalupe, who was worshipped throughout the continent. She was named as the patron saint of all Latin America, although eventually her cult spread to the northern continent as well.

It is worth pointing out that the mother concept represents for the Mexicans a totality, from its most sublimated representations such as the Virgin mother-creator who gives life and protects men (which is precisely the image of the Virgin of Guadalupe), all the way to the image of the fallen woman. In this sense, it would not be an exaggeration to think that the Spanish evangelizers gave enormous importance to Coatlicue-Tonantzin by associating her with the Black Madonna, knowing that her presence in the consciousness of the indigenous community could not be replaced by another goddess. By an extraordinary synthesis, the two sets of beliefs – Christian and Aztec – each totalitarian in its own way, are made to merge: the Aztec goddess and the European virgin are indispensable and irreplaceable.

There are many other forms of religious synthesis in America. For example, consider the Christian-animist practices that still take place in some parts of the Antilles where the black element, of African origin, dominates. Consider also the religious faith of the North American blacks, which is a mixture of African religious elements and Anglo-Saxon Protestantism.

There are practically no limits to cultural synthesis in America, whether it is in the Latin or Anglo-Saxon tradition. It has even spread beyond the confines of the continent. Throughout the twentieth century part of the world has danced to the rhythm of music imported from America, from the tango at the turn of the century and its present-day updates in the form of the salsa and lambada, to the different rhythms of swing and jazz, where the black influence is obvious. The bossa nova and samba of Brazil, the cumbia of Colombia, the cha-cha-cha of Cuba and many other dances are the results of compositions and reinterpretations of a range of cultural elements. They are rhythms which did not exist in Europe or Africa or pre-Columbian America, but which stem from the process of miscegenation in America.

Cross-fertilization is also evident in the preparation of food. Gourmets are well aware that *mole*, a Mexican combination of chicken with cocoa, is one of the supreme successes of international cuisine. The Antilles have a huge range of local variations on dishes generally described as creole, which include gastronomic delights which are again hybrid in origin. And in Europe, especially along the shores of the Mediterranean, cookery was effectively reinvented through the inclusion of products that had originated in the New World, such as tomatoes, potatoes and maize.

In architecture, Peruvian and Mexican Baroque have given rise to buildings which are as different and beautiful as those based on their European parent. In terms of art and craftsmanship, America has produced extraordinary works in a very distinctive style, such as can be found in the paintings of Tamayo or Botero. Similarly, some forms of artistic expression have resulted in what is known in Europe as 'naive' or 'primitive' art.

Finally, in the field of literature, American miscegenation has produced one of the most distinctive and astonishing styles in the world, known as 'magic realism': a way of looking at the real and interpreting it which goes far beyond the cold formal models of realism. This imaginary representation of reality mixes reminiscences of the past with fantasies from the life of the individuals involved; *One Hundred Years of Solitude*, by Gabriel García Márquez, is undoubtedly the most accomplished novel in this style.

The new America

Towards the end of the eighteenth century the democratic and anti-monarchic tendencies, which had appeared in Europe a century earlier, gained a more rapid hold in the American colonies and eventually prevailed. In little less than a quarter of a century America was *de facto* independent of Europe. This brought about an increase in the existing miscegenation, because the over-rigid social systems, like those of castes, were no longer applied. The complex social structure that had been put in place by the Spaniards in Latin America duly collapsed and left in charge of these budding nations the sons of Europeans who had been born in America: creoles. In the Antilles the departure of the Spanish left a social vacuum which was then filled by creoles, a minority group in a context where the black and mulatto population represented an enormous majority, and where a Caribbean identity with strong African roots was now in the process of emerging.

But neither the North Americans nor the Caribbeans nor the Latin Americans could consider themselves European. They needed a new identity that was based on identification with their native land: they felt and knew and 'made' themselves Americans.

After the independence of the American colonies was won a new wave of European immigration began. Attracted by the 'dreams' of the New World, crushed by wars and poverty in Europe, seeking new frontiers and convinced of the importance of their role in creating new young republics, thousands of Europeans set sail for America throughout the nineteenth century and at the start of the twentieth century. Successive waves of immigrants from every part of the old continent landed in the United States to settle and exploit the huge land that the British had left. North America now witnessed widespread ethnic

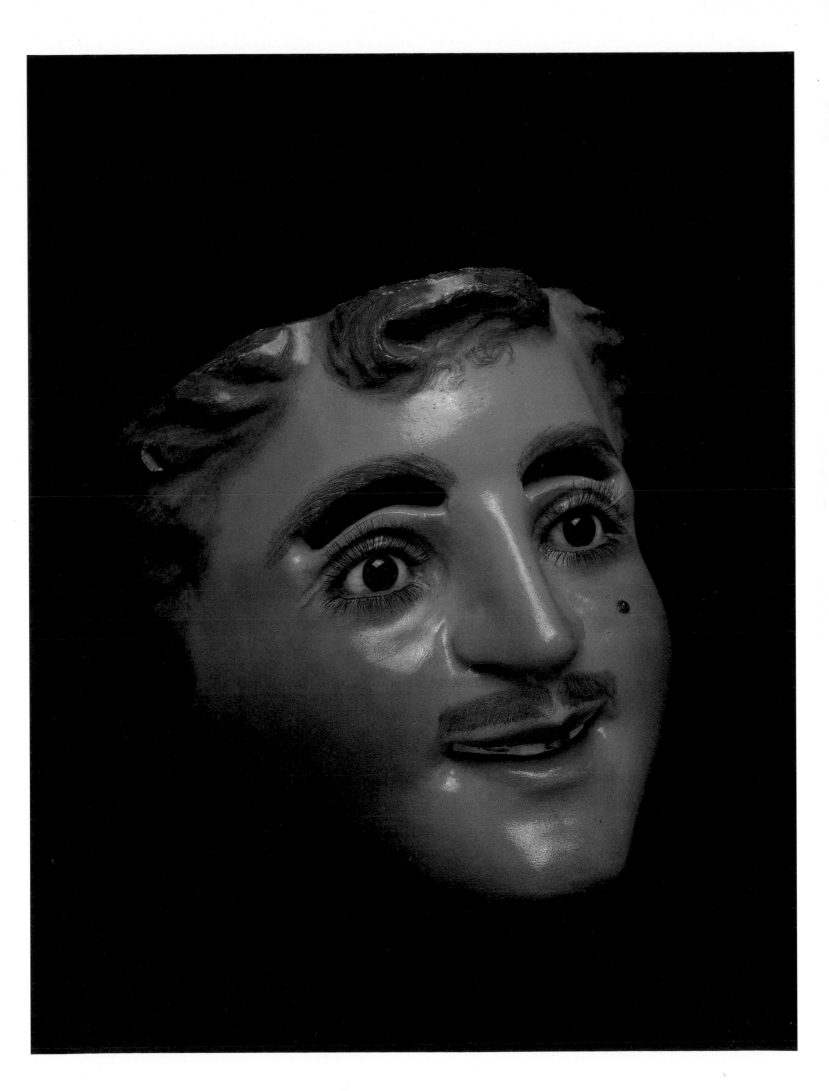

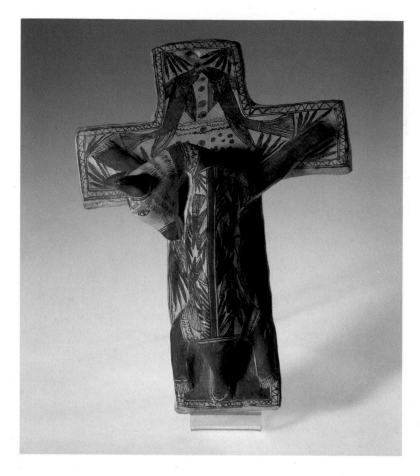

Crucified stag, *on painted earthenware. This artefact reflects the syncretism in Mexican beliefs: the deer, with connotations of the sun, is crucified (sacrificed) on the symbol of supreme Christianity. The animal's body is decorated with fish, another Christian symbol. Mexico, Mahua Indians, Guerrero. [Musée de l'Homme, Paris]*

miscegenation among the immigrant Europeans, excluding the black and native Indian population.

There was also extensive European emigration to other parts of the American continent, but the countries concerned were those most sparsely populated, such as Argentina, Chile and Uruguay. There the governments welcomed the newcomers warmly and undertook several expeditions with the sole aim of exterminating the Indians, who were still very numerous in these vast lands. Nonetheless, even though certain social classes in these countries claimed to represent 'pure European stock', in South America they now accept and acknowledge themselves as Latin American, simply because of the pressure of miscegenation.

American independence and the new wave of European immigration revealed two important realities about the new continent. On one hand there was the North American situation with an Anglo-Saxon population which considered itself to be the heir of new and better European traditions; in the North American social scheme, black and indigenous populations were marginalized. And then there was the Latin American situation where

the creoles, at the head of nations inherited from the Europeans, could not legitimize the European image because they themselves wanted to break free from the Old World and so based their independent attitude on a philosophy proclaiming liberty and equality among men. They looked for their roots in the American past, therefore accepting, symbolically at least, the mixed ancestry of the societies at whose head they had remained. Even so, these creole elites tended to preserve a 'provincial' attitude, for their ideal was still epitomized by the large cities of Europe and especially North America.

Although some people still use racist criteria to minimize the importance of the blacks, Indians and now the Latin Americans, it is undeniable that the future of North America depends on acknowledging its mixture of races. If this does not happen, the racial conflicts in the ghettos and the problem of ethnic minorities will continue to stifle harmonious socio-cultural development.

Latin America is no longer a place where the majority of the population is indigenous Indian, nor is it European; it is of mixed race. The way ahead, for both it and the Antilles, can be summed up in the ideal of the revolutionary Simon Bolívar – a famous man, whose grandmother was black – which proclaims union of the whole continent of Latin America without class or caste distinction: a genuine confederation of ethnic groups and races which respects the right to be different. In contrast to North America and its strong economy, hope in Latin America lies in its richness and extreme cultural diversity.

Today it is no longer possible to talk of pure cultures: in the strictest sense of the phrase, they no longer exist, although certain features of their past may reappear and be re-created in new contexts. For Indian, Anglo-Saxon, Latin and Afro-Caribbean America, acknowledgement of its hybrid multi-racial culture, with all the enrichment which it provides, represents the only path into the future, so that it can face up to the formidable challenges to the world at the dawn of the third millennium.

FROM
THE ENCOUNTER
TO UTOPIA

MIGUEL LEÓN-PORTILLA

Interminable mountain ridges, immense tropical forests, vast deserts and great temperate regions, endless coasts, rivers which seem like arms of the sea: a unique continent extending from the south to the north, from one end of the world to the other – this is where the drama is going to unfold. Far from being unoccupied, these lands, even their smallest islands, are filled with men and women, old people and children, both inhabitants of their sacred worlds and inhabited by symbols. There are songs, music and dances everywhere in festivals which seem never-ending. There are also images of protecting spirits, made of wood and clay, on the altars of small communities, and imposing pyramids, stone representations of gods, paintings and inscriptions in villages and cities. A sacred universe, full of symbols, which has flourished down through the centuries.

But something extraordinary is happening. It is said that several people of this land have suddenly been confronted by strange signs, which they take to be omens of misfortune. And shortly afterwards, strange beings, never before seen, arrive from across the sacred and immense sea. Scenes follow one another with disconcerting rapidity. Suddenly – there is no doubt about it – the land is witness to invasion, subjugation, destruction of the images of the gods, the pyramids, even whole towns, forced conversions, labour in the mines, unknown diseases, deaths by the million. The conquered people are aware of the scope of the drama and offer their own vision of it. The conquerors have already made theirs known through the printed word.

The Emperor, the Pope and those who are concerned with things Christian, including its economics, power and glory, worry about what is happening. The other sovereigns, who have not been included in the share-out of riches, prepare to act. For their part, the *conquistadores,* who never stop talking of their prowess and their suffering, as well as those attracted by the labour force of the vanquished peoples, often complain that their gains are being reduced to nothing.

Nevertheless, among the new arrivals a debate begins about the good and evil of events thus far. They feel obliged to denounce everything they have witnessed: the horrors of the invasion, the plundering, the capture of the lands from their natural owners, the forced labour, and finally the destruction and death. They become the conscience of a people, the same people who invaded and who now are looking for grounds to justify their actions. By their denunciations they become the real glory of Spain, and truthfully no one else has ever been involved in a more desperate and ceaseless struggle. The names of those who 'cried in the wilderness', as one of them said, but who eventually were heard by the Emperors will never be forgotten. Their denunciations and the controversies they fuelled brought them harassment and victimization. Founders of the rights of man, they were priests of total goodness. Among them must be acknowledged António de Montesinos in Santo Domingo, Bartolomé de Las Casas and Vasco de Quiroga in Mexico, Domingo de Santo Tomás and Luis de Morales in Peru.

But in spite of all their efforts and struggles, the accumulation of suffering and misery during these centuries grew enormous, arising from the new capital cities where ruled the conquerors, their descendants and so many others come to join them. In the shanty towns, and everywhere in the impoverished regions in which the endangered cultures had exiled themselves, only a few songs rang out. It was the muffled dialogue with our Mother Earth and Our Father in heaven. One who gives life and one who preserves it. That is the life today of forty million Indians, the survivors of the drama which began in 1492. Everything is both history and enduring reality .

These are events which can reasonably be called recent. From greatest antiquity until only five hundred years ago both sets of human beings were divided by the oceans, one in the 'eastern' hemisphere, the Old World, the other in the 'western' hemisphere, America. We were isolated from each other in a most radical fashion. We were two worlds on one planet.

The inhabitants of each hemisphere did not even know all the others who lived there. It is true that the shores of the luminous Mediterranean were like windows, out of which the peoples of Europe, Africa and Asia used to lean. They spoke of *œcumene,* a superb term which means 'inhabited places', where men live. From the Euro-African Mediterranean and from Asia Minor to the borders of the great Asian continent flourished great cultures such as those of Egypt, Mesopotamia, China, Greece and Rome. But not the Europeans, the Africans nor the Asians knew about everything which actually existed in the hemisphere in which they lived. And, moreover, they knew nothing about the other half of the globe.

Preceding page
An Inca warrior. *The meeting between cultures rapidly turned into conflict between the invaders and warriors such as the one depicted on this* quero, *or Inca vase. [Museé de l'Homme, Paris]*

The same goes for the other great continent on the other side of the wide Atlantic Ocean, completely isolated up until five hundred years ago. Its inhabitants too had created brilliant cultures, such as that of *Cemanahuac*, the 'lands surrounded by water' where the Aztecs, Mixtecs, Mayas and other peoples lived; and *Tawantisuyu*, the universe 'in four directions' of the Quechuas and the Aymaras. But, from Alaska to Tierra del Fuego, these nations did not all know each other and did not even suspect the existence of other men across the immense sea.

The landing of Christopher Columbus with about a hundred Spaniards in 1492 on the island of Guanahani – or whatever island you wish – in the Bahamas, followed by his entry into the Caribbean Sea, no less sparkling than the Mediterranean, marked the moment when many thousands of years of isolation drew to their end. We know now that it was then that the process of the universalization of man and his history started. We also know now that, for the Europeans, it was the discovery of a New World, America. For the inhabitants of the continent on to which the Spaniards had stepped, it was the arrival of those men, whom at first they took to be gods, only to discover afterwards that they were nothing but *popoloca*, that is to say 'barbarians'.

Taking the broad view, we can see that what in fact had happened was the establishment of a permanent relationship between the inhabitants of the two hemispheres. It was the encountering of two worlds.

This word 'encounter' (*encuentro* in Spanish) denotes several things. It can mean things or people coming together in the same place. It can express the idea of combat between two opposing forces, an engagement, a duel. Finally, it can also mean 'to meet', 'to have a meeting', to come together, including actual contact, or fusion. To speak, as was the fashion, of 'discovery' is to limit oneself to the European perspective only. The concept of encounter takes into consideration 'the others', those who were invaded, besieged, 'colonized'. It is also to acknowledge that both peoples, in permanent contact, eventually in many cases mingled and through this brought about a fusion of cultures.

Those of us who are descended from those who encountered each other, whether indigenous or European, have wondered if there are good reasons for commemorating such an event – an event during which, as we have said, the beginning of the universalization of humanity and its history took place. If it is really a question of commemorating it, we must ask ourselves how we should evoke this historic fact which it is impossible to separate from the successive invasions and their associated barbarity. The first conclusion that we reached was this: it was necessary to take account of the views of the inhabitants, then and now, the actors and victims in the great movement of encounter.

In the most open manner possible, we have to listen to the words of the Amerindians against whom were perpetrated – and continue to be perpetrated – aggression, conquest and invasion, destruction of culture, death of languages, the loss of ancestral lands. Parallel with this we have to take into account the scandal of slavery, which, from the time of the encounter, was the fate of millions of Africans – as well as the colonization which existed then and its new, modern forms. Equally, we cannot leave to one side the reciprocal forces which, from the first moments of the encounter and for five centuries afterwards, have acted with ever greater strength on the peoples of the earth, with cultural synthesis, the appearance of new nations brought about by miscegenation, the creation of a new geographical image of the whole world – all of them transformations which have led to full universalization of humanity.

In the light of this concept of an encounter, a commemoration rather than a celebration might allow the expression of different ideas and opinions. Dialogue is necessary, even more so if reflection and analysis, starting from past experience, are focussed on the present and the possibilities for the future. Universal reconciliation among men may be a reality, but there still exist numerous ethnic minority groups who are oppressed, and whose cultural identity and language risk disappearing. National states sometimes revert to forms of internal colonization, even though their duty should be to pave the way for all those who wish to preserve their language and their own customs.

Striking contrasts exist in other respects between countries in this world which is supposed to be unified. While some live in opulence and sometimes try to reinforce their hegemony, other states – the great majority – are undergoing a serious crisis, almost paralysed by their crushing debts. It seems that we have not succeeded, even now, either in respecting ethnic minorities or in putting an end to neo-colonialism, which is much more subtle and thus more pernicious.

We are, at the dawn of the twenty-first century. Undeniably, the history of humanity, which only began to be aware of its completeness five hundred years ago, invites reflection on our present and our future. What will be the situation of the inhabitants of the different countries of the planet in a hundred years from now, when people other than us will be preparing to commemorate the six-hundredth anniversary of the vital historical process begun in 1492?

That is why the New World – even with all its differences, sometimes appalling – has already become the symbol of that which might one day be the destiny of all humanity. Today, alongside the forty million descendants of the indigenous American peoples, live hundreds of millions of men and women of very diverse origins. Some are the great-grandsons of the invaders and the Spanish, Portuguese, English and French conquerors. Others are descendants of immigrants originating from

Right-hand page
A devil's mask, *in painted wood, Chichicastenango, Guatemala. The popular arts were a manifestation of cross-cultural fertilization. This devil's mask depicts a snake; could it be the biblical serpent, or perhaps the creature seen in several representations of the old indigenous gods? [Musée de l'Homme, Paris]*

Germany, Scandinavia, Italy or Poland. Others have Arab, Chinese, Japanese or Filipino ancestors. Today, a large number are the children of those Africans who came, reduced to slavery, as part of one of history's most dramatic crimes against humanity and who, through their presence, their capacity for work and their love of music, song and dance, have contributed so much to fashioning the cultures of the Americas. Through the centuries, men and women from all these diverse origins have mixed together, and so it is that in the Americas, as in no other continent, new faces and new hearts have appeared. The first people to have noticed what was happening – albeit with a discriminatory view of colonial societies which were becoming more and more mixed – spoke of 'castes': half-breeds, mulattos, 'coyotes' and other grotesque local epithets.

Nowadays, although other forms of discrimination still remain, certain realities have begun to impose themselves. Not only in Latin America but also in the United States and in Canada – side by side with the Indians who have managed so far to preserve their identity – one meets men and women whom one can state belong to what is becoming, in truth, the great family of the people of the earth, human beings who have ancestors from the four cardinal points of the globe.

Some members of this large family have already created new forms of culture out of the legacy of the indigenous peoples, the Europeans, the Africans and others. These are now very different creations, but they are just as much indigenous to the New World as were those extraordinary creations of the people of America before the encounter.

To feel that one is an 'earth person' does not mean losing any sense of identity. One may be proud of one's roots, be they Maya, Aztec, Algonquin, Inca or whatever; and, at the same time, share in a wider sense the awareness of belonging to the world of the Indians. And, on another level, one can also acknowledge that one is both Indian and Mexican, or Indian and Canadian. Moreover, as a member of a national state of the American continent, where Europeans, Africans, Asians and Amerindians coexist, frequently intermixed, one may have relationships with human beings other than those of one's own country. In this way it is possible to recognize another level of identity, more generic, but true, as in the remarkable case of the Latin Americans. Almost everywhere in the Americas there exist people who obviously symbolize in their very beings the coming together of communities. They may feel themselves both children of the New World and children of the whole world.

Despite all the violence, sorrow and slavery, the encounter of the peoples of the two hemispheres, in the East and the West, has brought this new reality to history. Are we now on the threshold of a world where, notwithstanding the differences in languages and identities, we may feel equal as humans, ready, not to kill each other or to exploit each other, but to work together for common happiness, without making any distinction as to whether we belong to the 'first', 'second' or 'third' world?

Is all this utopia? Or was it not said that men like Thomas More conceived of their utopias, inspired by what they had heard about the lands on which Columbus and others had landed?

It is true that today crises are worsening in many regions: minorities become engaged in bloody struggles in order to preserve their own identity and, sometimes, what they consider their own territorial rights.

Faced with these violent confrontations, we should ask ourselves how we may speak of the world view of humanity, not just as an idea, but as if it were actually a reality. Will this world view, instead of favouring mutual understanding between humans, have to coexist for ever with so much hostility stemming frequently from ancient prejudice and ill will?

When the fifth centenary has passed there is a lesson to be learnt from history. In the Americas, where hundreds of millions of men and women of different origins have met whatever might have been or will be in terms of confrontations and murderous struggles, life has taught that it is possible to take on totally different identities whilst acknowledging that they are not incompatible. It is as if there was a stratigraphy of identity. I have just said that to acknowledge that one is Indian or to feel that one is of mixed origins does not exclude a sense of sharing a national identity. And it is possible to go even further by perceiving affinities with other people, sometimes of the same language or beliefs, or sometimes with quite different cultural traits.

So the crucial question is reached, almost certainly utopian for some, but from which we should not shirk, if, in the final analysis, we wish the species to survive. Will we humans succeed in safeguarding our most intimate identities – for each of us is unique in that respect – by finding at the same time the means to participate on equal terms in everything which signifies communion with other people of the earth? Can we afford to wait for the day to dawn when so many utopias come to pass, inspired by what was called the New World, but which must be extended into the fullness of a *new world*?

CHRONOLOGY

AMERICA		THE REST OF THE WORLD	
1492: Christopher Columbus reaches the Bahamas	1500	1492	The end of the *Reconquista* of Spain
		1462	Start of the reign of Ivan III in Russia
The Inca empire stretches from southern Colombia to the River Maule (central Chile)	1400		
1325: The founding of Mexico-Tenochtitlan by the Aztecs	1300	1389	Ottoman victory at Kosovo in Serbia
The Incas establish themselves at Cuzco		1275	Marco Polo's voyage to China
	1200	1167–1227	The empire of Gengis-Khan
Chanchas, capital of the state of Chimu, founded in northern Peru	1100	1163–1275	Construction of Notre-Dame, Paris
		1096–1229	Period of the Crusades
The Vikings reach the coast of the New World		1066	William the Conqueror wins the Battle of Hastings
	1000		
The height of Toltec civilization in Mexico		950	Khajuraho period in India
	900		
	800		Coronation of Charlemagne
The height of Huari-Tianasco civilization in Peru		732	Defeat of the Arabs at Poitiers
	700		
Period of classical civilization in Mexico: Teotihuacan, Zepotèpus, Mayas	600	624	The Islamic era begins: Hegira
		570–632	Reign of Mahomet
Period of regional cultures in Peru: Mochica, Recuay, Nazca	500	482–511	Reign of Clovis, King of France
	400		
	300		
	200		
	100		
	0	58–51	Caesar conquers the Gauls
Construction of the Pyramid of the Sun at Teotihuacan		73–71	Slaves' revolt, led by Spartacus
Mohican culture dominant on the north coast of Peru	100		
Nazca culture dominant on the south coast of Peru			
	200	218	Hannibal crosses the Alps
Paracas culture dominant on the south coast of Peru		332	Alexander the Great conquers Egypt
	400	447–438	Construction of the Parthenon, Athens
	600		
		750	Homer writes the Odyssey
	800	753	The founding of Rome
The height of Chavín civilization in Peru			
	1000	996–926	Solomon, King of Israel, orders the construction of the Temple of Jerusalem
The height of Olmec civilization in Peru			
	1500		
		1600–1150	Mycenaean period in Greece
	2000		
First ceramic plastic art at Valdivia (equatorial coast)		2650–2190	Construction of the Pyramid of Saqqarah and the Pyramids of Giseh
	3500		
The first evidence of agricultural practice			
	4000		
Beginning of the domestication of llamas in the Andes			
	6000		
	8000		Neolithic period
	10000		Mesolithic period
First settlers begin to populate the American continent			
	40000		Paleolithic period

AMERICA AND THE ENGLISH RENAISSANCE
Shakespeare's 'Tempest' (1611)

M I C H A E L   B A R R Y

Cruel Aristotelian symbolism, similar to that defended by the conservative clergy of the Spanish colonial empire, may well underlie the imagery of the greatest literary work of the European Renaissance inspired by the encounter with the New World: Shakespeare's *Tempest* (1611).

The English were late-comers indeed to New World exploration – notwithstanding the landfall on the Newfoundland coast in 1497 by the Venetian navigator Giovanni Caboto ('John Cabot') sailing under letters patent of Henry VII. When Elizabethan sea-power truly began to assert itself in the second half of the sixteenth century, planetary ocean communications, and all maritime gateways both to India and to the New World, appeared locked in the grip of Portugal and Spain (King Francis I of France protested in 1522 that he wanted to see the clause in Adam's will dividing the world between Lisbon and Castile), and the English, like their immediate rivals the French, had no recourse but to prey as corsairs on Spanish and Portuguese shipping, or to search perilously for the northernmost possible sea passages towards the east or west around the top of the Eurasian and American landmasses so to avoid the dangerous waters dominated by the two Iberian powers.

'Seeing that the wealth of the Spaniards and Portuguese, by the discovery of new trades and countries was marvellously increased, supposing the same to be a course and mean for them also to obtain the like, they thereupon resolved upon a new and stange navigation': thus wrote Richard Hakluyt in his monumental *Principle Navigations, Voyages, Traffiques and Discoveries of the English Nation* in 1589, concerning the first English attempt to sail around Muscovy in 1553 in order to reach the fabled East. No less 'a new and strange navigation' were Martin Frobisher's American probes into what is now Hudson Bay to find a Northwest passage to Cathay between 1576 and 1578. But Elizabethan England's main effort in the New World consisted in poking for weaknesses in colonial Spanish defences with daring (and profitable) pirate raids, like Sir Francis Drake's stinging attacks on Cartagena and Puerto Bello in the Caribbean ('the Spanish main') in 1572, then up the coasts of Chile and Peru (and as far as California) in 1577, then again in the Caribbean in 1585 and 1595. While Drake robbed, Sir Walter Raleigh sought for geographical gaps in the Spanish Empire where he might plant English colonies – none of which took root in the sixteenth century – in Virginia in 1584–1585 and Guiana in 1595. When Raleigh returned to Guiana in 1617, the Spanish were in occupation, and in 1618 King James I executed the poet-explorer in London: among other reasons as a sop to Spain with whom England was now at peace. Hence the sixteenth-century English have little to tell us of American Indians – this was the Spaniard's age.

The decline of Iberian naval power left England free in the seventeenth century to establish outposts in the Caribbean and along the North Atlantic coast with her tobacco planters at Jamestown in Virginia in 1607, her Puritan emigrants in the Boston area from 1620 onwards, and finally her slave-colony of Jamaica seized from the Spanish in 1655. England eliminated rival Northern European empire-builders when she took New Amsterdam (founded in 1624) away from the Dutch in 1644, renaming it New York, and in the same year absorbed the Swedish colony of Delaware (founded in 1638), thus consolidating her hold along the Atlantic strip. But the French remained formidable opponents to the English, hemming them close to the coast and prohibiting them from pushing into the interior: it was the seventeenth-century French who explored and occupied the continent's waterways from the Gulf of the Saint Lawrence through the Great Lakes down to the

Mississippi delta, and France's riverborne North American trade empire drew into its commercial network – whether directly or indirectly – virtually every indigenous nation between New Orleans and Quebec. Hence, for the seventeenth century, the primary sources for North American ethnography are still not English, but French. Ultimately, however, numbers told; the scattered French along the St Lawrence and the Mississippi never amounted to more than 75,000 individuals by the first half of the eighteenth century, whereas pressure to expand built up in the same period in the English colonies where the population soared to 900,000. Britain's military capture of the gateway to French Canada, Acadia – whose cession by Louis XIV was confirmed by the Peace of Utrecht in 1713 – foreshadowed the fall of New France herself and the extension of the English-speaking people's sway over the entire North American continent after the middle of the eighteenth century.

Englishmen may have been penned up on the periphery of American affairs in the sixteenth and seventeenth centuries, but their cultural attitudes towards Native Americans hardly differed from that of their more successful European rivals in this period – notwithstanding modern sentimental tendencies to exaggerate the supposed contrast between warm-blooded, religiously dogmatic but merrily miscegenating Latin Catholics in the South, and cold, racist, priggish Anglo-Saxon Puritans in the North. Despite very real and bitter sectarian and political differences, all four colonial European nations in America essentially drew upon the same common cultural legacy of Latin Christianity and its set of prejudices. Their attitudes towards non-Europeans were more often than not pragmatically dictated by circumstances. To begin with, all four took African slavery for granted. Also, their reactions to their very first encounters with the materially primitive Indians of the Atlantic seaboard were remarkably similar, and it is arresting to compare the writings of the Hispanicized Italian Columbus in the Antilles (1492), the Portuguese sailor Pêro Vaz de Caminha on the coast of Brazil (1500) and the English sea-captain Arthur Barlowe in Virginia (1584). All three betray almost identical wide-eyed wonder before naked, innocent people living in what they took to be a state of nature, corresponding to their common European myth of a Golden Age before the Fall: 'very handsome and goodly people, and in their behaviour as mannerly and civil as any of Europe', as Captain Barlowe put it.

But attitudes hardened when Europeans settled down to business. Like Columbus or Cartier, Barlowe himself thought nothing of kidnapping two Virginia Indians to take back to England to train as interpreters and also to show as curiosities ('they will not give a doit to relieve a lame beggar, they will lay out ten to see a dead Indian', Shakespeare's Trinculo cynically comments in the *Tempest*, II, ii). Miscegenation of the type we think

of as Spanish-American and aristocratic (Cortés and Malinche, Don García Lasso de la Vega and the Inca princess Chimpu Ocllo), occurred in the early years of the Virginia colony also. Forty members of the first group of settlers married Indian wives and John Rolfe wedded the daughter of the local chief Powhatan, Pocahontas (who died of tuberculosis in England in 1616). With the arrival of white women from England, British colonial authorities came to frown upon such marriages amongst gentry. Even more disapproving the supposedly non-racist Spanish colonial authorities (an edict of Philip II specifically excluded *mestizos* or mixed-bloods from taking Holy Orders as early as 1580). Throughout the seventeenth century, English colonials relied on vital alliances with certain Algonquian tribes and especially the redoubtable Iroquois, whom they rewarded with trade goods and muskets to stave off and harass the French. They paid cash to their Indian auxiliaries for scalps taken from the heads of enemy tribesmen or even Frenchmen, and the French in turn dealt with their own friendly tribes at English expense.

For their part, just as in New France, the technologically Neolithic Algonquian tribes on the English borderlands came to depend heavily on English trade goods, obtainable with furs for which they ransacked their forests, their Stone Age way of life inevitably disintegrated in contact with seventeenth-century European Iron Age civilization. Captain Barlowe in Virginia saw the writing on the wall as early as 1584: 'We exchanged our tin dish for twenty skins, worth twenty crowns, or twenty nobles: and a copper kettle for fifty skins worth fifty crowns. They offered us good exchange for our hatchets and axes, and for knives, and would have given anything for swords: but we would not depart with any.' Barlowe also noticed that 'they have no edge-tools'; but then a European ship was wrecked by a tempest on their shore, 'out of whose sides they drew the nails and spikes, and with those they made their best instruments.'

What doomed the Indians in the English colonies was white population pressure. The Spaniards in the rural highlands of Mexico and Peru kept a place for Indians in their society: as serfs (that 20 per cent of the once-teeming indigenous peasantries of these two highly civilized zones survived the initial onslaught of the conquest is nothing, one should think, for Hispanic apologists to be proud of). The handful of French also desperately relied on their own Indians as essential military auxiliaries and trading partners down to the bitter end of New France. But any social role for Indians decreased dramatically in late seventeenth-century New England as homesteaders in multiplying numbers drove native tribes off land they wanted for their own farms. The ghastly comment of a Puritan bigot like Cotton Mather (1663–1728) after the slaughter by settlers of six hundred Pequot Indians resisting encroachment of their territory – 'on this day we have sent six hundred heathen souls to hell' – may be offset by the kindliness of his contemporary William Penn (1644–1718) when he purchased from a local tribe the land on which he intended to found Philadelphia in 1682: 'We may all live in love and peace one with another... we who are His workmanship.'

But the two main culprits which decimated Indians under English rule were the same that ravaged the Spanish Antilles or French Huronia: social disintegration and European disease. As early as 1634, John Winthrop in Massachusetts observed, apparently with pleasure, that in his area, 'the natives are near all dead of the small pox, so as the Lord hath cleared our title to what we possess.' By 1675, when the uprising of the Narragansott Indians was crushed by armed force, European settlers already outnumbered Native Americans by about two to one in the New England colonies (40,000 to 20,000) and 'Providence was visible thinning the Indians to make room for the English' (according to a later seventeenth-century Rhode Island governor quoted by George Howe, *Mount Hope*, New York 1959). But at least one Englishman deliberately used sickness to clear a region of unwanted native peoples: Lord Geoffrey Amherst, successor to General Wolfe (conqueror of Quebec in 1759), who took blankets from a smallpox ward in the military hospital at Fort Pitt and distributed them in 1763 to the starving Indian tribes (former French allies) in the region around Detroit. Mercifully, this crime, perhaps the most heinous ever committed under English auspices against the native peoples of the New World, lies beyond the time-limit set by this book.

That English views of North American peoples at the turn of the sixteenth and seventeenth centuries resembled those of other European nations – and grimly so – clearly emerges from a dispassionate examination of Shakespeare's *The Tempest*: a masque-like play contemporary with the first permanent settlements in Virginia and thought to borrow directly from reports of a shipwreck in the Bermudas in 1609 by Sir Thomas Gates, Sir George Somers and William Strachey. But Shakespeare's sources go beyond such topical references to draw on the wider literature of both the English and continental Renaissance dealing with the New World. The Italianate framework is provided by Thomas' *History of Italy* (1549). Mandeville's geographical fables are pillaged (Gonzalo's 'when we were boys, who would believe... that there were such men whose heads stood in their breasts....', III, iii, compares closely with Raleigh's 1595 relation on Guiana: 'They are reported to have their eyes in their shoulders, and their mouths in the middle of their breasts, and that a long train of hair groweth backward between their shoulders. Such a nation was written of by Mandeville, whose reports were held for fables for many years, and yet since the East Indies were discovered, we find his relations true of such things

as heretofore were held incredible'). As is well known, Shakespeare also borrows from Montaigne's amused essay (1588) on utopian equality which favourably compared the simple cannibals of the New World with the refined decadence of contemporary Europe, 'Des Cannibales', (*Essais*, I, xxxi), translated from the French into English in 1603 by the Italian Protestant refugee in London, John Florio.

But the single most important literary influence appears to have been the treatise *De Orbe Novo* ('On the New World') by the Milanese official chronicler to the court of Spain, Peter Martyr of Anghiera (1455–1525), containing the first reports of Columbus' and Magellan's voyages, and a work taken extremely seriously by Renaissance Englishmen: Richard Hakluyt issued an edition of the original Latin text during his stay in Paris in 1587 and successive English versions were brought out by Shakespeare's acquaintance Robert Eden in 1577 and 1612 (the poet may have seen the second of these in manuscript). Peter Martyr yields such details as the name of Caliban's devil-god 'Setebos' – which clinches the proof of his influence – but more important, he provides a key to the play's thinking. More eloquently and indeed more chillingly than any other Christian intellectual of his age, Peter Martyr formulated the official reasoning of Spain's ruling class regarding the unfolding human reality – and tragedy – both in the New World and in the Old (in his *De Babylonica Legatione*, he typically calls the kingdom's expelled Jews 'an infected pestilent and contagious herd, *morbosum, pestiferum contagiosum pecus*'). Concerning the American Indians, Peter Martyr's point of view evolves, over the thirty years covered by his writings, from considering them innocent children of the Golden Age (*aurea aetate viventes*, 'they live in the Golden Age, without laws, without accusing judges, without books, they pursue their lives happy in nature'); to disquiet as he transcribes from European language derived from the name of the Carib Indians of the Antilles (*Canibales arbitrati – sic truculentos illos, sive Caribes, vocant*); to cold contempt as a people fit only to be enslaved: 'They eat human flesh, they are more sodomite than any other human nation, they know no justice, go naked, respect neither love nor virginity..., get drunk, are brutal, observe no obedience, their young respect not the old nor sons the fathers, they cannot be taught lessons, punishment is wasted on them, traitorous, cruel, vindictive, grudging, hostile to religion, lazy, thieving, abject and low in their judgements, observing neither faith nor law.'

This is the portrait of Caliban, a Carib cannibal as his name suggests, and as every rebellious line he utters in the play confirms. And this unfortunate Caribbean Indian out of the pages of Peter Martyr is twisted to fit into the scheme of Shakespeare's own well-known preoccupation to link the misfortunes of the outer world to the turmoil inside a man's soul (Brutus' 'state of man,

Caravel on a stormy sea. *Detail from the maps painted by Ygnazio Danti on the walls of the Gallery of Geographical Maps. [Vatican Museum. Photo G. Tomisch, © Arch. Photeb]*

like to a little Kingdom, suffers then the nature of an Insurrection'), a perceived correspondence between the outer macrocosm and the inner microcosm which was indeed one of the philosophical commonplaces of the age. Thus Raleigh: '(God) vouchsafed unto man both the intellectual of angels, the sensitive of beasts, and the proper rational belonging unto man, and therefore, saith Gregory Nazianzen, "Man is the bond and chain which tieth together both natures". And because in the little frame of man's body there is a representation of the universal, and by allusion a kind of participation in the parts thereof, therefore was man called *microcosmos*, or the little world.' If, in addition to bearing in mind this theory of the microcosm, one also scans Shakespeare's play in the light of so much European Renaissance thinking on the New World cast in a ferocious Aristotelian mould – with the naked Indian slave forced to the bottom rung in the hierarchy of mankind – one might suggest the following reading of the *Tempest*:

Shakespeare's exiled magician-duke Prospero is a character derived from the historical Prospero Adorno, a Genoese doge, tributary to Milan in the fifteenth century, who was overthrown by a plot hatched between his brother Antonio and the Aragonese King Alfonso I of Naples, father to King Ferdinand or Ferrante I (who also appears in the play as Miranda's lover).

In the play, Prospero, transported by a spell to an island in the Bermudas ('the still-vex'd Bermoothes'), acquires, thanks to his white magic which symbolizes the power of his intellect, omnipotence over all elements on his island microcosm and primarily over the native Caliban, a symbol of lower and sensual nature and of the beast in man, whose instinctive revolt must be mercilessly crushed by the ducal Intellect and whose fate can only be total enslavement: 'Thou most lying slave, whom stripes may move, not kindness!' To this Caliban can only retort: 'You taught me language; and my profit on't is, I know how to curse.' The egalitarian and unrealistic remarks, dangerously Utopian in their folly, made by the kind but naive Aragonese councillor Gonzalo, would be entirely lost on such a creature as Caliban who must be pitilessly subdued.

Indeed Caliban and every other character in the play must be brought back under Prospero's firm control, for each represents a potentially dangerous tendency of the human soul, from immoral ambition (the three princes Alonso, Antonio and Sebastian) to bestial lust and drunkenness (the sailors Stephano and Trinculo and most especially Caliban), not excepting even the lovers (Ferdinand and Miranda must curb their sensual desire before marriage under Prospero's stern admonition). Having overcome the rebellion of Caliban and the evil princes, Prospero regains full sovereignty over his duchy, similar to the Intellect in the well-balanced microcosm, and may prepare for death as a sage, for 'we are such stuff as dreams are made on' and 'every third thought shall be my grave'. Prospero's closing words find their parallel in the Renaissance English version of Thomas à Kempis as rendered by Richard Whitford in 1530: 'Command the winds and the tempest of pride to cease; bid the sea of covetousness to be at rest; and charge the northern wind – that is the devil's temptation – not to blow. Then great tranquillity and peace shall be within me.'

But why must the tragedy remain Caliban's alone?

BIBLIOGRAPHY

MEXICO

Georges BAUDOT, *Les lettres précolombiennes,* Toulouse, Private, 1976; *Utopie et Histoire au Mexique,* Toulouse, Private 1977.

Georges BAUDOT and Tzvetan TODOROV, *Récits aztèques de la conquête,* Paris, Le Seuil 1983.

Hernan CORTES, *Cartas de relación,* Mexico, Porrua 1971.

Christian DUVERGER, *La Fleur létale, économie du sacrifice aztèque,* Paris, Le Seuil 1979; *l'Origine des Aztèques,* Paris, Le Seuil 1983; *La Conversion des Indiens de Nouvelle-Espagne,* Paris, Le Seuil 1987.

Miguel LEÓN-PORTILLA, *Mexico-Tenochtitlán, su espacio y tiempo sagrados,* Mexico, Instituto nacional de antropologia e historia 1978; *La Pensée aztèque,* Paris, Le Seuil 1985.

Eduardo MATOS MOCTEZUMA, *Muerte a filo de obsidiana,* Mexico, Secretaria de Educación Pública, SEP/INAH 1975; *Vida y Muerte en el Templo Mayor,* Ediciones Oceano, 1989; *El Rostro de la Muerte,* Mexico, G.V. editores 1987; *Les Aztèques,* Paris, La Manufacture 1989.

Jacques SOUSTELLE, *La Vie quotidienne des Aztèques à la veille de la conquête espagnole,* Paris, Hachette, 1955; *L'Univers des Aztèques,* Paris, ed. Hermann 1977.

PERU

Louis BAUDIN, *La Vie quotidienne au temps des derniers Incas,* Paris, Hachette 1955

Maria Concepción BRAVO, *El tiempo de los Incas,* Madrid, ed. Alhambra 1986.

Henri FAVRE, *Les Incas,* Paris, P.U.F., coll. Que sais-je? No. 1504, 5th ed. 1990.

Inca GARCILASO DE LA VEGA, *Commentaires royaux sur le Pérou des Incas,* Paris, François Maspéro 1982 (3 vols).

Felipe GUAMAN POMA DE AYALA, *Nueva corónica y buen gobierno* (1613), Institut d'ethnologie, Paris 1936.

Federico KAUFFMANN DOIG, *Manual de arqueologia peruana,* Lima, Promoción editorial Inca S.A. 1978.

Daniele LAVALLÉE and Luis LUMBRERAS, *Les Andes: de la préhistoire aux Incas,* Paris, Gallimard, coll. L'Univers des formes 1985.

John MURRA, *Formaciones económicas y politicas del mundo andino,* Lima, Instituto de Estudios Peruanos, 1975; *La organización económica des estado Inca,* Mexico, Siglo XXI 1978.

Nathan WACHTEL, *La Vision des vaincus, les Indiens du Pérou devant la conquête espagnole,* Paris, Gallimard 1971.

NORTH AMERICA

Atlas of Great Lakes Indian History, University of Oklahoma Press 1987.

Dictionnaire Biographique du Canada, Laval, Presse de l'Université 1966-1969.

Handbook of North American Indians, vol. 15, Washington, Smithsonian Institute 1978.

History of Indian-White Relations, vol. 4, Washington, Smithsonian Institute 1989.

Les Voyages de Samuel de Champlain, Saintongeais, père du Canada, Paris, P.U.F. 1951.

The History and Culture of Iroquois Diplomacy, Syracuse University Press 1985.

The Jesuit Relations and Allied Documents: Travels and Explorations of the Jesuit Missionaries in New France, 1610–1751, Cleveland 1896– 1901.

Relations Inédites de la Nouvelle France, vols I and II, Montreal 1974.

James AXTELL, *The European and the Indians. Essays in the Ethnohistory of Colonial North America,* New York, 1981; *The Indian People of Eastern America,* Oxford University Press 1981.

J.-B. BOSSU, *Nouveaux Voyages en Louisiane 1751–1768,* Paris, Aubier, coll. Étranges Étrangers, 1980.

J. de BREBEUF, *Les Relations de ce qui s'est passé au pays des Hurons, 1635–1648,* Geneva 1957.

CABEZA DE VACA *Naufrages,* Paris, Fayard 1980.

Jacques CARTIER, *Relations,* Critical edition by M. Bideaux, University of Montreal Press 1986.

Pierre CHAUNU, *Conquête et exploitation des nouveaux mondes,* Paris, P.U.F., coll. Nouvelle Clio 1969.

Louise DECHÊNE, *Habitants et Marchands de Montréal au XVIIIe siècle,* Paris 1974.

Denys DELAGE, *Le Pays renversé, Amérindiens et Européens en Amérique du Nord-Est, 1600–1660,* Montreal 1985.

Pierrette DESY, *Trente ans de captivité chez les Indiens Ojibwa,* Payot 1980.

Olive DICKASON, *The Myth of the Savage and the Beginning of French Colonialism,* University of Alberta Press 1984.

Patricia DILLON WOODS, *French Indian Relations in the Southern Frontier, 1699–1762,* Chicago 1979.

William ECCLES, *The Canadian Frontier, 1534–1761,* Toronto 1969.

Claude FOHLEN, *Les Indiens d'Amérique du Nord,* Paris, P.U.F. coll. Que sais-je? 1985.

Daniel FRANCIS and Toby MORANTZ, *Partners in Furs: A History of the Fur Trade in Eastern James Bay, 1600-1870,* Mac Gill University Press 1983.

Patricia GALLOWAY, *La Salle and His Legacy, Frenchmen and Indians in the Lower Missisipi Valley,* University Press of Mississipi 1982.

Marcel GIRAUD, *Histoire de la Louisianne française,* Paris 1953–1974; *Le Métis Canadien, Son Rôle dans l'Histoire des Provinces de l'Ouest,* Paris 1945.

Conrad HEIDENREICH, *Huronica. A History and Geography of the Huron Indians, 1600–1650,* Toronto 1971.

Wilbur JACOBS, *Dispossessing the American Indians: Indians and Whites in the Colonial Frontier,* University of Oklahoma Press 1972.

Philippe JACQUIN, *Histoire des Indiens d'Amérique du Nord,* Paris, Payot 1976; *Les Indiens blancs, Français et Indiens en Amérique du Nord, XVIe-XVIIIe siecles,* Paris, Payot 1987; *La Terre des Peaux Rouges,* Paris, Gallimard, coll. Découverte, 1987; *Une journée chez les Iroquois,* Paris, Payot 1987; *Une journée chez les Iroquois,* Paris, Flammarion 1992.

Cornelius JAENEN, *Friends and Foes, Aspects of French-Amerindian Cultural Contacts in the Sixteenth and Seventeenth Centuries,* Columbia University Press 1976.

Marc LESCARBOT, *History of New France,* (3 vols), London, Greenwood Press 1969.

Calvin MARTIN, *Keepers of the Games: Indian-Animal Relationships and the Fur Trade,* University of California Press 1988.

Jacqueline PETERSON and Jennifer BROWN, *The New Peoples: Being and Becoming Metis in North America,* University of Nebraska Press 1985.

Arthur RAY, *Indians in the Fur Trade, Their Role as Hunters, Trappers and Middlemen in the Lands Southwest of Hudson Bay, 1660–1870,* University of Toronto Press 1974.

André THEVET, *Singularités de la France antarctique autrement nommée Amérique,* Paris, ed. du Temps 1982.

Bruce TRIGGER, *The Children of Aataentsic: A History of the Huron People to 1660,* Mac Gill University Press 1976; *Les Indiens, la Fourrure et les Blancs,* Paris, Le Seuil 1990.

GENERAL

Claude d'ABBEVILLE, *Histoire de la mission des pères capucins en l'isle de Maragnan et terres circonvoisines,* Paris 1614 (facsimile Gratz 1963).

Jean de LERY, *Histoire d'un voyage faict en la terre de Brésil, autrement dite Amérique,* Geneva, Droz 1975.

Alfred METRAUX, *Religions et magies indiennes d'Amérique du sud,* Paris, Gallimard 1967.

MONTAIGNE, *Essais, Des Cannibales,* Paris, Gallimard, coll. La Pléiade.

Hans STADEN, *Nus, Féroces et Anthropophages, 1557,* Paris, A.-M. Métailié 1979.

André THEVET, *Histoire d'André Thévet Angoumoisin...de deux voyages par lui faicts aux Indes australes et occidentales...1585.* Manuscrpt of the B.N, France no 15454, Paris.

THE COLONIAL PERIOD

Georges BAUDOT, *La Vie quotidienne dans l'Amérique espagnole de Philippe II, XVIe siècle,* Paris, Hachette 1981.

Jacques LAFAYE, *Les Conquistadores, 'Le temps qui court',* Paris, Le Seuil 1962.

189

INDEX

All vernacular names are in *italics*, as are the titles of published works. The page numbers in **bold** refer to illustrations, while those in *italics* refer to the notes found in page margins or in the boxes at the bottom of pages.